Rev. Edmund P. Joyce, C.S.C., Rev. Theodore M. Hesburgh, C.S.C.

We thank you for the lights
That you have kindled

Rev. Edmund P. Joyce, C.S.C.   Rev. Theodore M. Hesburgh, C.S.C.

We thank you for the lights
That you have kindled

# The University of Notre Dame
*A Contemporary Portrait*

# The University of Notre Dame
*A Contemporary Portrait*

by
Robert Schmuhl

University of Notre Dame Press
Notre Dame, Indiana

Copyright © 1986 by
University of Notre Dame Press
Notre Dame, Indiana 46556
All Rights Reserved

*Library of Congress Cataloging-in-Publication Data*

Schmuhl, Robert.
   The University of Notre Dame.

  Bibliography: p.
  1. University of Notre Dame—History.  I. Title.
LD4113.S35  1986        378.772'89        86-40246
ISBN 0-268-01916-9

Manufactured in the United States of America

*For my Mother and Father
for nurturing a love of Notre Dame
and for so much more*

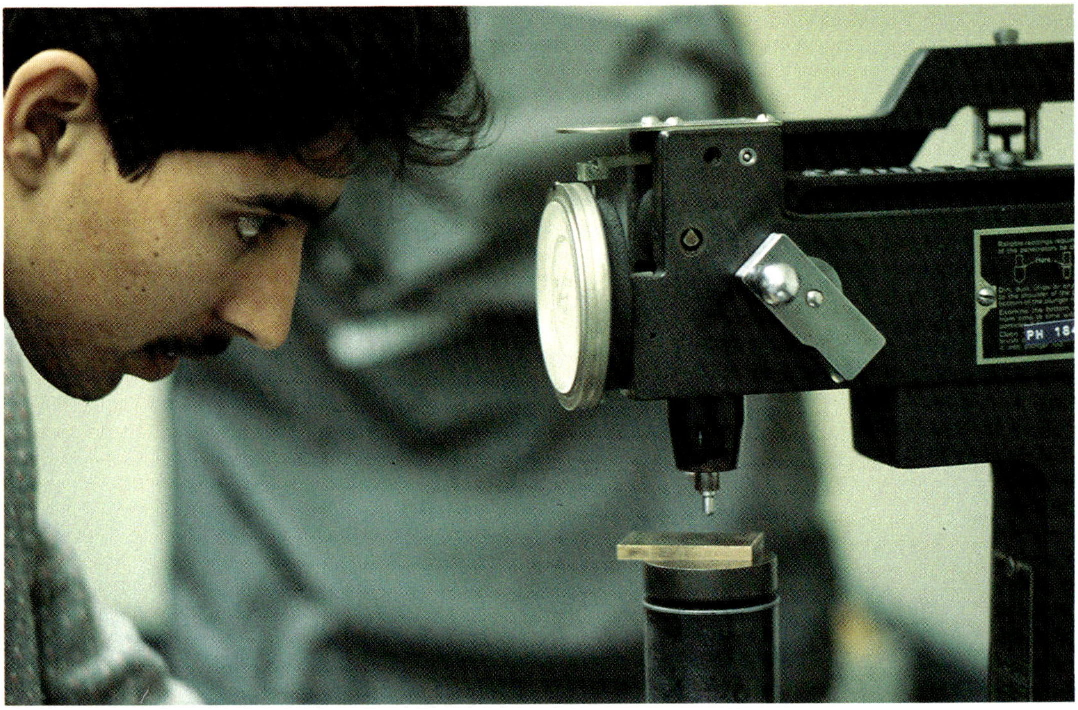

# Table of Contents

Introductory Note  ix

Yesterday and Today  1
Profile of Rev. Theodore M. Hesburgh, C.S.C.  18
Profile of Timothy O'Meara, Provost  28

The College of Arts and Letters  34
Profile of Michael J. Loux, Dean  62

The College of Science  66
Profile of Francis J. Castellino, Dean  78

The College of Engineering  82
Profile of Roger A. Schmitz, Dean  95

The College of Business Administration  100
Profile of Frank K. Reilly, Dean  113

The Law School  116
Profile of David T. Link, Dean  130

The Graduate School  133
Profile of Robert E. Gordon, Vice President  140

Tomorrow  143

Acknowledgments and Sources  147

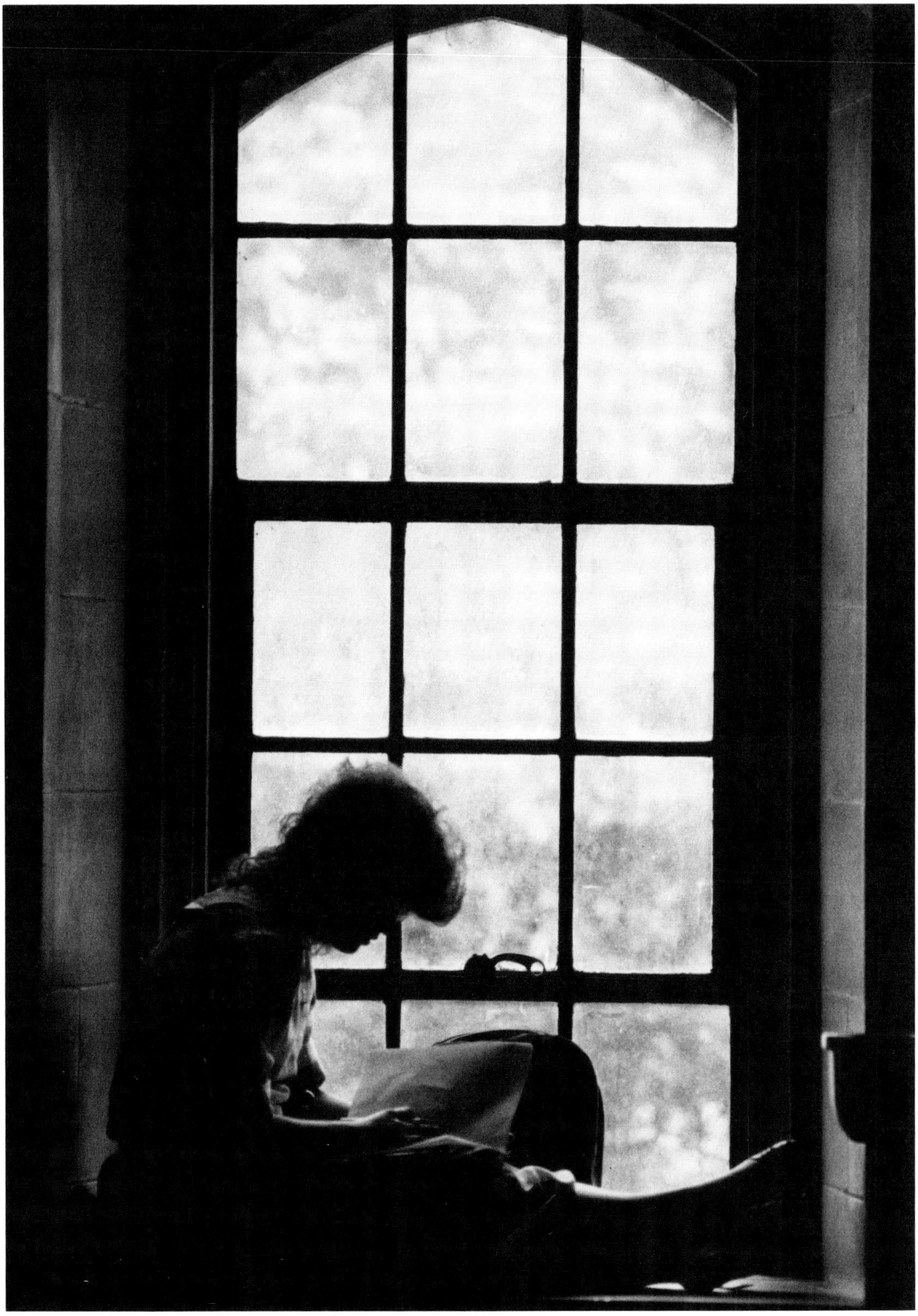

# Introductory Note

THE WORDS AND PICTURES in this book provide a portrait of the University of Notre Dame as it exists today. Although each chapter considers both the past and the future, the focus throughout the volume is on what's happening at Notre Dame now in the 1980s. The book discusses—at least in passing—all aspects of life on the campus. The paramount concern, however, is the intellectual life of the University—the teaching and scholarship occurring within the individual departments, colleges, and institutes.

Given this emphasis, each of the four colleges —Arts and Letters, Science, Engineering, and Business Administration—along with the Law School and the Graduate School receive separate chapters. Much of the text is descriptive, explaining and underscoring specific areas of concentration and specialization. Besides this factual treatment, several professors and administrators leaven the narrative by providing their personal views on the University as it approaches its 150th anniversary.

By combining facts and opinions, this book seeks to be an accurate and realistic picture of contemporary Notre Dame. Viewed from a distance, a university—any university—frequently appears to be the most tranquil of places, as placid as a small lake on a calm day. This stereotype of everyone going about his or her work in collegial harmony is, for good or ill, often at odds with reality. Like any institution, a university is involved in a continuing process of development and definition. This natural and human process creates crosscurrents, opposing ideas and viewpoints that bring vitality to an institution and ripple its water as they converge. In such an academic setting, these crosscurrents can become sources of tension, argument, debate. Several crosscurrents flow through Notre Dame today, as it develops (in the eyes of most observers) into being a preeminent Catholic university. To be both realistic and comprehensive, this book discusses how several crosscurrents are affecting and shaping one contemporary university.

Notre Dame's existence and identity come from the joining together of many different interdependent elements. Everything that has occurred since its founding in 1842 creates a foundation for the present and serves as prologue for the future. In years to come, certain aspects of the University will, undoubtedly, change. New priorities will emerge; some current concerns will become subordinate or disappear. For the moment, though, this is Notre Dame.

D. O. M.
HOC IN MEMORIAM
EDUARDI SORIN
SUP. GEN. C.S.C.
NOSTRAE DOMINAE UNIVERSITATIS
FUNDATORIS
QUI APOSTOLICIS VIRTUTIBUS CLARUS
CATHOLICAE AMERICANAE
EDUCATIONIS STUDIOSISSIMUS
NAT. ID. FEB. A. D. MDCCCXIV. NATUS
A. LXXVIII M. V. VIXIT.
DISCIPULI ALUMNI AMICI
VENERATIONIS GRATITUDINIS

# *Yesterday and Today*

AT 11 O'CLOCK on the morning of April 23, 1879, shouts of "Fire! Fire! The college is on fire!" reverberated through the campus of the University of Notre Dame. Three hours later, most of the buildings, furnishings, library holdings, and historical documents of the thirty-seven-year-old school lay in ruins. On April 27, Father Edward Sorin, founder of the University and at that time Superior General of the Congregation of the Holy Cross (besides being chairman of the school's Board of Trustees), returned from Montreal to survey the damage and to decide what to do. Seeing the still-smoldering debris stiffened the sixty-five-year-old priest, and he assembled the teachers, students, and staff in Sacred Heart Church, one structure which had been spared.

Speaking with the confidence that comes from single-minded resolve, Father Sorin wasted no time in making plans. Characteristically, he placed himself and the University's namesake at the center of his new dream: "The fire was my fault. I came here as a young man and founded a university which I named after the Mother of God. Now she had to burn it to the ground to show me that I dreamed too small a dream. Tomorrow we will begin again and build it bigger, and when it is built, we will put a gold dome on top with a golden statue of the Mother of God so that everyone who comes this way will know to whom we owe whatever great future this place has."

In less than four months, after over three hundred laborers worked from dawn until sunset, the new Administration Building—with its classrooms, offices, and dormitories—was ready for the fall semester. The golden dome with its statue was completed later in the 1880s. In *Notre Dame: Reminiscences of an Era*, Richard Sullivan remarks: "I think indeed it might be said that Sorin not only founded Notre Dame on a cold winter day in 1842 but refounded it on a fresh April Sunday in 1879." The principal policymaker for the University until his death in 1893, Father Sorin began a line of dreamer-builders who have guided Notre Dame during its development from a small "frontier school" that was hardly a college into a true university, with distinct Colleges of Arts and Letters, Science, Engineering, and Business Administration, a Law School, and a Graduate School.

Several of Father Sorin's successors as president—notably Fathers John W. Cavanaugh, James A. Burns, John F. O'Hara, John J. Cavanaugh, and Theodore M. Hesburgh—shared the founder's dream and worked to build a university with a strong academic reputation and a commitment to religious principles. As time has passed, the original dream has been sharpened and refined. During the nineteenth and early twentieth centuries, Notre Dame offered (in addition to the collegiate curriculum) elementary and high school programs as well as a vocational institute, called the "Manual Labor Training School." Some campus leaders, like Father Andrew Morrissey, president from 1893 to 1906, defended such precollegiate activities and opposed University growth, because he did not think Notre Dame could "compete with all those schools so heavily endowed." Others, like Father John Zahm, provincial of the Holy Cross order from 1898–1906 and the first scientist of note on the Notre Dame faculty, challenged the idea that the non-collegiate programs should receive emphasis. He wanted Notre Dame to become "the intellectual center of the American West."

After considerable discussion and debate, the elementary school (for what were called "the minims"), the preparatory school, and the vocational school were discontinued so that the University could concentrate on undergraduate and graduate education as well as scholarly research. The period between 1917 (the last year for the Manual Labor Training School) and 1932 (when the Graduate School was formally organized) is particularly significant in the history of Notre Dame. During these years, all the lower-level educational efforts were abandoned, with "the minims" the last to go in 1929. In addition, from 1919–1922, the University experienced, in the phrase of the late historian and Notre Dame archivist Rev. Thomas T. McAvoy, C.S.C., "the Burns Revolution."

Named for Father James Burns, the first president to hold a doctoral degree, the "revolution" gave structure and direction to modern Notre Dame. Father Burns, the country's leading authority on the history of Catholic education in America, divided the University into separate colleges, appointing deans to direct these colleges and chairmen to lead each of the departments within a college. He established the Academic Council, composed of administrators and faculty members, to help shape programs and make policy decisions. He sought and obtained the first support from foundations Notre Dame ever received. Realizing that prudent financial management was essential to future success, he created an endowment fund, the interest from which was earmarked to raise faculty salaries and to pay for other expenses. Overseeing the investments for the endowment was a lay Board of Trustees made up of experienced financiers who were both alumni and non-alumni friends of the University.

What the brief yet influential "Burns Revolution" began continues today. The collegiate and departmental structure remains firmly in place, and the Academic Council formulates scholastic policies and regulations as well as requirements for admission to and graduation from the University. Foundation support has grown from grants in 1921 of $12,500 from the General Education Board (which later became the Rockefeller Foundation) and $75,000 from the Carnegie Foundation to annual support of nearly $20 million for research and sponsored programs. The University endowment of $22,000 in 1920 stood at over $300 million in 1986, giving Notre Dame's endowment a ranking of twenty-second of all the colleges and universities in America. Lay involvement in the Board of Trustees took on much greater meaning in 1967, when priests of the Congregation of the Holy Cross voted to place University governance in the hands of an independent board of lay and clerical members. Notre Dame was the first major Catholic university to be governed by a predominantly lay board. (Of the some fifty trustees serving in 1986, only seven are Holy Cross priests.)

As Notre Dame evolved and developed its modern identity as a true university, it still retained several of the defining characteristics from the early days. These qualities, which contribute to the ethos and spirit of Notre Dame, took root in the nineteenth century and help provide what historians and contemporary observers refer to as "the sense of place" the University possesses. This "sense of place" cuts across time, levels of education, and academic disciplines, with the result being a distinct experience linked to a common purpose. Outsiders with but a passing acquaintance with Notre Dame use a word like "mystique" to describe the reactions of people toward the University. Those more knowledgeable—students, alumni, faculty, staff—realize that what many consider intangibles are, in fact, institutional qualities shaped over time by human decisions. Notre Dame's evolution from a frontier school (that emphasized pre-baccalaureate education) to a college (that focused on the teaching of undergraduates) to a university (that balances undergraduate and graduate instruction with scholarly research) has meant that profound changes have occurred since 1842. These changes, though, have taken place within an environment that not only values but nurtures continuity and tradition.

The cornerstone of continuity, of course, is the Catholic character of Notre Dame. From Father Sorin to the present, religious practices and principles have permeated life across the campus to create a spiritual or moral atmosphere that one writer called the University's "surrounding climate." During the nineteenth and early twentieth centuries, Notre Dame's Catholicity was most evident in the participation by students, faculty, staff, and others in the rituals and devotions of the faith. Attending Mass, receiving Communion, saying the rosary, going on retreats, reading the *Religious Bulletin,* and taking part in other spiritual activities played an important role in the Notre Dame experience, enhancing the educational and religious formation of the young men on campus. (The University became co-educational in 1972.)

Earlier in this century, the formal study of religion and theology entered the curriculum, and another dimension of Notre Dame's Catholicity began. Scholar-teachers, particularly priests and in most cases members of the Congregation of the Holy Cross, provided students with an academic foundation of religious thought and principles. Many of these faculty members also wrote books and articles to advance the understanding and thinking of the church for people outside the University. Today the Department of Theology is one of the strongest departments at Notre Dame, and the University has been referred to as the place where the Catholic Church does its thinking. Moreover, several scholars in disciplines other than theology contribute to Catholic thought and teachings. For example, economists and business professors from Notre Dame assisted American bishops as they prepared the recent pastoral letter about the United States economy. Such scholarly contributions help to serve the Church.

The University also annually recognizes the achievements of an American Catholic man or woman through the awarding of the Laetare Medal. Inaugurated in 1883, the Laetare Medal honors a lay person or member of the clergy (in the words of one citation) "whose genius has ennobled the arts and sciences, illustrated the ideas of the Church, and enriched the heritage of humanity." Recipients of what is generally regarded the most prestigious award conferred on an American Catholic include Al Smith, George Meany, Clare Boothe Luce, George Shuster, John Kennedy, Dorothy Day, Monsignor John Tracy Ellis, and Helen Hayes.

Besides the explicitly religious activities that take place, a concern for values and ethics pervades the University, enriching its spiritual dimension. This concern, which dates back to the past century and an early interest in cultivating the moral conduct of all students, has no disciplinary or professional boundaries. In varying degrees, ethical considerations enter teaching and research in all of the Colleges, the Law School, and the Graduate School. Unlike other universities, which try to stress ethical neutrality or a value-free approach, Notre Dame places moral questions at the forefront. Debates occur over the validity of varying ethical viewpoints, but not whether ethical deliberation is an appropriate academic activity. In a 1981 address to the faculty, "A Great Catholic University: A Persistent Dream," Father Hesburgh said: "If the vision of this institution is special and unique, it is because we cherish faith and values. Absent or present both of them, education and life are different. Most universities, for a wide variety of reasons or circumstances, do not share this special vision. Some of them are probably better than we are, right now, as universities. Whether we are better ultimately will depend in large measure how seriously we pursue our quest for excellence, both as a university and as Catholic." The many dimensions of "this special vision" provide unity and coherence to Notre Dame, regardless of the discipline or endeavor. Intellectual concerns and ethical considerations go hand in hand.

Another aspect of Notre Dame life that contributes to its distinctive ethos is the University's emphasis on what it calls "residentiality." Since the school's founding, the vast majority of students along with a sizable percentage of faculty, particularly priests, have lived on campus. In early years, young men in the collegiate program resided in large, multi-bed dormitories in the Administration Building. The construction of Sorin Hall in 1888 marked the beginning of a new approach to campus life. Sorin Hall, still a popular residence hall, was the first dormitory with private rooms for male students built at any Catholic college or university.

In subsequent years, other residence halls were constructed, and Notre Dame became known

4   *Yesterday and Today*

*Sorin Hall, dedicated in 1889 and the oldest residence hall*

*Yesterday and Today* 5

throughout higher education in America as a pioneer in establishing the concept of the residential university. Symbolic of Notre Dame's commitment to residentiality was the building program of the 1920s that featured the construction of Morrissey Hall, Lyons Hall, and other residence halls. A shortage of living space had forced students to live off-campus. As a result, in the words of Rev. Arthur J. Hope, C.S.C., in *Notre Dame: One Hundred Years,* "the indefinable Notre Dame spirit was being lost," and it had to be re-captured.

At Notre Dame, however, residentiality has always meant more than occupying or sharing a room in close proximity to classes. Each residence hall includes a chapel, where Mass is offered daily and other religious services take place. Many of the rectors and assistant rectors are priests, brothers, and sisters, and they serve as counselors when a student faces personal questions or problems. Several observers have likened the residence halls to small Catholic parishes, with the spiritual dimension of hall life enriching the religious atmosphere of the University. Over ninety percent of the undergraduates, the largest group of students living in residence halls, are Roman Catholic.

In addition to deepening the religious character of Notre Dame, residentiality also plays a role in the intellectual life of the University and in the development of students outside of the classroom. Halls sponsor public forums about contemporary issues, programs that bring faculty members into the dorms on a regular basis, and similar projects. Through the office of Student Affairs, which is responsible for residence life and many extra-curricular activities, students in residence halls (as well as those who live off-campus) can enhance their education by attending lectures, dramatic presentations, films, and other events or by participating in such work as the campus media.

As Rev. David T. Tyson, C.S.C., the Vice President for Student Affairs and himself a resident of Grace Hall as well as a faculty member in the Department of Management, says: "We are teachers in the residence halls, and we are involved in an educational endeavor. I would like to see residence life and academic life linked even more closely than it is now."

Earlier this century, it was quite common for faculty members, both clerical and lay, to live in the halls and to talk with students about their classes and intellectual interests. For many years, prominent, unmarried lay professors—Colonel William J. Hoynes, Thomas P. Madden, Frank O'Malley, Joe Ryan, and Paul Fenlon—were known as "the bachelor dons" of the campus. Until Fenlon's death in 1980, Sorin Hall was home for at least one of the bachelor dons for ninety-one consecutive years. The era of the avuncular bachelor don has passed, but Father Tyson and others are working to revive and strengthen the relationship between residentiality and intellectual life. "When rectors went out of the classroom, we lost something special, and we're trying to bring it back," Father Tyson explains. He believes that the stricter standards for faculty tenure and promotion have been a factor in the decline of academics serving as rectors and assistant rectors in the halls. The time required to teach effectively, to conduct research, and to publish scholarly findings makes it difficult for younger faculty members to become actively involved in residence life.

Father Tyson also notes that the changing standards of students have had an impact on reducing the connection of residentiality to the intellectual concerns of undergraduates. "The academic life has become so competitive that the faculty is now often viewed as the enemy." Father Tyson hopes that new programs in the halls as well as additional activities organized by Student Affairs will create links between residential and intellectual life that compares to the ties between residential and religious life.

Although the feeling of community that comes from residentiality is one of Notre Dame's hallmarks, a concern for the world outside the campus animates the University and extends its work. Father Sorin and the four Brothers of Saint Joseph who accompanied him to Northern Indiana in 1842 were missionaries from France. Father Sorin himself crossed the Atlantic between Europe and America fifty-two times in his lifetime, establishing ties between people and institutions (educational and religious) abroad. Later, at the urging of Father John Zahm, Notre Dame cultivated relationships with citizens and schools of South American countries, and at one point early in this century over ten percent of the student body came from Latin America. The University's involvement in the "Good Neighbor" policy was also reflected in the curriculum. Influenced by Father John O'Hara, who had lived and worked in Uruguay and Argentina, Notre Dame in 1917 became the first American University to offer a four-year course in foreign commerce. Many graduates from this program subsequently worked for multinational companies in South America and Europe.

During the 1930s and 1940s, the arrival of foreign-born scholars to Notre Dame created a more cosmopolitan atmosphere on campus and broadened the community's awareness of international affairs. Such academics as the mathematicians Emil Artin and Karl Menger, the physicists Arthur Haas and Eugene Guth, and the political scientists Waldemar Gurian and F. A. Hermens, sought refuge from Nazism and Communism, and their teaching and research enhanced the University's reputation both in America and abroad. In the opinion of Father Hesburgh, a Notre Dame student in the 1930s and a faculty member in the 1940s, "Perhaps more than any other single event, this open-arms policy nudged us into national academic prominence. Virtually overnight Notre Dame took on the flavor of an international university. By providing refuge to European scholars who were seeking to retain their own freedom, Notre Dame liberated itself to enter the ranks of the world's major universities. In doing so, it strengthened its own sense of intellectual purpose and anchored itself even more firmly in its religious tradition."

More recently, and primarily as a result of the work and example of Father Hesburgh himself, University activities outside the United States have proliferated. In 1964 Notre Dame inaugurated a Sophomore Year Abroad Program at the University of Innsbruck in Austria. Twenty years later foreign study programs for undergraduates exist at Innsbruck; Angers, France; Tokyo, Japan; Mexico City, Mexico; London, England; Cairo, Egypt; Jerusalem, and the People's Republic of China. Undergraduates are also able to study in Rome, Italy, and Maynooth, Ireland, in programs conducted by St. Mary's College, while third-year students in Notre Dame's School of Architecture are required to participate in the Rome Program of Architectural Studies, which was initiated in 1969. Moreover, the College of Arts and Letters sponsors a one-semester program in London for its students, the Law School operates its unique London Law Centre, and the College of Business Administration offers the opportunity of a semester of study in London as part of its Master's in Business Administration. The London programs in law and in business stress the international dimensions of legal and corporate life. The undergraduate programs are designed to introduce foreign cultures and languages.

In addition, following a suggestion from Pope Paul VI to Father Hesburgh, the University in 1972 formally established the Ecumenical Institute for Advanced Theological Studies, which is located between Jerusalem and Bethlehem. Inspired by the ecumenical initiatives of Vatican Council II, the Institute brings together scholars of several disciplines—religion, history, and archaeology—and faiths—Catholic, Orthodox, and Protestant—to study all aspects of theology. The scholars who come from North and South America, Europe, Asia, and Africa work on specific research projects during their residence at the Institute. In 1983 the Interfaith Academy of Peace was established at the Institute. The Academy, which sponsors international conferences for theologians and scientists as well as individual scholarship, focuses on the dilemma of the arms race and the problems caused by regional warfare. Discussing the creation of the Academy and its objective, Father Hesburgh said: "It has become clear to me that if we don't do something about the issue of disarmament, and pretty soon at that, there won't be any issues left—not the Middle East or Afghanistan or anything else, because the whole earth will be incinerated."

Besides the many foreign study programs and the Ecumenical Institute, there are other facets to Notre Dame's international involvement. The Helen Kellogg Institute for International Studies conducts several programs bringing foreign scholars to campus and also sending scholars from Notre Dame abroad, particularly to Latin America. The College of Business Administration is engaged in a long-term Program on Multinational Corporations and Third World Development, which involves academics from numerous disciplines, international executives, religious leaders, and government officials. Since 1980, the University and Katholieke Universiteit Leuven in Belgium, regarded as one of the world's great Catholic universities, have participated in a continuing exchange of faculty members.

The growth of international programs of various kinds is but one manifestation of the diverse intellectual activity that has been taking place at the University in recent years, and contributed to the recognition it has received. For much of the first half of the twentieth century, Notre Dame was primarily known to the vast majority of Americans as a school with a successful athletic program. Especially in the realm of intercollegiate football, the exploits of Knute Rockne, George

Gipp, the Four Horsemen, Frank Leahy, Angelo Bertelli, Johnny Lujack, Leon Hart, and many others made Notre Dame, these coaches, and players household words across the country. Popular books were written and movies were produced celebrating their feats. A national following of so-called "subway alumni" joined actual alumni, students, and staff in a spirit of allegiance that no other school in the United States has ever enjoyed.

Although achievement in athletics remains an integral element in the University's history and tradition, the years since 1952, when Father Hesburgh assumed the presidency, are more notably marked by efforts to improve other aspects of Notre Dame, especially the intellectual life with its several different dimensions. During the past three decades, there has even been greater concern for academic accomplishment among University student-athletes than ever before. Notre Dame's system of monitoring the classroom performance of athletes and the rate of graduation for athletes (ninety-eight percent) have received considerable attention and merited several honors, including the Academic Achievement Award of the College Football Association in 1982 and 1983. The University is a leader in the number of post-graduate scholarships awarded by the National Collegiate Athletic Association. Notre Dame ranks first among universities around the nation for recipients of graduate scholarships from the National Football Foundation and Hall of Fame.

The differences between 1952 and the present are, indeed, striking. The annual operating budget then was $9.7 million. Today the yearly budget approaches $200 million. The number of buildings on campus has risen dramatically. The replacement value of physical facilities was $24 million. Now it's over $450 million. Support for research and sponsored programs used to be less than $1 million per year. Recently grants in excess of $17 million underwrite research annually. The amount of the University's endowment has jumped from $9 million to $300 million. The number of people on campus has grown, too. The student body has doubled—there are now some 7,500 undergraduates and 2,000 graduate and professional students. The faculty has almost tripled since 1952. The number now approaches one thousand, with the vast majority holding doctorates. In the early 1950s, only about one-third of the faculty had doctorates.

In addition to enlarging the number, strength-

*The Marching Band, the oldest university band in the United States*

ening the faculty throughout the University has been a principal objective and activity during the past thirty years. In the late 1960s, Notre Dame announced a major focus of faculty development would involve the creation of endowed professorships. By 1971, the University had established four such professorships, one in each of the Colleges —the George and Winifred Clark Chair in Biology, the Frank M. Freimann Chair in Electrical Engineering, the John Cardinal O'Hara Chair of Philosophy, and the C. R. Smith Chair in the College of Business Administration. As of 1985, some sixty-five other endowed chairs for distinguished teacher-scholars have been either completely funded or partially supported. Almost half of the chairs, which exist in all of the Colleges and in the Law School, are occupied. Many of the chairholders come to Notre Dame after earning scholarly recognition at universities elsewhere. They and Notre Dame professors awarded endowed chairs do not only contribute to their disciplines through their research, publication, and teaching; they also serve as models for faculty colleagues of the type of professor the University now seeks —the academic who understands the values of the University and is able to combine effective classroom instruction with respected scholarship. While the "bachelor don" was something of a symbol of the Notre Dame professor of an earlier era, the endowed chairholder represents the contemporary University, its work, and its aspirations.

Improving the faculty extends well beyond appointing established scholars to endowed professorships. The standards for hiring, promoting, and awarding tenure have changed dramatically in recent years, particularly since the 1970s. When University leaders decided to seek academic excellence across the University, they realized that a school's stature was, in large part, determined by the scholarly reputation of individual faculty members in their respective disciplines. Such recognition comes primarily from the outside—from the appraisal of others about the quality of research being conducted at an institution. Conference papers, articles, and books serve as yardsticks that measure someone's place in his discipline. Administrators, including deans and department chairmen, sought people who would continue Notre Dame's heritage of effective teaching and also contribute to the intellectual life of their fields. Academics selected to join the faculty were expected to meet the internal responsibilities of undergraduate and graduate education and the external responsibilities of advancing their disciplines through research and scholarship.

The transition to a single faculty who balance teaching and research has not occurred without tension and debate. Some professors, especially those who came to Notre Dame when undergraduate instruction was the primary focus, worry that teaching will suffer by emphasizing scholarship. There is a fear that the distance between the faculty and the student body will become greater. Other professors counter by stressing that achieving equilibrium between the traditional commitment to teaching and the newer one to research will help Notre Dame improve its standing as a university. They also note that having an active research agenda contributes vitality to classroom lectures and discussion periods. The debate between the older and newer definitions of Notre Dame is a continuing crosscurrent that, to varying degrees, affects each of the Colleges and the Law School.

As the requirements and standards have changed for the faculty, so, too, have the rewards they receive. The compensation for all levels— full, associate, and assistant professors as well as instructors—now ranks in the top twenty percent of all universities in the United States, according to a survey conducted by the American Association of University Professors. The average salary at all academic levels was ranked twenty-seventh nationally in 1984–85. Six years earlier, most of the salary rankings were only in the top sixty percent of schools surveyed.

As the standards for faculty members have become more strict, requirements for admission to the student body have also increased. On both the undergraduate and graduate levels, Notre Dame chooses students with greater selectivity than ever before. In recent years applicants to the freshman class have outnumbered admittances by almost three to one, and seventy-five percent of entering freshmen have attained cumulative grade averages of A or A− in high school as compared to thirty-three percent nationally. Incoming students —thirty-five percent of whom are ranked in one of the top five places in their graduating class— average a total of 1,200 points on the combined portions (verbal and mathematics) of the Scholastic Aptitude Test. This amount is 300 points above the national average. To a greater degree than at most other colleges and universities, students accepted by the University exhibit leadership potential—typically some thirty-five percent of the freshmen were presidents of their student bodies, classes, or a major school club — and they are active outside the classroom, with seventy percent involved in volunteer work or community service and over sixty percent engaged in varsity high school athletics. On the graduate level, admission for advanced study is also selective. One in three degree-seeking applicants is accepted by the Graduate School, while one in eleven gains admittance to the Law School.

Despite the more rigorous requirements for admissions, Notre Dame students have retained certain characteristics over the years. Historically, the student body has been composed of residents of all of the states and numerous foreign countries, as many as sixty-five in a given year. (In 1984, when Jose Napoleon Duarte was elected President of El Salvador, it marked the first time a Notre Dame graduate became a head of state. Duarte received a bachelor's degree in 1948 in engineering. Besides being national and international in composition, the students who come to Notre Dame to a remarkable degree stay at Notre Dame. The attrition rate of students who leave American colleges and universities in their first year is approximately thirty percent. At Notre Dame about one percent leaves for illness, academic, or disciplinary reasons. The success of the Freshman Year of Studies, inaugurated in 1962, is a principal factor in maintaining such a high level of retention. A broad curriculum of classes in the humanities, mathematics, natural sciences, and social sciences as well as elective classes allows students to receive a foundation in liberal education and to sample a variety of disciplines before declaring a major area for study. The Freshman Year office also sponsors counseling and advising services and tutorial programs to help in providing the transition to upper-level academic work. Emil T. Hofman has served as the Dean of the Freshman Year of Studies since 1971. A professor of chemistry known widely for his accomplishments as a teacher, he was named one of the nation's top ten professors in 1985 in competition sponsored by the Council for Advancement and Support of Education.

In addition to suggesting that the selection process yields students with a strong possibility of graduating, the high rate of retention (almost ninety-three percent from freshman through senior years) also indicates a sense of loyalty among the men and women who choose Notre Dame. In many cases, this loyalty carries over into their lives after they leave the campus. The Alumni Association, with its network of some 165 clubs throughout the country, provides a continuing link between the University and those who have graduated. Alumni activities vary from club to club, but several include continuing education programs involving guest speakers from Notre Dame as well as social occasions. The University also publishes *Notre Dame Magazine,* a quarterly with a circulation of 100,000, almost seventy percent being alumni. Formerly called *The Alumnus, Notre Dame Magazine* combines information about the University, its people, and its programs along with essays and articles by prominent writers about significant social, political, and religious issues. For over a decade, the magazine has consistently been selected as one of the ten best university periodicals in the country in judging sponsored by the Council for Advancement and Support of Education. Alumni allegiance extends beyond participating in local clubs and reading *Notre Dame Magazine.* In the percentage of alumni making financial contributions to their alma mater, Notre Dame usually ranks in the top five. Nearly fifty percent of the alumni donate to the University annually. The first annual fund drive at Notre Dame in 1942 brought in $35,000 from the alumni. In 1984 alumni gave $15.4 million to the University.

A portion of each year's contributions from alumni and others supports the University's libraries. Realizing that the quantity and quality of a university's library holdings are a significant factor in attracting and keeping faculty members and students (especially graduate students), administrators at Notre Dame have in recent years sought to improve the research collections on campus. The University has a library system of six specialized libraries—architecture, chemistry-physics, engineering, law, life sciences, and mathematics—as well as the main, thirteen-story Memorial Library, which upon completion in 1963 became the largest collegiate library building in the world. Today the University libraries have over 1.5 million volumes, and they subscribe to almost 13,000 current serials. In a survey conducted by the Association of Research Libraries in 1983–84, Notre Dame placed 101st in quantitative comparisons among American and Canadian universities and colleges. Despite this ranking, a source of concern for many scholars at the University, the Memorial Library has what are acknowledged to be strong collections in philosophy, theology, and medieval studies. To improve the holdings in specific areas, benefactors of the University have contributed endowments to support certain collections, such as the Miller Collection in Science, the Phalin Collection in English, the Ryan Collection in Fine Arts, the Abrams Collection in Hebrew and Jewish Studies, the Williams Collection in Ethics in Business and Society, the Eck Collection in Chemical Engineering, the Gibbons Collection in American History, and the Pilliod Collection in International Marketing and Finance. The Kresge Law Library, located in the Law School and recently enlarged to accommodate over 300,00 volumes, has major holdings in jurisprudence and in civil rights that draw scholars to the campus from this country and abroad.

Another collection of manuscripts and other materials that brings numerous researchers to Notre Dame is the University Archives, housed on one of the floors of the Memorial Library. In addition to being the repository for University records and the personal papers of several administrators and professors, the Archives have extensive holdings pertaining to the history and development of the Catholic Church in the United States. During the late nineteenth century, James F. Edwards, a Professor of History and University librarian, began collecting diocesan records and the papers of prominent clergymen and lay people. An estimated half-million items—from the bishops and archbishops of New Orleans, Cincinnati, Detroit, Hartford, and elsewhere as well as the papers of Orestes Brownson, Richard Henry Clarke, and James McMaster—document the growth of the American Catholic experience. In the current century, the Archives continued to build this collection, acquiring the papers of members of the Church hierarchy, Catholic organizations (like the Christian Family Movement), religious orders (the Xavarian Brothers), and religious press (such as *Commonweal* and *National Catholic Reporter*). For several years, beginning in 1961, the Archives has received from the Vatican microfilmed copies of the official documents of the Sacred Congregation for the Propagation of the Faith detailing the development of the Church in North America from 1662 until the early twentieth century. Formally called *Propaganda Fide*, this Vatican office had control over all missionary activities in the New World. The collection of microfilmed documents, the only one of its kind in the U.S., is widely used by researchers.

In recent years, the Archives has also acquired several significant collections of papers documenting the changing nature of religious life since the Second Vatican Council of the 1960s. Religious organizations and communities as well as prominent theologians have made Notre Dame the repository of their records.

Today, with an elaborate computer system that helps locate four million items in manuscript, microfilm, graphics, or tape format, the Notre Dame Archives is recognized by historians and other scholars as a leading center for primary research about Catholicism in America. In addition to the records and documents about the University and the Catholic Church, the Archives houses other notable collections, such as the papers of General William Tecumseh Sherman.

Besides the holdings of the Archives, the University of Notre Dame Press fosters research in American Catholic thought and history through its series "Notre Dame Studies in American Catholicism" and other books it publishes. Established in 1948 as an expression of the University's desire to advance scholarship, especially in the humanities and social sciences, the Press has become the world's largest Catholic university press, and it ranks in the top third of U.S. academic presses, based on number of books published. Averaging some thirty-five new titles annually (selected from more than 600 manuscripts and proposals each year), the Press currently has over 750 books in print. Professors at more than 200 colleges and universities in the United States use books from the Press in their classes.

In its early years, the Press received considerable recognition for the publications produced by Notre Dame's Committee on International Relations, under the direction of Stephen Kertesz. More recently, the Press has achieved publishing prominence for its volumes in philosophy, ethics, and Mexican-American studies. Publication of such books as Alasdair MacIntyre's *After Virtue*, considered a landmark study of moral philosophy, and Mario Barrera's *Race and Class in the Southwest*, winner of the American Political Science Association's Ethnic and Pluralism Award in 1980, gave additional stature to the Press. In addition, the work of leading theologians—Nicholas Lash, Charles Curran, John S. Dunne, Thomas O'Meara, Stanley Hauerwas, and many others—regularly appears from the Press, strengthening its contribution to religious understanding. Moreover, noted Jewish writer Elie Wiesel, honored for his literature about the Holocaust, is the author of two Press books—*Five Biblical Portraits* and *Four Hasidic Masters and Their Struggle Against Melancholy*. Besides publishing contemporary theological scholars, the Press also reprints classic works of Catholic thought by St. Thomas Aquinas, St. Anselm, John Henry Cardinal Newman, Etienne Gilson, and Jacques Maritain.

In addition to the recognition it receives in philosophy, theology, and Mexican-American studies, the Press over the years has developed and maintained a strong list of books in political theory, economics, and sociology. Several works in these fields (as well as others) have been translated into foreign languages for editions printed outside the United States. Currently almost a third of all of the books issued by the Press each year appear in Spanish, German, French, or Japanese. British publishers also frequently work with the Press for co-publication of books in the United Kingdom.

The Notre Dame Press extends the intellectual vitality of the University and contributes to the spirit of free inquiry that Notre Dame seeks to engender. For example, some books critical of the Church or its hierarchy (like *Power and Authority in the Catholic Church: Cardinal Cody in Chicago*) have themselves been the object of criticism from Catholic readers displeased with probing treatments of religious subjects. However, the Press, which uses faculty members as authors, manuscript referees, and members of the Editorial Board, adds a tangible dimension to the University's commitment to serious scholarship. Moreover, the adoption of Press books as texts has considerable impact in classrooms across the country. The creation of the Alumni Book Club in 1980 also enables the Press to participate in a program of continuing education for former students.

Although several books appeared sporadically before 1948 under the auspices of the University, the founding of the Notre Dame Press provided institutional support for the regular publication of noteworthy studies in several fields. The establishment of the Press occurred during the presidency of Rev. John J. Cavanaugh, C.S.C., who served from 1946–52. Credited with bringing Notre Dame into the modern era, Father Cavanaugh built much of the foundation for intellectual development that has taken place since Father Hesburgh succeeded him in 1952. In a memorable speech delivered in Washington, D.C., in 1957, Father Cavanaugh said: "Even casual observation of the daily newspapers and the weekly news magazines leads a Catholic to ask, where are the Catholic Salks, Oppenheimers, Einsteins?" During his tenure as president and subsequently as director of the Notre Dame Foundation, he tried to provide human answers to that question. Among his accomplishments as president, he enlarged the Graduate School by over 450 percent, and he authorized the establishment of the Institute of Medieval Studies, the germfree Laboratories of Bacteriology at the University of Notre Dame (LOBUND), the Committee on International Relations, and the Natural Law Institute. In a structural reorganization reminiscent of "the Burns Revolution" of the early 1920s, Father Cavanaugh created four distinct vice presidencies—academic affairs, business affairs, student affairs, and public relations and development—to direct the principal areas of University administration. Seeking, in his words, "to break Notre Dame out of the monastic mentality," he was particularly concerned with finding sources of financial support necessary to improve the intellectual life of campus through, in particular, the hiring of distinguished professors, offering scholarships to worthy students, and expanding research facilities and resources. In 1947 he established the Notre Dame Foundation, the first formal and continuing fund-raising program in the University's history. After leaving the presidency, while directing the Foundation, he helped Notre Dame to develop as he desired it would.

The Cavanaugh years of dreaming and building were a prelude to the Hesburgh years and to the Notre Dame of today. Physically, over thirty new buildings symbolize the growth that has taken place on campus since Father Hesburgh took office. Intellectually, the pursuit of excellence now encompasses all of the academic areas in which the University is involved. A key factor in Notre Dame's recent development has been its ability to secure financial resources to support educational and scholarly endeavors. "In the last thirty years, we have become far more conscious of the absolute necessity of fund-raising," states Rev. Edmund P. Joyce, C.S.C., who has served as Executive Vice President and Treasurer of the University since 1952. "If we're not able to do this both now and in the future, we will die. Any private university—if it's not able to raise a lot of money from its alumni, friends, corporations, foundations, and almost anybody that has money—is going to wither on the vine. This is our life line, and we all recognize how terribly important it is to us."

Father Joyce, who has worked closely with both Father Cavanaugh and Father Hesburgh on all financial matters related to the University, recalls a ten-year campaign to raise $25 million between 1948 and 1958 "sounded astronomical" when it was first proposed. That effort, however, was successful, and it was the beginning of what Notre Dame would continue to do from the 1950s to the present day. Father Joyce notes that the University received a grant for $3 million from the Ford Foundation in 1957 for its academic programs. "That was the biggest windfall we had ever gotten from anybody," says Father Joyce.

"But the most important thing that ever happened to Notre Dame to my mind and what was really responsible for us skyrocketing in every respect was another program of Ford. They came back to us in 1960 and said: 'We have selected six schools in this nation that we think are capable of moving up to the very top ranks. What we want to do is give you $6 million in cash with the proviso that you raise $12 million in cash during a three-year period.' Pledges wouldn't count. We had to have $12 million in cash within 36 months. At that time we were up to where we were raising in total gifts about $1.5 million a year. This meant we were going to have to move that up to $4 million a year. We were going to have to do it overnight. This was an inspired program by Ford for this reason: This forced a university that was willing to use the energy to get behind something like this to really lift its sights way above anything we had thought of previously."

That campaign was successful, allowing the University (among other things) to build the Memorial Library. At the end of the three-year period, the Ford Foundation offered to repeat this challenge grant program for Notre Dame. "We were successful again," comments Father Joyce. "That raised another $18 million, and that's a total of $36 million in six years. The money was important; it enabled us to do many things academically. But the big thing was it showed what could be done with this kind of all-out effort." Two more capital campaigns between 1966 and 1981 raised $243 million.

Father Joyce credits the fund-raising activities with allowing Notre Dame to make numerous academic advances across the University. He also sees their impact in the lives of many students. "The academic entity is an insatiable animal," he observes. "If we had twice what we have now, we could use it almost overnight. It's a balancing act and always has been. But I think the fact that we have been as successful as we have been in fund-raising has enabled us to grow without putting undue pressure on tuition. As a matter of fact, our tuition — compared to the Ivy League schools with whom we're competing in many respects — is really much lower. That's a matter of some satisfaction to me. There are others who say we ought to be charging the same thing they are, but I don't believe that. We're not dealing with a very wealthy constituency in our student body. About seventy percent of them get some kind of financial aid, and that's a pretty good indication that the need is there."

Writing about Father Sorin and the dream he had for Notre Dame, Father Hesburgh once noted: "The French priest aimed to build a kind of institution that had eluded the fledgling American civilization and that, fourteen decades later, eludes it still. He envisoned an institution of the first rank that explored great issues within the context of the Catholic faith, a place where leading scholars discuss moral and ethical issues — in short, a great Catholic university." Building a great Catholic university (in fulfillment of the founder's dream) is the driving force and preoccupation of Father Hesburgh's presidency. Although the objective is clearly defined and frequently articulated, obstacles — in their way as threatening as the fire of 1879 — have been, and remain, formidable.

Many years ago, George Bernard Shaw remarked that "a Catholic university is a contradiction in terms." This tart aphorism represents a cast of mind that, to varying degrees, has existed in this country and abroad throughout the past two centuries. Underlying this thinking is the idea that Church authority and teaching conflict with the spirit of free and open inquiry that a university seeks to achieve in any scholarly endeavor. In "Notre Dame: Our First GREAT Catholic University?," a 1967 cover story in *Harper's* magazine, Peter Schrag posed some of the fundamental questions that Shaw's satiric jab implied: "Can a university be 'free' and Catholic at the same time? Can it be open to all points of view, all modes of inquiry, without jeopardizing its Catholicism? Doesn't the presumption of some sort of Catholic wisdom foreclose the possibility of giving all other views equal time?"

During the past three decades, and particularly since the early 1970s, Notre Dame has been coming to terms with these issues, attempting to resolve such questions by maintaining the delicate balance between its commitment to intellectual accomplishment and to spiritual principles. Achieving this equilibrium involves a considerable amount of time and the systematic integration of human knowledge, religious faith, and philosophical understanding into a coherent whole. The effort does not only embrace Father Sorin's dream but also the ideal of a Catholic university envisioned by John Henry Cardinal Newman: "I wish the intellect to range with the utmost freedom, and religion to enjoy an equal freedom; but what I am stipulating is that they should be found in one and the same place, and exemplified in the same persons. . . . I want the intellectual layman to be religious, and the devout ecclesiastic to be intellectual."

The Notre Dame of today is vastly different from what it once was. The school that Father Sorin founded in an untamed area of Northern Indiana and that focused almost entirely on instruction — everything from the primary grades to the collegiate level — has matured into a true university concerned not only with teaching but with the discovery of new knowledge and the communication of that knowledge through research and published scholarship. Despite the many changes over the years, traditions that developed in the past continue to contribute to the University's ethos and vitality in the present. In the words of a group of outside academics and administrators asked to evaluate the University in 1984 for the North Central Association, "there is a certain excitement at Notre Dame at this time. It is the excitement of being part of an institution which not only makes promises about excellence, but seems capable of mastering the will and the resources . . . to enable the realization of these promises."

16  *Yesterday and Today*

*Stepan Chemistry Hall*

## PROFILE

## REV. THEODORE M. HESBURGH, C.S.C.

## UNIVERSITY PRESIDENT

AT THE UNIVERSITY CELEBRATION in 1977 honoring Rev. Theodore M. Hesburgh, C.S.C., for his first twenty-five years as the school's President, Thomas Stritch, a professor at Notre Dame since 1935, delivered remarks on behalf of the faculty. Recalling the earliest statements Father Hesburgh made when he assumed the Presidency in 1952, Stritch said: "The call to excellence he sounded then was a brave and courageous call, and few could have given it much chance of success. But it worked, and it worked, I think, largely because Father Hesburgh made it work by working himself to become a shining exemplar of all he meant. His own reputation grew nationally with that of Notre Dame; they became mirrors of one another."

During the years since 1977, the reputations of Father Hesburgh and Notre Dame have continued to grow, increasingly so in the international realm. The mirrors—and the reflections they cast—have taken on new dimensions. As Father Hesburgh prepares to leave the Presidency in May of 1987, he looks back on the last thirty-five years with a sense of both satisfaction and anticipation. In his view, what has been accomplished in the past is a prelude to a future of even greater possibility.

Father Hesburgh became President at the age of thirty-five, after serving three years as Executive Vice President in the administration of Rev. John J. Cavanaugh, C.S.C. Father Hesburgh credits Father Cavanaugh's six years in the Presidency as being the time when Notre Dame began to take the goal of University-wide academic excellence seriously. At the outset of his Presidency, Father Hesburgh realized that how Notre Dame was perceived in the educational community and by the public at-large was crucial to future success in its teaching, research, and service programs. "I knew that we had to change the image of the place from what was sometimes called a 'football factory' to an academic image," he says.

Father Hesburgh vividly remembers one of his first series of press conferences as President. "The first trip I made to the West coast, out of Los Angeles and north to Seattle and Vancouver, every single press conference we had was totally populated by sports writers. I asked if they wanted to talk about education. When they said 'no,' I said, 'Well, then this news conference is over.' I figured that would never happen again, and it never has. From that time on, I said we're going to talk about education. I'm not going to talk about football. I have never professionally talked about football or any other kind of athletics. Not that I don't think they're important. They are. It's important that they be very good. Everything we do we ought to do well, but it shouldn't be the central focus of the place, and isn't."

Improving the academic programs throughout the University became the principal concern of Father Hesburgh and Rev. Edmund P. Joyce, C.S.C., Executive Vice President and Treasurer of Notre Dame since 1952. Father Hesburgh recalls that he and Father Joyce, the chief financial officer, faced three distinct yet related problems in their efforts to have the University more highly regarded as an educational institution. "The first problem was we had a miserable operating budget of under $10 million," notes Father Hesburgh. "That needed to be increased about twenty times if we were going to have decent salaries and decent living conditions. That was the first big challenge: How to generate enough money from tuition and from other sources to be able to grow? On top of that, there was a second problem that we needed about a quarter of a billion dollars worth of buildings. We needed twice as many buildings, square-foot capacity, than we had at that time, mostly academic buildings but many others as well. The third thing was we had an almost non-existent endowment. The endowment began here in 1920 and took fourteen years to get to

$5 million, and it took another seven years to get to $10 million, which is about where we got in. That needed to be greatly increased for the long range. That was the third problem, because we had to do the other two first. In fact, we had to do them all together, but we mainly put the emphasis on enlarging the academic budget and getting salaries up, on the one hand, and getting the facilities into place, on the other. What was left went into endowment.

"The net of it was that the under $10 million operating budget went to $167 million in 1985–86, and the buildings were built and paid for. There is almost no debt on the University, except a little long-range debt, forty years at three percent, which I consider a gift. And the third priority, the endowment, went from under $10 million to the vicinity of $330 to $340 million today, depending on where the market is."

Solving these three major problems has dramatically changed Notre Dame during the past thirty-five years, with the changes enhancing the University's academic stature in this country and abroad. Comparing Notre Dame of 1952 to the University today, Father Hesburgh identifies several factors as contributing to this new standing. "First of all, when I came here we had a library that was jam packed with 250,000 books. You couldn't get more in there for love or money. Today we have a library that has a capacity of 3 million books, and it's better than half full. There are about 1.6 million volumes, plus a million items in microfilm or microfiche, including extensive materials from Europe's first public library, Milan's Ambrosiana. We had good students in those days, but we have superb students today; seventy percent of our incoming freshmen are in the top ten percent of their graduating classes. Today we have twice as many students and three times as many faculty, which means the faculty-student ratio has improved a great deal. Faculty were being paid at the bottom of the scale then nationally. Now they are at the very top of the scale — the top fifteen or twenty out of 3,000 schools. Research then was almost non-existent. We did over $20 million in 1984–85, with virtually all of it coming with support from the outside; half our proposals are funded. Today's endowment reflects two things I am very proud of. First, we had no endowed professors in 1952. We have over sixty fully endowed today, with twenty more partially endowed. We'll have twenty more to add to that very soon. Before I leave, we hope to have one hundred fully endowed. Second, we had $100,000 endowed in scholarship money then. We have over $50 million today, with $6 or $7 million for minorities. I hope to have more than $100 million before I get out of here."

Besides the growth in academic stature, Father Hesburgh finds a different attitude among students today, and he sees Notre Dame graduates becoming more involved in public service and significant leadership roles than ever before. "There's a whole spirit today. I don't know how many students back in 1952 were working for the less fortunate. But if there were any doing so, I didn't know about them. Today about a third of our student body is working for the less fortunate, and about ten percent of our graduates are going into such work for a year or two of their lives after they graduate. On top of that we have over 3,000 graduates today working in higher education, including about 35 presidents of colleges or universities. We have hundreds of priests and sisters and dozens of bishops who have been educated here. We have an astronaut; we have generals and admirals; we have over 800 CEO's or senior officers of corporations large and small across the land. We have thousands of lawyers (and a growing number of federal judges), as well as thousands of medical doctors. One of them, James E. Muller, was a cofounder of the International Physicians for Prevention of Nuclear War, which won the 1985 Nobel Peace Prize.

"I can remember in those days people used to say: 'Who are your outstanding graduates?' One would cough and say, 'Well, there is Frank Walker, who was Postmaster General.' Then one might cough again and, if he were fairly liberal, say: 'George Shuster, President of Hunter College.' Then it would stop about there. Knute Rockne might be mentioned or something of that sort, but I can recall very well it was not easy in those days coming up with a distinguished list. Today, we are one of a handful of universities with a statistically significant number of undergraduate alumni in *Who's Who in America*. Outside America, we have the president of a country, Jose Napoleon Duarte, President of El Salvador."

Father Hesburgh's thirty-five years in office surpass by approximately thirty years the average tenure of university presidents today, and they constitute a record for the fifteen Holy Cross priests who have led Notre Dame since its founding in 1842. (Rev. Edward Sorin, the school's founder, was president from 1842 until 1865, with his term of twenty-three years ranking second in length of time.) Looking back at his tenure, Father Hesburgh is particularly proud of two changes that have occurred at the University: the transfer of governance from the Congregation of the Holy Cross to a predominantly lay Board of Trustees in 1967 and the admission of women to the undergraduate program in 1972. "I think those two changes will be seen as substantial enhancements of the quality of life and of academic excellence at the University."

Recalling the early years and what he imagined Notre Dame might become, Father Hesburgh says without any hesitation: "It's probably better than I envisioned it might be. We've been very, very fortunate. We've had generous benefactors and first-rate leadership. During this long time I've been President, there have been four or five vice presidents in every one of the sectors, and they have all served with distinction. Some of them burned out by giving all they had. Many peo-

*Steeple of Sacred Heart Church*

ple have been involved in the march forward. You tend to get a lot of the credit if you are up at the head of the procession. The fact is that your achievement rests on the efforts of others."

Reflecting on his administrative experience, Father Hesburgh emphasizes that leadership involves articulating a vision and getting others to own it as their own, especially colleagues. "The secret is really to get the very best people you can get, even if they are better than you are and to get them in the right slot. But once you get them appointed to that slot and get their agreement to do the work, then leave them alone. Don't try to second-guess them. Don't try to say who is going to be their assistant and who is going to work with them. That's their problem. I always told them: 'You do your work, and I'll do mine. Whatever you do, you are going to get the credit for it, and whatever you do I'll back you on it. Unless you make an absolute mess of it, I'm with you all the way.'

"As a result, people know that they have their own bailiwick that they are going to run themselves. They are going to pick their people, and they are going to have a reasonable freedom to have their own particular vision within the bigger vision. My responsibility is to have the overall vision, but others have to have goals, too, for a wide variety of things from academics to athletics; to maintaining buildings; to providing security; to making books available; or to having a computing system that works. Administrators who don't make it are fussy administrators who are constantly sticking their noses into other people's business and telling them how to do things. A much better system is to get people who know much more about a specific area than you do and let them go. Again, you also have to make sure that if something good happens they get the credit for it. You can get an awfully lot done if you don't care who gets credit for it. My job, I think, is to see that the person who did it gets the credit for it."

Although Father Hesburgh comments that "it would take me twenty minutes to name all the people that have been an integral and important part of advancing the vision of a great Catholic university," he singles out Father Joyce for special praise. Not only has Father Joyce been responsible for all of the financial matters relating to Notre Dame, he has also served as chairman of the Faculty Board in Control of Athletics and of the University Building Committee. Of his colleague and friend, Father Hesburgh comments, "He and I are quite different. He is very good with numbers, and I'm better with words. He knows finances. I think of other things and hardly ever think of finances directly. I spend money, and he has to raise and conserve it and make sure the balance sheet comes out even at the end of the year. Despite some tough times in the national economy, we have had only one year in the red in thirty-three years. I give him the credit for it because he is in charge of the budget. He has brought to Notre Dame everything that I couldn't bring to it. I include our national reputation for an athletic program with integrity. What he does often is kind of invisible, while I'm always giving the speeches and getting my picture taken and being visible. Whatever was accomplished during the last thirty-three or thirty-four years, Ned Joyce deserves credit for a half share of any praise."

Besides his position at Notre Dame and his other work related to higher education, Father Hesburgh has become nationally and internationally known for his service to the government, the Catholic Church, and several institutions in the private sector. Since he was named to the National Science Board in 1954 by President Dwight Eisenhower, Father Hesburgh has held fourteen Presidential appointments. He was a charter member of the U.S. Commission on Civil Rights, created in 1957, and he served as Chairman of the Commission from 1969 to 1972. He was, to use his word, "fired" from this post by President Richard Nixon for his criticism of the Nixon Administration's civil rights record. In 1974 President Gerald Ford appointed Father Hesburgh to be a member of the Presidential Clemency Board, which decided how to deal with the civilians and military personnel accused of violating civilian or military law during the Vietnam War. From 1977 through 1979, Father Hesburgh held the rank of U.S. Ambassador, the first priest to serve in a formal diplomatic role for the American government. The rank was a result of Notre Dame's president being appointed by President Carter to lead an eighty-person delegation to a 1979 United Nations Conference on Science and Technology for Development in Vienna. During the last two years of the Carter Administration, Father Hesburgh was the Chairman of the U.S. Select Commission on Immigration and Refugee Policy. The Commission, composed of four cabinet members, eight members of Congress, and four other people appointed by the President, advocated new legislation for immigration reform. In 1982 President Ronald Reagan named Father Hesburgh to be a member of the U.S. Official Observer Team for the strife-torn El Salvador Elections. The memory he carries away from that experience is not helicoptering between rural villages to check balloting, but the chance meeting of a funeral cortege carrying a young victim of the country's civil war to burial. The procession lacked a priest. Father Hesburgh comforted the mother of the deceased, blessed the casket in Spanish, and gave the mother a rosary. The incident was a reminder that he thinks of himself, first and foremost, as a priest.

In one capacity or another, Father Hesburgh has served every President since Eisenhower. During the past thirty years, he has also received appointments from four Popes. From 1956 until 1970, at the request of Pius XII, John XXIII, and Paul VI, Father Hesburgh was the permanent Vatican representative to the International Atomic Energy Agency in Vienna. In 1972 Paul VI asked Father Hesburgh to create an Ecumenical Institute for Advanced Theological Studies in Jerusalem. He serves as Chairman of the Institute's Academic Council, which continues its work under the auspices of the University. John Paul II named Father Hesburgh to the Pontifical Council for Culture in 1983.

In addition to his service to the government and to the Church, Father Hesburgh has also been actively involved in organizations in the private sector. He was appointed to the Board of Trustees of the Overseas Development Council in 1971. He chaired the Council, which supports efforts to help people of the underdeveloped world, from 1971 until 1982. In 1979–80 he was Co-Chairman of the Cambodian Crisis Committee, a group which raised $70 million to avert mass starvation in Cambodia. Father Hesburgh was the first priest to be named a trustee of the Rockefeller Foundation. He was on the Board of Trustees from 1961 until 1982, the last six years as its Chairman. He was also the first priest to serve on the Board of Directors of the Chase Manhattan Bank.

In the realm of higher education, Father Hesburgh has been the President of the International Federation of Catholic Universities and of the Association of American Colleges. As President of the International Federation of Catholic Universities from 1963 to 1970, he led a movement to redefine the nature and mission of the contemporary Catholic university in the world. He has served on the boards of trustees of several other education-related organizations, including the Carnegie Commission on the Future of Higher Education and the Institute of International Education. He is currently the Chairman of the Business-Higher Education Forum (BHEF) of the American Council on Education. BHEF brings together college and university presidents with the chief executive officers of some of the nation's largest corporations.

Of all of his activities outside the University, Father Hesburgh believes his experience on the Commission on Civil Rights was the most challenging and most rewarding. "We literally changed the face of the nation," he explains. "We took a three-hundred-year-old geographical apartheid and eliminated it overnight in 1964 with the Omnibus Civil Rights Act. Then we changed for all times voting patterns, when six million blacks were given the vote in 1965. With the entry of blacks into the state schools in the South; with the dismantling of legally mandated separate education for all black youngsters in the South; with the opening up of equal job opportunity; with a dramatic change in the all-white administration of justice; with the total elimination of de jure prejudice—that had to be the high-point of my federal service."

In the private sector, Father Hesburgh views his years on the Rockefeller Foundation as ones of landmark significance for agriculture and education in developing countries. "We sponsored the Green Revolution that saw six times as much food produced on the same land and by the same farmers. World hunger lingers as a massive problem, but it would be a lot worse without the Green Revolution. We had more ships on the sea bringing food to India during Lyndon Johnson's Presidency than were going across the English Channel on D-Day. Today, India is exporting food because of the Green Revolution. The same would be true of many other countries in the

Orient. We also spurred education throughout the Third World through a $150 million program. Some of the universities have not developed as quickly as we would have liked, but at least that was a beginning."

Father Hesburgh says he has refused ten invitations of outside appointments for each one he has accepted. For example, he turned down the chance to be Administrator of NASA as the Apollo Program to the moon was being launched under President Johnson, and he declined an offer of President Nixon to become Director of the War on Poverty Program. Overtures to run for the Vice Presidency and for the Senate from his native state of New York were also turned aside. "I always refused to do something unless I could do it wholeheartedly as a priest and as a person in higher education. I felt those were my two tasks in life, and I didn't want to get distracted."

Despite the diversity of his various activities, Father Hesburgh sees a unifying pattern to all of them. As a priest-educator, he wants "to see the Kingdom of God spread throughout the world. I think the Kingdom of God curiously in our age may spread faster through education and development activities than through other activities." In addition, Father Hesburgh believes that his outside endeavors contributed much to his work as President of the University, notably in such areas as science, human rights, and developmental concerns. "Those outside experiences are all re-enforcing; you establish a national, in fact, a worldwide network. A lot of the work overlapped, intensifying my own education and giving me ideas about intellectual inquiries Notre Dame ought to foster. Human rights overlap with world development; that overlaps with food problems around the world, the Green Revolution; that overlaps with university development of the Third World, and so on."

His participation in off-campus activities also enriched the resources for research at Notre Dame. The papers, documents, and books related to his public, private, and religious service have been given to the University for use by scholars. As a result of his tenures on the Commission on Civil Rights and on the Select Commission on Immigration and Refugee Policy, Notre Dame has the most comprehensive archives on civil rights and immigration in the United States.

Since the early 1980s, Father Hesburgh has markedly reduced his activities outside the University. He is devoting as much time as possible to trying to make plain "the nuclear threat to humanity." Although interested in the subject for decades, he became alarmed in 1981 about the possibilities and consequences of using nuclear weapons. "It suddenly struck me—I knew it all the time, but there is a difference between knowing something and being struck by it—that everything else that I've been working on all my life would literally be wiped out by a nuclear attack. It would be the end of everything. It would be the end of all the great institutions, such as the universities, governments, libraries, and families. Everything would be gone. Our future would be gone and with it everybody else's future—the future's future, if you will. If we don't solve this problem, the rest of our problems simply become irrelevant. Without human beings you don't even have the concept of problem."

In his work on the nuclear dilemma, Father Hesburgh has devoted much of his time to bringing together representatives of the world's religions and noted scientists from the five major nuclear powers including the United States and the Soviet Union. It is an attempt to bring together two groups at odds since Galileo, but Father Hesburgh is unbothered. "Scientists fashioned the nuclear monster, and they bring that credibility to the discourse. Religious leaders have a moral standpoint. To facilitate the conversation we began by setting up a program for peace studies in Jerusalem, where we can join it to the Ecumenical Institute. More recently, with Joan Kroc's generous help, we set up an Institute for International Peace Studies at Notre Dame."

Father Hesburgh believes that his past work inside and outside the University prepared him to become so involved in seeking peace, an endeavor he plans to pursue when he leaves the Presidency. As with earlier activities, he views this effort as being part of his mission both as a priest and as an educator. He, however, considers his vocation to the priesthood—after theological studies in Rome he was ordained in Sacred Heart Church at Notre Dame in 1943—as the stimulus that has driven him to lead such a busy life. "I can't remember a time when I didn't have about ten concurrent jobs," he says. Despite all he has done and continues to do, he is above all a priest. "I offered Mass every morning or at night or whenever I could do it when I had time. When you're traveling you can't always control your time, but I said Mass every day except once, when I was stuck in a hospital. Secondly, I said my breviary every day. I thought it was a bit of a drag when it was said in Latin, but now that it's in English, I find it a delight. I've also probably said the rosary almost every day. I've never passed up a chance to be a priest and anything that might involve. It often involved counseling, or talking to people, or helping people in the unique way that you can as a priest, sacramentally or otherwise. I think that's the common thread that kept me going, and I simply cannot view my life apart from being a priest, whether it's my past life or my future life. I don't really want to be anything else. There were a couple of times that I could have been a bishop, but I felt at the time what I was doing and the demands that had to be met couldn't be met if I didn't keep at them, so I didn't think that was much of a temptation. I've been far enough on the fringes at times, probably that temptation has been removed permanently from my life."

Even with the crowded schedule he has kept since joining the Notre Dame faculty in 1945 as an Assistant Professor of Religion—he received his doctorate in sacred theology from the Catholic University of America earlier that year—Father Hesburgh has written several monographs and books. His most recent books include *The Humane Imperative: A Challenge for the Year 2000*, published by the Yale University Press, and *The Hesburgh Papers: Higher Values in Higher Education*, published by Andrews and McMeel.

Father Hesburgh's achievements inside and outside of education have brought considerable recognition to him and to Notre Dame. More than one hundred institutions of higher learning in this country and abroad have awarded him honorary degrees, the most ever received by one person. In 1964 President Johnson bestowed on him the Medal of Freedom, the nation's highest civilian honor. He received the Meikeljohn Award from the American Association of University Professors in 1970, an honor for upholding academic freedom. In 1982 he won the Jefferson Award given by the Council for Advancement and Support of Education. More than fifty different national and international organizations have given him special awards.

Looking to the future and his retirement from the Presidency of the University, Father Hesburgh says he plans to stay away from the campus for a year to give his successor "a free track" in beginning his administration. After that year, he will return to become what he calls "a utility outfielder" on behalf of the school. "Notre Dame has been my whole life, and I'm certainly willing to do anything I can do. But I don't want any job that has any line authority going with it. I don't want a position or a title, except that I suppose that academic tradition would anoint me President Emeritus. I don't want anybody sitting where I'm sitting now thinking he's got to use me, or that I'm an anchor around his neck, or that I'm a rival of his in some way."

Throughout his career as President of Notre Dame, an abiding vision has animated Father Hesburgh's leadership. That vision—of creating a great Catholic university—is much closer to realization today than in 1952. How Father Hesburgh describes that vision and what it encompasses will remain pertinent in the years ahead: "I've always said without equivocation that I want it to be a great university that is also a great Catholic university. That's a dual goal. It's much easier to be a great university than to be a great Catholic university. It's no great secret how to become a great university, if you can get the resources for it. You have to have an intellectually curious student body, an intellectually competent faculty, and classrooms, laboratories, museums, and libraries where they can get together. But a great Catholic university goes beyond that. We need people who have a commitment to the philosophical and theological implications of all the great questions of our times. We need people who inquire about transcendentals and not just temporary things. We need people who are concerned with the moral and the spiritual as well as the intellectual formation of students. You have to have people who can speak to values and whose life professes them. Such teachers are rare, and that is why becoming a great university is easy compared to becoming a great Catholic university."

26  *Yesterday and Today*

*Formal opening of the academic year*

Yesterday and Today 27

PROFILE

TIMOTHY O'MEARA

UNIVERSITY PROVOST

SINCE COMING TO NOTRE DAME in 1962, Timothy O'Meara has played an increasingly important part in the University's efforts of attaining academic excellence and maintaining its Catholic character. In quite specific ways, modern mathematics and contemporary Notre Dame are different because of him. But contemplating the past takes up little of O'Meara's time. He's more concerned with the present and in deciding how he can translate new ideas into realities. "The concept that Notre Dame should be a truly excellent university is well established," O'Meara says. "We are now making that happen."

A South African by birth who became a naturalized American in 1977, O'Meara is the Howard J. Kenna, C.S.C., Professor of Mathematics and the University's Provost. Named to the Kenna Chair in 1976, he became one of the first holders of an endowed professorship at Notre Dame. He was appointed Provost in 1978. As Provost, he has responsibility under the President for the administration, coordination, and development of all academic activities and functions of the University.

O'Meara came to Notre Dame as a full professor after several years as a faculty member at Princeton University. While at Princeton, from which he received his doctorate in 1953, he also spent three semesters as a member of the Institute for Advanced Study. O'Meara notes that "Father Hesburgh's unequivocal commitment to excellence" and "the Catholic ethos of the University" were principal reasons for his coming to Notre Dame. From his experience as a professor, provost, and parent of five Notre Dame graduates, he believes that the religious dimension should not only be preserved but strengthened in years to come.

"We have to build on three separate foundations," O'Meara states. "Undergraduate education is the first; graduate and professional education with research and scholarship is the second; and the third is the Catholic character of the institution. All of these have to continue to evolve, and they all have to interact with each other. The one that will be most difficult to preserve, in the light of what has happened at other institutions with religious origins, is the Catholic dimension."

Always the mathematician, O'Meara describes these three fundamental components by using a geometrical metaphor. He sees them as a triangle with equal sides. As the sides intersect, they influence each other in the process. "On the undergraduate level our Catholic character clearly and obviously is of influence in the formation of students. But the Catholic dimension of the University must also make us distinctive on the graduate-professional research level. As a university we have a role to play in influencing the professions and in the advancement of knowledge. As a Catholic university we have an additional role to play—that of influencing our society through our Catholic values. Our voice must be heard on ethical and moral questions. Within the church we must participate in and contribute to the development and evolution of Catholic thought. Our perceptions and ideas are always expanding through research. We all know that this is true of science. It is true of knowledge. It is also true of theology. Yesterday's theology of the just war will not serve tomorrow's threat of nuclear annihilation."

O'Meara completes his sketch of the Notre Dame triangle by explaining the links between the two levels of instruction at the University: "I am a strong believer in the ideal of having the kind of faculty in which every individual professor excels as a teacher of undergraduates, as a teacher of graduate students, and as a scholar and researcher," he says. "In this way the excitement that comes from exploration and discovery in research can be transmitted to the next generation in the classroom."

Assessing the development of Notre Dame, O'Meara views the years since the Second World War as being the most important in solidifying and deepening the three foundations. He is characteristically candid in offering his analysis: "When the University was founded in 1842, it was called the University of Notre Dame. But it was a university in name alone. During the Hesburgh era, there has been a transition to a university in fact as well as in name. A true university has a balance between undergraduate education and advanced studies—by advanced studies I mean graduate and professional education as well as research and scholarship. Our history, of course, is that we provide an excellent undergraduate education. That must not suffer in the transition, rather it must be enhanced. There are some schools where the emphasis is so heavily on the side of research that undergraduate education is weakened in the process. That must not happen at Notre Dame."

O'Meara recognizes that some important advances in knowledge occurred as a result of research conducted at Notre Dame before the 1950s. He cites work in aerodynamics and also the basic research that led to the discovery of synthetic rubber as examples of notable accomplishments. These discoveries, however, happened sporadically.

"Since the Second World War, the premise has been that research must be done systematically and integrated into the life of the University," O'Meara states. "What has happened is that we are now indeed a real University. We provide, in my opinion, an excellent undergraduate education to excellent students. The nature of our involvement on the graduate level and in the area of research varies from department to department. Some departments are very strong. Just to pick one doctoral program from each College, I would say that Chemical Engineering is very strong on the doctoral level in Engineering; Philosophy in Arts and Letters; and Mathematics in Science. In Business Administration, we still don't have a doctoral program, but we anticipate that we will in the 1990s. In the meantime we are moving forward with the development of MBA programs of different types. The last thirty or forty years have been a period of remarkable transition. Our goal now is to make the University as strong across the board on the advanced level as it is on the undergraduate level. That is what I see as our most immediate challenge." Returning to his metaphor of the triangle, O'Meara sees this challenge as being inextricably connected to the Catholic heritage and commitment of the University.

O'Meara remembers that back in the early 1960s several academicians looked askance at him for wanting to join the faculty of a Catholic university. He does not think the same reaction would occur today. In fact, for many professors of all faiths on both junior and senior levels the Catholic character of the school is proving to be a major attraction; it is a primary reason for being at Notre Dame.

According to O'Meara, preserving the religious dimension of the University and, in his words, "not being ashamed to say it," has helped define Notre Dame in the minds of the academic community as well as the public at large. "Some Catholic schools in adapting to what they thought would be the best way to obtain resources from public agencies have tried to neutralize or camouflage their heritage. We have not. Interestingly enough, the very fact that we have maintained our self-confidence in what we are has proved to be a positive factor in enabling us to find the resources we need."

In discussing the significance of Catholicism at Notre Dame, O'Meara is positive in articulating the role which those who are not Catholic play in the intellectual and spiritual life of the University. "I do not believe that the faculty at Notre Dame should consist only of people who are professed Catholics. That is too narrow an idea of a University. Nor, to take the other extreme, do I believe that we would have a Catholic university if there were no Catholics on the faculty. We must be ecumenical in spirit while maintaining a predominant Catholic presence on the faculty. All of us should be concerned with the centrality of values in education. Ultimately it is not just what we profess that is important, but also what we do."

The importance of the University's religious nature and commitment is a subject that O'Meara frequently addresses when he speaks to students, professors, alumni, and others. For instance, in "Illumination and Freedom in a Catholic University," the homily he delivered in Sacred Heart Church to open the 1985–86 academic year, O'Meara noted: "Recently at a Washington meeting on education for values I was struck by how the word 'values' has been so neutralized out of deference to pluralism that it has lost its meaning. Heaven knows, these days a course on the value of money could be construed as a course on education for values! Use of the word 'virtue,' on the other hand, is as popular as the plague. We really have to renew our meanings of virtue, morality, ethics, and character, and, quite frankly, we have to recognize that the values of the Scriptures cannot be taught unless they are exemplified in the lives of those who teach them."

O'Meara is dedicated to the ideal of a university-wide academic community of teacher-scholars who are able to balance classroom instruction with published research and participation in their disciplines or professions. According to O'Meara, having a "single faculty" will help Notre Dame retain its heritage of effective undergraduate education and lead to greater recognition and respect in the scholarly world as well as the society at large.

"My primary concern is the quality of the faculty," says O'Meara. "As provost, I'm actively involved in the decision-making process for new appointments as well as for promotion and tenure. Yes, we're insisting on high standards. At the same time we're recognizing outstanding accomplishments through hefty salary increases and rapid advancement."

In 1985 the American Association of University Professors reported that the salaries of faculty members of all ranks at Notre Dame were in the top twenty percent of the country. By contrast, in 1979 salaries at Notre Dame in all but one rank (associate professor) were classified in the top sixty percent, while those at the level of associate professor were in the top forty percent. Commenting on the new salary scales, O'Meara says: "We now have faculty compensation commensurate with our academic aspirations." He adds: "In the better paying disciplines, like accountancy or electrical engineering, our salaries are driven by market forces. In the lower paying disciplines, like philosophy, our salaries actually exceed market value. We have to be sure that the salaries we pay are in conformity with the rhetoric we use about, for example, the significance of the humanities or the life of learning."

O'Meara believes in "strong leadership at all levels" of the University, in the faculty as well as the administration. "If administrators are to be truly effective, they themselves have got to symbolize the ideals of the people whom they represent. You don't become a strong dean by going to management school; you become a strong dean by being respected in your own discipline—and of course by having a certain amount of common sense! I believe that our deans really represent the kind of faculty who should be at Notre Dame."

O'Meara realizes that developing a strong faculty in all of the different disciplines requires time and considerable resources. From his perspective, the progress of recent years provides an essential component for future advancement. "In addition to continuing to strengthen the faculty, we must now strengthen graduate studies at the University—in terms of the programs we offer, in terms of the doctoral work that is done here, in terms of the quality of the students we attract. That is our next step."

Although throughout his tenure as provost O'Meara has insisted on the standards of "excellent teaching, distinguished research, and compatibility with the goals of the institution," he does not believe that he has been confronted with "any serious morale problems" by the faculty. He has, however, perceived a certain amount of anxiety, for example on the part of professors who came to Notre Dame before the recent emphasis on research and advanced education. "Any institution has to change if it is to maintain its fiber, vitality, and ultimate survival," observes O'Meara. "When there is change there is uncertainty, and when there is uncertainty there is anxiety. Some faculty think: 'I've never done research, and now research is a central issue!' We must be aware of these human concerns. But we must also move forward."

Even with his responsibilities as provost, O'Meara continues to engage in his own scholarly activities as the Kenna Professor of Mathematics. He is currently completing his fourth book. Since the summer of 1981 he has delivered several academic lectures at leading universities and scientific institutes in the People's Republic of China. These lectures have not only enabled O'Meara to present his research discoveries to new groups of mathematicians—over the years he has held visiting positions at many American, Canadian, and European universities—but they have also helped him to establish ties between Notre Dame and Chinese universities and research centers.

O'Meara, who is particularly interested in modern algebra and the theory of numbers, sees the type of mathematics he does as "an art rather than a science." New mathematical ideas (what's called in academic circles "pure mathematics") are his province, and he realizes that "for the average man or woman it's difficult to know what we do. Many think mathematics is just solving problems. To be a true mathematician one has to have original ideas." Shortly after O'Meara arrived at Notre Dame in 1962, he published his first book, *Introduction to Quadratic Forms*, which was the culmination of his first ten years of research. The volume, which integrated and advanced certain fundamental concepts in this branch of algebraic number theory, was published by Springer-Verlag, the German publisher, in its celebrated "Yellow Series" of distinguished studies in mathematics.

The response to this book, which has gone through several printings, enhanced O'Meara's international reputation. He decided, however, to change the focus of his research, so that he could study a new but allied field—the theory of the classical groups. His concepts led to the publication of two books, *Lectures on Linear Groups* (1974) and *Symplectic Groups* (1978), both of which have been translated into Russian, and to a major breakthrough in a branch of modern algebra that is called "the isomorphism theory of the classical groups."

Early in 1983, Springer-Verlag invited O'Meara to write his fourth book. The underlying structure of the book is based on the concepts discovered by O'Meara in the 1960s and 1970s, and the volume is a successor to the definitive work in the area written by the famous French mathematician Jean Dieudonne. The book is co-authored by Alexander Hahn, Professor of Mathematics at the University, who has also made extensive research contributions to the area. O'Meara readily admits that with his responsibilities as provost he would not have been able to undertake such a vast project on his own. The manuscript was completed in 1986, with the final book encompassing between 450 and 500 pages.

In talking about his research, O'Meara acknowledges that its abstraction and lack of immediate application make it difficult for the layman to comprehend. He is philosophical, however, in explaining the value of such thought: "The relationship between good mathematics and reality is something mysterious. Think of the theorem of Pythagoras. You can rest assured that it was not proved for the advancement of technology in its day—about 500 B.C. Consider the lines, triangles, squares, and circles of Euclid. These are forms that occur to us because of our experiences in nature. People then study relationships between these forms in increasing degrees of abstraction based only on the intrinsic harmony which we find in the relationships that unfold. Centuries later some of the relationships derived in pure abstraction come back to earth and allow us to explain nature or even to change it. There is this intrinsic harmony then between mathematical forms, nature, and the mind. That is what is mysterious."

O'Meara has received nine major grants for his research from the National Science Foundation. He was an Alfred P. Sloan Fellow from 1960 through 1963. He credits his scholarship with helping him understand the duties of the provost: "My background in mathematics has certainly influenced how I see things in administration. On the one hand, it clearly plays an important role in my thought processes as I analyze things in making decisions. On the other hand, my own teaching and research have influenced my own expectations of what a faculty member should be."

Another factor that has affected O'Meara's thinking about education has been the experience of watching one son and four daughters become graduates of Notre Dame. The professional interests of the children—architecture, photography, television writing, sculpture, and the theatre—made O'Meara concerned for quite some time about the fine arts and literature. "I am especially delighted by the fine arts and literature requirements that have been added in the recent curriculum revision," he notes. Undoubtedly the most influential factor of all has been his close relationship with his wife, Jean, and her interests in literature, the fine arts, and the Church.

As a mathematician and as provost, O'Meara takes the long view. Tomorrow will use—and judge—today's efforts. He already sees many differences from the past that indicate the kind of progress he sees for the future. "Since coming to Notre Dame in 1962, I've seen many of our disciplines grow to national recognition and indeed some of them to national prominence. We are a fine university, a fine Catholic university, and we have a firm commitment to excellence in the years to come."

*Sculptures by Ivan Mestrovic in the Snite Museum of Art*

# The College of Arts and Letters

THE COLLEGE OF ARTS AND LETTERS as it exists today grows out of the original academic program designed by Father Edward Sorin when he founded the University in 1842. Originally called the Collegiate Course, the curriculum in the earliest days featured a classical education: Latin, Greek, philosophy, and history, with some attention to mathematics and science. As Notre Dame became more established in the middle decades of the nineteenth century, academic offerings grew to include classes in composition, literature, and modern languages. The first course in what came to be known as the social sciences, "Political Economy," was given in 1872.

The contemporary College takes its organizational shape from administrative changes that were made in 1920. Until this time, the College was responsible for departments of commerce, foreign commerce, and engineering administration as well as programs in the humanities, fine arts, and social sciences. Establishment of the College of Commerce helped to advance business education at Notre Dame, and it also allowed development within Arts and Letters. The College of Arts and Letters was composed of ten departments in the 1921–1922 academic year: classics, philosophy, letters, modern languages, history, economics, education, journalism, music, and library science. Individual courses in art, religion, and sociology evolved into distinct departments by the middle of the 1920s, and there was also a combined department of economics and politics.

During most of its first century, the College devoted itself almost exclusively to undergraduate teaching. The faculty stressed the fundamentals of the liberal arts, seeking to produce students with a well-rounded education. As a result of this approach and emphasis, Arts and Letters has always been known as the College responsible for providing every undergraduate with a foundation in the humanities, social sciences, and the fine arts. Serving the University in this manner led to a commitment to effective teaching that became—and remains—a hallmark of the College. In fact, the most prestigious honor given by the College to a member of its faculty is the Charles A. Sheedy Award for Excellence in Teaching. The award is named for Rev. Charles Sheedy, C.S.C., the Dean of the College from 1952 until 1968 and a major figure in its development. Several of Notre Dame's most distinguished (and in some cases legendary) teachers—Charles Phillips, James A. Withey, Rev. Charles Miltner, C.S.C., Frank O'Malley, Rev. Leo R. Ward, C.S.C., Rev. Leo L. Ward, C.S.C., Joseph Evans, Willis Nutting, Thomas Stritch—served on the Arts and Letters faculty and brought classrooms to life in imaginative ways. Students learned to think, to write, to analyze, to evaluate, and they also experienced the exhilaration of learning about the arts, letters, and the social sciences.

Until the late 1920s and early 1930s, many observers likened the College to a young man's boarding or finishing school. The education was solid, but there seemed little interest in going beyond rudimentary facts or principles of any discipline in Arts and Letters. This situation began to change when University and College administrators decided to bring to the campus as either guest lecturers or regular faculty members writers and scholars noted for the contributions they had made to the arts, to letters, and to the social sciences. For example, in the fall of 1930 G. K. Chesterton, one of Great Britain's leading men of letters and the most famous Catholic in the English-speaking world, delivered a series of literary and historical lectures on the Victorian Age. Contemporary accounts of these "intellectual performances" note that Washington Hall was always packed and that the lectures awakened an enthusiasm for literature and history never seen before at Notre Dame.

Other prominent European thinkers followed Chesterton later in the decade. The French philosophers, Jacques Maritain and Etienne Gilson, lectured frequently at Notre Dame, while their colleague and countryman, Yves Simon, helped establish the University's graduate program in Philosophy during his ten years (1938–1948) on campus. The famed French literary critic and translator, Charles Du Bos, came to South Bend in 1937 to begin teaching at both Notre Dame and St. Mary's College. His arrival in America merited a picture in *The New York Times*. Two political scientists from Germany, Waldemar Gurian and F. A. Hermens, joined the Arts and Letters faculty in the late 1930s, and they (along with Father Leo R. Ward and Frank O'Malley) founded *The Review of Politics* in 1939. *The Review*, a quarterly journal, was the first continuous scholarly publication of significance with links to the College, and the international reputation it gained in the 1940s brought considerable recognition to the College and to the University as a whole.

During the three decades after 1930, over forty European scholars sought refuge from either Nazism or Communism by joining the Notre Dame faculties of Arts and Letters and Science. In *The University of Notre Dame: A Portrait of Its History and Campus,* Thomas J. Schlereth notes that these professors "enlarged Notre Dame's participation in the wider American academic community via the sponsorship of symposia, their outside lecturing and publishing, and their personal contacts with refugee scholars in other havens such as Princeton's Center for Advanced Study and the Committee on Social Thought at the University of Chicago. Notre Dame's foreign-trained faculty also brought a new cultural heterogeneity to the campus, helped make research and publication an integral part of University life, and contributed greatly to the expansion of the Graduate School."

Foreign scholars were by no means completely responsible for the new intellectual spirit that animated the College of Arts and Letters after 1930. During this decade, four Holy Cross priests—Father Charles Miltner, Dean of the College, Father Leo L. Ward in English, Father Leo R. Ward in Philosophy, Father Philip Moore in Medieval Studies—were instrumental in fostering a concern for scholarship as well as teaching. In the case of Father Moore, a principal architect of graduate studies for the University, he edited and contributed to *Publications in Medieval Studies.* This series of book-length studies, which began in 1936, launched Notre Dame's interdisciplinary work in medieval studies and ultimately led to the creation of the Medieval Institute in 1946. Father Leo L. Ward, himself a prolific writer, brought the well-known novelist, editor, and literary critic John T. Frederick to the English faculty in 1930. Frederick, who in 1915 founded one of America's most distinguished literary magazines, *The Midland*, taught at both Northwestern and Notre Dame for several years, but he subsequently became a full-time professor at this University.

What these scholars and others accomplished between 1930 and 1960 was a harbinger of what would later happen throughout the College. Beginning in the 1960s and particularly since the mid-1970s, greater emphasis has been placed on enriching the teaching and educational mission of Arts and Letters through research and scholarly publication. The Center for the Study of Contemporary Society was established in 1961 with the primary objective of stimulating and promoting research in the social sciences and the humanities. The creation of endowed professorships in the late 1960s and their growth in number in the 1970s and 1980s brought noted scholars to Notre Dame to serve as models and to contribute to the intellectual vitality of the campus. Most of the departments in the College have at least one endowed chair.

In 1984 the University established the Institute for Scholarship in the Liberal Arts. A major undertaking to enhance teaching and research in the humanities, fine arts, and social sciences, the Institute is different from other academic centers and institutes—like Stanford's Humanities Center or Virginia's Center for Advanced Studies—which sponsor year-long research fellowships as their central activity. Notre Dame's Institute for Scholarship in the Liberal Arts has several different facets and does not operate as a separate research center. For example, the Institute supports faculty development by providing grants for research, for travel to conduct research, and for designing new (particularly interdisciplinary) courses and academic activities. The Institute also helps faculty members to seek outside support from private foundations and public agencies, and it brings prominent academics to campus to participate in its "Distinguished Visiting Scholars Series." Nine different series, involving almost forty visitors and encompassing such topics as "Philosophy of Language," "War and Society in the Twentieth Century," "Advances in Sociological Research," and "Visual Narratives," took place in 1985–1986.

The Institute for Scholarship in the Liberal Arts enhances the teaching and research of the College as a whole, and it strengthens the academic work being done within the individual departments. Today fifteen departments make up the College of Arts and Letters:

American Studies
Anthropology
Art, Art History, and Design
Communication and Theatre
Economics
English
Government and International Studies
History
Modern and Classical Languages
Music
Philosophy
Program of Liberal Studies
Psychology
Sociology
Theology

Traditionally, Arts and Letters has had the greatest number of departments, faculty members, and student majors (both undergraduate and graduate) within the University. Of the fifteen departments, only three—Anthropology, Communication and Theatre, and Liberal Studies—do not offer at least one master's degree program. Doctorates can be earned in Economics, English, Government and International Studies, History, Medieval Studies, Philosophy, Psychology, Sociology, and Theology.

Despite the size, variety, and levels of academic programs, common concerns unify the College and contribute to its coherence. Notre Dame requires a larger core of liberal arts courses for all of its undergraduates than most other universities. This curricular commitment grows, in part, out of a long-standing desire to provide students with an education that combines technical proficiency in a specific major with critical and qualitative thinking derived from the liberal arts. This dimension of service to the University draws some of its strength and direction from the heritage of effective undergraduate teaching and its continuing significance. In addition, and more specifically, examining the ethics, the values, and the religious aspects of the humanities, fine arts, and social sciences pervades the teaching and research in Arts and Letters. This concern, of course, is most visible and pronounced in Philosophy and Theology. However, other departments have specific ethical and religious interests. For example, the Department of Government and International Studies addresses the values and moral foundations of politics; the Department of History has as one of its fundamental concerns the history of Christianity in Western Europe and in America; the Department of Economics explores questions of morality and justice related to development; the Department of Music offers several programs in sacred and liturgical music, and the Department of Sociology provides a concentration in the sociology of religion. This thread of concern binds the disparate departments of the College together and contributes to the moral and religious character of the University as a whole.

In "The Vision of the Catholic University in the World of Today," an essay written in 1967 to celebrate the 125th anniversary of Notre Dame, Father Hesburgh observed: "Catholic means universal and the university, as Catholic, must be universal in a double sense: first, it must emphasize the centrality of philosophy and, especially, theology among its intellectual concerns, not just as window dressing, not just to fill a large gap in the total fabric of knowledge as represented in most modern university curricula. . . . Both philosophy and theology are concerned with the ultimate questions, both bear uniquely on the nature and destiny of man, and all human intellectual questions, if pursued far enough, reveal their philosophical and theological dimension of meaning and relevance." Philosophy and theology, especially as they embody and enhance the Catholic character and tradition of Notre Dame, serve as cornerstones for the University, and, as a result, they play a special role within the College of Arts and Letters. Quantitatively, in terms of faculty members and course offerings, the two departments are the largest in the College. Qualitatively — and of greater significance — Philosophy and Theology are recognized in this country and abroad for their accomplishments in scholarly research and graduate education.

The roots of the Philosophy Department extend back to the first series of classes conducted at Notre Dame after its founding. Today — with a faculty of 35, a graduate program of 50, and between 150 and 200 undergraduate majors — the department is one of the biggest in the United States. Its size and the mixture of specialties on the part of professors results in a department that is both pluralistic and comprehensive. One of the first philosophy departments at a Catholic university to pursue analytic as well as Thomistic philosophy, the current areas of concentration include the history of philosophy, contemporary European philosophy, metaphysics, epistemology, ethics, political philosophy, philosophy of science, philosophy of religion, philosophy of language, and formal logic. In their teaching and scholarship, faculty members examine different figures

---

*ALVIN PLANTINGA*
*Dept. of Philosophy*

*What is it for Notre Dame to be a Catholic, or (as I should prefer to put it) a Christian university? Obviously this means many things. Here I shall mention just one; one that seems to me as difficult as it is important. To be a proper* **Christian** *university, Notre Dame must offer the opportunity to consider the various disciplines — not just philosophy (my own discipline), but also history, literature, psychology, sociology, economics, and the like — from an explicitly Christian and theistic perspective. We must offer students the chance to think about, not just how to be a historian or philosopher, but how to be a Christian historian or Christian philosopher.*

*We must explore the question how to be a Christian in philosophy and history, we must ask how Christianity bears on the theory and practice of history and philosophy, psychology and literary theory, economics and sociology, mathematics and biology. This is monumentally difficult, because we have no precedents to emulate and no trails to follow; it is nonetheless of the first importance.*

and movements from a variety of methodological perspectives, and this approach leads to an openness and diversity not found in most other philosophy departments in this country. In 1982 the doctoral program in Philosophy received the highest rating of all of the graduate programs in the humanities, social sciences, and fine arts at the University. The evaluation, conducted by the Conference Board of Associated Research Councils, ranked Notre Dame ahead of any other American Catholic university and among the best private and public schools in the United States.

Since the 1970s inquiry into the philosophy of religion has become a dominant concern. Neglected as a field of study for many years, work in philosophy of religion now flourishes within the discipline, with Notre Dame playing a significant part in advancing the subject. The Center for Philosophy of Religion, established in 1976, sponsors conferences, summer institutes for college teachers, a visiting scholars program, and a series of books, "Notre Dame Studies in the Philosophy of Religion," which is published by the University of Notre Dame Press. The director of the Center is Alvin Plantinga, John A. O'Brien Professor of Philosophy. Plantinga, who joined the faculty in 1980, is considered by most philosophers to be the single most influential teacher-scholar in the philosophy of religion.

Notre Dame's efforts in this area, which is appropriate given the tradition and direction of the University, go well beyond the activities of the center. Several other faculty members pursue this specialization, and nearly half of the graduate students seeking doctoral degrees select philosophy of religion as their concentration. To enhance the program, Philip Quinn, who formerly occupied the William Herbert Perry Faunce Professorship at Brown University, came to Notre Dame in 1985 to assume the second John A. O'Brien Chair in Philosophy. He is a specialist in classical philosophical theories of religion and the philosophy of science. Another University strength that contributes to comprehensiveness in this area is its long-standing and continuing commitment to the examination of medieval philosophy, especially Thomistic thought. Ralph McInerny, an acknowledged authority on St. Thomas Aquinas, is the Michael P. Grace Professor of Medieval Studies. Much of the teaching and research about the philosophy of the Middle Ages is conducted in conjunction with Notre Dame's Medieval Institute, an interdisciplinary center with extensive research holdings in medieval philosophy and theology. Certain aspects involved in the study of epistemology, metaphysics, and ethics also contribute to philosophical activity in the philosophy of religion.

Besides the philosophy of religion, the department for many years has had an active and multifaceted program in the philosophy of science. Work in this area—classes, conferences, visiting scholars, and publications—was enhanced in 1985 with the establishment of the John J. Reilly Center for Science, Technology, and Values. The Center, under the direction of Rev. Ernan McMullin, the John Cardinal O'Hara Professor of Philosophy, and an international authority on Galileo and the philosophy of science, stresses humanistic understanding and evaluation of scientific thought and phenomena. Father McMullin, the only person ever to hold the presidency of the four major United States philosophical associations, is also the director of the University's graduate program in the History and Philosophy of Science. This program, which draws on Notre Dame's resources in philosophy, history, theology, and the natural and social sciences, allows students to explore the interaction between the philosophy and the history of science.

The intellectual life of the Philosophy Department and the University is enriched through its "Perspectives in Philosophy" series. Each year four prominent philosophers from this country and abroad spend a week on campus, delivering lectures and conducting classes on a specific theme established for the year. Topics of recent series include "The History of Philosophy," "Current Issues in the Philosophy of Mind," "Epistemology," and "Philosophy of Law." Most major contemporary philosophers have visited the campus since the series was inaugurated in 1966. In addition, two journals of considerable reputation are published from the department. The *Notre Dame Journal of Formal Logic* is one of the foremost English language publications on symbolic logic, the history and philosophy of mathematics, and the philosophical underpinnings of logic. *The New Scholasticism*, the journal of the American Catholic Philosophical Association, has been published at Notre Dame since 1967.

During the early years of the University, there was no formal study of theology. Religious practice—going to Mass, participating in the sacraments, attending special prayer services—encompassed the religious instruction carried out on the campus. Later, individual classes entered the curriculum, and in the mid-1920s students for the first time were able to major in what was then called "Religion." The Department of Theology has grown dramatically during this century, and it currently has the largest number of faculty members in the College of Arts and Letters and the most graduate students of any department in the University.

*(REV.) EDWARD A. MALLOY, C.S.C.*
*Dept. of Theology*

*For me, Notre Dame is a place, a heritage, and a vital reality. It is a university where scholarship of the highest order is fostered and where teaching is respected as a privileged profession. It provides an open forum in which the truth can be pursued with enthusiasm and zeal. In addition, Notre Dame is a Catholic university. It attempts to elevate the human spirit by the exposure of paths of goodness and forms of beauty in the context of community. It presents worship of God and service of the needful as integral components of a faith-filled life.*

One observer called Notre Dame the place where the Catholic Church does its thinking. This designation to a great degree grows out of the work being carried out within the numerous teaching and research programs in Theology. The classes, publications, lectures, and conferences provide a broad foundation for the scholarly exploration of the dimensions of religious faith and of the relationship of human life to the transcendent. Besides offering a full complement of undergraduate classes for majors and the student body at-large, Theology has two master's programs — a general master's in theology and, since 1968, the ministerial and academic Master of Divinity.

The three specialty areas of the doctoral program highlight the principal intellectual concerns of the department. Liturgical studies, the examination of Christian worship in its historical and theological context, served as the initial focus of graduate education, when it began in 1947. Traditionally, this specialization has received national recognition within the academic and religious community, particularly since a curriculum leading to a doctorate in liturgical studies was established in 1966. The department and the University consider the formal study of Christian worship to be central to Notre Dame's mission. In addition, and more recently, the specialties in Christianity and Judaism in antiquity and in the theological inquiry (which embraces systematic theology, ethics, and church and ministry) have developed and become strong. The department now has several respected scholars of the Old and New Testaments and of the writings of the Church fathers. In 1975 the University established the Center for the Study of Judaism and Christianity to advance the study of Jewish religious thought and the history of contact between Jewish and Christian traditions.

Of considerable significance to the development of the Theology Department and to its reputation has been the appointment of chaired professors. Rev. Richard P. McBrien, the author of twelve books including the landmark, two-volume study, *Catholicism*, came to Notre Dame in 1980 as the Crowley-O'Brien-Walker Professor of Theology and as chairman of the department. Rev. Charles Kannengiesser, S.J., internationally known as a scholar of historical theology, joined the faculty in 1982 as the Catherine F. Huisking Professor of Theology, coming from the Institut Catholique in Paris. Two faculty members within the department were awarded endowed chairs in

1985. Joseph Blenkinsopp was named the John A. O'Brien Professor of Old Testament Studies, and Rev. Thomas F. O'Meara, O.P., became the William K. Warren Professor of Catholic Theology. In addition to these chairs, Theology regularly brings distinguished scholars to campus on a visiting basis. For example, the John S. Marten Program in Homiletics and Liturgies has as one of its activities the support of a visiting professorship whose purpose is to advance the study and practice of preaching.

The University's efforts in teaching and research in theology are enriched through the department's involvement with Notre Dame's Institute for Pastoral and Social Ministry. Founded in 1976 as a center committed to bridging the gap between the Catholic Church and the modern world, the Institute sponsors several educational programs for clergy and lay people that taken collectively is unique in Catholic higher education. Placing the resources of the University at the service of the Church is a principal objective of the Institute, and many activities involve the continuing education and renewal of priests, sisters, brothers, choir directors, organists, and active parishioners. Specific programs of a continuing education nature are the Center for Pastoral Liturgy, the Center for Continuing Formation in Ministry, the Programs for Church Leaders, and Retreats International. Each program has several components. For instance, the Center for Pastoral Liturgy, one of four centers established by the American bishops after the Second Vatican Council, promotes liturgical life and Catholic worship at the national, diocesan, and parochial levels through research, publication, conferences, workshops, and lectures. Another dimension of the Institute's work is the Center for Social Concerns. With a goal of making students, faculty, administrators, and alumni more aware of social problems and issues of justice, the Center for Social Concerns sponsors programs that allow students and others to learn about contemporary concerns through direct involvement (experiences in urban areas of America and developing regions of Latin America) and through formal course work and discussions.

Service to and scholarship about the Catholic Church are fundamental interests of the Theology Department, but they exist alongside the academic commitment to study the wide spectrum of religious tradition, thought, and belief. Several non-Catholic theologians are members of the Theology faculty, and more non-Catholics than Catholics participate in the department's doctoral program. This diversity exists for a purpose. Father Hesburgh told the National Catholic Educational Association in 1969 that ". . . theology in the Catholic university must enjoy the same freedom and autonomy as any other university subject because, otherwise, it will not be accepted as a university discipline and without its vital

---

*PHILIP GLEASON*
*Dept. of History*

*As graduate student and faculty member I have been at Notre Dame for more than thirty years. There have been many changes in that time, but the underlying aim has always been the same. That aim is to combine loyalty to our own Catholic heritage with openness to other traditions of learning, and to cultivate excellence in teaching and scholarship, sensitivity to moral issues, concern for the personal needs of students, and a commitment to serve the larger community.*

presence, in free dialogue with all other university disciplines, the university will never really be Catholic." The extent to which the department emphasizes its Catholic character became an issue in the 1980s. Some professors who preferred a more ecumenical approach believed that instead of "a theology department in a Catholic university," Notre Dame was creating "a department of Catholic theology." The continuing concern about this issue is significant because it not only raises some fundamental questions for the department but also for the University at large. A few such issues include: Does Notre Dame's Catholic character conflict with its quest for academic excellence? Is it possible for free intellectual inquiry to take place at an institution that upholds specific religious beliefs? Are faculty appointments unduly affected by the religion of the applicant?

Philosophy and theology are central and defining disciplines within the College, and their influence reaches outward to embrace the entire University and the wider world of academic scholarship and religious service. Many of the concerns that animate philosophy and theology also affect the other disciplines in Arts and Letters —most notably, of course, in the commitment to explore the moral, ethical, and spiritual dimensions of the humanities, social sciences, and fine arts. In addition, the humanistic approach of interpreting, evaluating, and criticizing a subject, which has roots in philosophy and theology, pervades the humanities programs and also exists to varying degrees in the social sciences and in the fine arts.

Although it is but one aspect of its academic program, the Department of History has long been recognized for its work in the history of American Catholicism. Instruction and research in this area are enhanced by the vast holdings of documents and papers related to the American Catholic experience in the Notre Dame Archives and the activities of the Cushwa Center for the Study of American Catholicism. Inquiry into the establishment and growth of the Church in the United States takes place within the department's wider examination of the history of Western Christianity, particularly the cultural context of theology and religious thought and the contours of popular religion.

In addition to the focus on religious history, the Department of History is noted for its interests in the social and political history of Europe and America. The appointment of Walter Nugent to be the Andrew V. Tackes Professor of History in 1984 strengthened the department's program in American history. Nugent, who came to Notre Dame from Indiana University, is an authority on the frontier experience and on the United States during the nineteenth and early twentieth centuries. The different specialty areas help form the foundation for the undergraduate and graduate classes offered by the department. On the doctoral level, for example, students concentrate on one of three specialties: medieval history, modern European history, or United States history. There are, of course, individual classes and scholarly activities being carried out in other areas as well, most notably in Latin American and Oriental history.

In their teaching and research, faculty mem-

*Jesus and the Samaritan Woman by Ivan Mestrovic in the Shaheen-Mestrovic Memorial*

bers in History use several different approaches. Some consider the preeminent figures and events of the past and assess their significance to political, diplomatic, intellectual, or religious life and thought. Others look at history more explicitly in its social context, interpreting the meaning of what has occurred in an earlier time by looking at specific groups of people involved in that experience. The combination of methodologies—the highly traditional and the more contemporary—fosters intellectual diversity within the department and bolsters the areas of specialization.

Since the late nineteenth century, Notre Dame's Department of English has possessed a reputation for distinguished teaching. Courses in language and literature from such professors as Maurice Francis Egan, Fred Myers, John T. Frederick, Father Leo. L. Ward, Frank O'Malley, and Richard Sullivan earned large followings of students from throughout the University. Today effective teaching remains a hallmark of the department. This dimension, however, now co-exists with a more sustained emphasis on the scholarship and creative writing of faculty members. The establishment of the William P. and Hazel B. White Professorship of English enhanced the department's classroom offerings as well as its commitment to scholarship. Gerald L. Bruns, who has taught and published in a variety of literary fields (modern literature, classical rhetoric, literary theory, Romantic and Victorian literature, and the Irish literary renaissance) assumed the White

Chair in 1985, after serving since 1970 on the University of Iowa faculty.

One of the most popular undergraduate majors in Arts and Letters, English allows students to select from a broad spectrum of courses. Each semester there are classes in British, American, and European literature, in expository and creative writing, and in rhetorical, linguistic, and literary theory. On the graduate level, such variety also exists. However, the majority of students working on master's and doctoral degrees specialize in medieval and American literature.

An abiding interest within the department is the relationship between religion and literature. Besides regular course offerings, the English Department sponsors an annual summer conference on this subject, and the department publishes *Religion and Literature.* Scholars from American and foreign universities contribute to this journal.

The English Department has had an active creative writing program throughout this century. Offering a large number of poetry and fiction writing classes as well as having several accomplished poets and novelists on the faculty make Notre Dame distinctive among Catholic colleges and universities in the United States. The department helps to recognize the significance of creative writing to the University by participating in the yearly Sophomore Literary Festival. Begun in the 1960s, the Festival has brought to campus such writers as Norman Mailer, Tennessee Williams, Joseph Heller, Kurt Vonnegut, and Tom Wolfe to speak and to meet with classes.

Although most of the teaching and writing about language and literature follows traditional approaches, the English Department has been doing pioneering work in the use of computers in literary research and language instruction. One program about computer aided instruction in English grammar and spelling has been used at some 500 schools in North America, Europe, and Africa.

The Department of American Studies is unique among other such departments in the United States. Unlike other programs of this kind which have relatively few interdisciplinary classes, Notre Dame's department offers several integrating courses each semester as well as student access to advanced classes about American subjects—like American history, literature, government, and economics—that are given by other departments in Arts and Letters. The department is also distinctive in the way it incorporates the study of journalism, broadcasting, book publish-

*ROSA MARIA OLIVERA-WILLIAMS*
*Dept. of Modern and Classical Languages*

*STEPHEN A. FREDMAN*
*Dept. of English*

ing, and other aspects of communication into its curriculum. Teaching and scholarship in these areas developed out of the work carried on by the Departments of Journalism and of Communication Arts that existed at the University until the establishment of American Studies in 1971. The new undergraduate department sought to provide students, not just those interested in careers in communications, with a diverse yet focused major.

The commitment of American Studies to interdisciplinary teaching and scholarship, especially with a literary dimension, is evident from its selections for its W. Harold and Martha Welch Chair. This endowed professorship is awarded on a rotating basis to distinguished people of letters, and their duties include public activities on campus as well as teaching and writing. Authors and syndicated columnists Max Lerner and Garry Wills and James O'Gara, the former editor of *Commonweal Magazine,* were the first occupants of the Welch Chair.

On the graduate level, Notre Dame has offered a master's degree in American Studies since 1953. Since the late 1970s, the graduate curriculum has included departmental classes in the theory and practice of American Studies and material culture studies as well as appropriate courses in allied departments, such as English, History, Government and International Studies, Economics, Philosophy, or Sociology. Interdisciplinary research for the master's thesis requires concentration in English, government, history, or material culture. The graduate program is known nationally for its work in material culture studies, the interpretation of past and present human activity through the analysis of physical evidence, such as buildings, technology, and domestic artifacts. The communications component on the undergraduate level and the emphasis on material culture in both the undergraduate and graduate curricula make Notre Dame's program the only one of its kind in the field of American Studies.

Besides the activities in communications carried out in American Studies, the College also has a Department of Communication and Theatre. An undergraduate department established in 1980, Communication and Theatre evolved from what for many years was known as the Department of Speech and Drama. The change of name reflects a broadening of concern about communication and a more comprehensive treatment of the various forms of communication. There are distinct programs in media studies, film and video, and theatre, and each program involves instruction in theory and practice. Although the approach is primarily humanistic in nature—with the aesthetic, historical, cultural, and ethical dimensions of communication and drama receiving emphasis—the department also has a strong performance component. Students and faculty members are actively involved in creating and presenting their own cinematic, video, and dramatic productions. The most popular concentration is film and video. This program and the campus community as a whole are enriched through the department's sponsorship of four continuous film series each semester. These series bring classic and noteworthy movies, produced in this country and abroad, to the University on an almost nightly basis. The study and appreciation of film has a strong heritage at Notre Dame. One of the first classes in cinematic criticism, "Film as Insight," was offered by Professor Edward Fischer in the early 1950s. His book, *The Screen Arts,* published in 1960, was widely used in colleges and universities as the interest in film studies mushroomed in the 1960s and 1970s.

The Department of Communication and Theatre is also responsible for sponsoring a season of plays and other dramatic productions each year. Some of the plays are original works by faculty members and students. Others are classical or popular dramas, which are directed and performed by professors and students. The extensive renovation of Washington Hall, which was completed in 1983, gives the University additional facilities to strengthen its program in theatre studies and to enhance cultural life on campus.

Some of the Communication and Theatre courses that focus on foreign films are cross-listed with offerings of the Department of Modern and Classical Languages. This inter-departmental cooperation, which exists in several different ways within Arts and Letters, suggests the breadth of Modern and Classical Languages. The department does not only have an extensive curriculum in elementary, intermediate, and advanced foreign language instruction, it also offers numerous classes in the literature, civilization, and culture of non-English speaking people.

Faculty within Modern and Classical Languages provide instruction in Arabic, French, German, Greek, Italian, Japanese, Latin, Russian, and Spanish. Several of the courses in these languages fulfill undergraduate and graduate requirements enhancing one's ability to communicate and to understand foreign life. Others serve as the foundation for a student's major or as preparation for one of Notre Dame's Foreign Study Programs. Many of the students who spend a year in Austria, France, Mexico, and elsewhere return to campus to pursue a double major in modern languages and another discipline.

In addition to developing programs in language instruction, the department since the mid-1970s has devoted greater attention to teaching and scholarship about foreign literature, civilization, and culture. The breadth of this work spans Egyptian hieroglyphics and Roman satire to the Russian novel and modern Arabic literature. In 1984 *Annali d'Italianistica*, an annual journal for scholars of Italian literature, was founded by the department. Besides an increasing number of faculty publications, other signs of the department's commitment to advancing the study of foreign literature and culture at Notre Dame are evident in its master's program in French, German, and Spanish and its participation in international conferences about Spanish and Latin American literature. One such Notre Dame conference on how social change in Mexico is reflected in contemporary fiction received a Creative Programming Award in 1982 from the National University Continuing Education Association.

The Program of Liberal Studies, which was established in 1950, is the only undergraduate department of an American college or university exclusively devoted to the study of the Great Books. Some schools, like St. John's College and Thomas Aquinas College, base their entire curriculum on the Great Books. Notre Dame is unique in offering such a program within the context of a multidisciplinary College and University. Rev. John J. Cavanaugh, C.S.C., Notre Dame's president from 1946 to 1952, was instrumental in founding the Program of Liberal Studies. The John J. Cavanaugh Professorship in the Humanities, which is located in Liberal Studies, is a memorial to his commitment to the Great Books and to liberal education. Frederick J. Crosson, who from 1968 until 1975 served as the first lay dean of Arts and Letters, assumed the Cavanaugh Professorship in 1984. Crosson, a specialist in phenomenology and existentialism, was the John Cardinal O'Hara Professor of Philosophy from 1976 to 1984.

Majors in Liberal Studies are able to select electives from any department to complement their study of classic works of philosophical inquiry,

*M. KATHERINE TILLMAN*
Program of Liberal Studies

*I take great pride and constant delight in being on the faculty of the Program of Liberal Studies where people are genuinely excited about the great conversations in which they participate: between the best of the tradition and our contemporary world, between enduring spiritual values and the rich varieties of cultural experience, among colleagues and students who really love good books and engaging ideas.*

literature, natural science, ethics, Christian thought, fine arts, and intellectual and cultural history. Relatively small seminars and tutorials serve as the foundation for the courses.

Despite this emphasis on teaching and counseling, professors within the program publish in their respective disciplines—philosophy, literature, theology, political science, history, and science. Being generalists in the classroom as well as specialists in a research field places demands on the faculty that are unique within the College.

A sense of camaraderie among students in

Liberal Studies has long been a feature of the Program. An indication of the collegiality and loyalty of graduates is evident in the volumes being published in the Notre Dame Series in the Great Books by the Notre Dame Press. Contributions from alumni help to underwrite the re-publication of significant works—like *Treatise On Happiness* by St. Thomas Aquinas and *The Idea of a University* by John Henry Newman—that have gone out of print. These books are used in classes at Notre Dame and are distributed to bookstores throughout the United States.

Although the University provided individual classes in politics, economics, and sociology in the late nineteenth and early twentieth centuries, serious academic development in teaching and research in the social sciences did not begin until the late 1930s. From that time until the 1960s, most members of the social science faculty approached their subjects from the perspective of a humanist—the theoretical, philosophical, historical, and moral dimensions of such disciplines as government, economics, and sociology were explored. This humanistic perspective remains strong, and it is a defining quality of the College of Arts and Letters as it exists today. Michael J. Loux, O'Shaughnessy Dean of Arts and Letters, notes: "There is a unique character to the social sciences at Notre Dame. What our social scientists have done historically is closer to what humanists here are doing than at most universities. That's helped to make us a real college. I have a suspicion that, at universities which don't have a tradition of strength in theory and in the qualitative approach to social phenomena, humanists, social scientists, and fine artists don't talk among themselves as well as they do here."

Even though the humanistic heritage is pronounced, quantitative methodological approaches —the scientific collection and interpretation of research data—are now integral factors in the social science disciplines at Notre Dame. The establishment of the Social Science Training and Research Laboratory in 1965 provided necessary resources for this work. The Laboratory offers faculty and students assistance in instrument design, questionnaire development, computerized research, data processing, analysis, and evaluation. The University is also a member of the Interuniversity Consortium for Political and Social Research.

The relatively rapid growth in the social sciences at Notre Dame has created some friction between social scientists and humanists within the College. Given the humanistic orientation of Arts and Letters, some social scientists wonder whether their work receives the attention it deserves. Is it possible, they ask, for humanists with qualitative methodological frames of reference to understand and to evaluate a behavioral or quantitative study? Some social scientists are also concerned whether Arts and Letters majors are required to take a sufficient number of courses in the social sciences and whether the views of social scientists are fairly represented on committees. This tension develops out of the natural conflict between newer research techniques and more traditional approaches to the social sciences.

The Department of Government and International Studies, which for several years has had the largest number of undergraduate majors of any department in Arts and Letters, grew out of the Department of Economics and Politics (until 1935), the Department of Politics (until 1945), and the Department of Political Science (until 1964). The current designation signifies the scope of interests and areas of emphasis for the department. On both the undergraduate and the graduate level, Government and International Studies allows for specialization in American government and politics, international relations, comparative and foreign government and politics, and political theory. A unifying element that links these specializations and binds the department as a whole is its concern for values and the moral foundations of politics.

Notre Dame's work in world affairs and political theory benefited greatly from the emigration of European Catholic scholars fleeing Nazism and Communism in the 1930s and 1940s. As noted earlier, Waldemar Gurian and F. A. Hermens helped to found *The Review of Politics* in 1939, and with contributions from such thinkers as Jacques Maritain, Hannah Arendt, Hans Morgenthau, Eric Voegelin, and Mortimer Adler, the *Review* attained an international readership interested in a philosophical and historical approach to political realities. In addition, and largely through the initiative of Stephen Kertesz, an Hungarian diplomat and international lawyer, the Committee on International Relations was established in 1949. Over sixty scholarly books have been published under the Committee's auspices. Graduate and undergraduate course offerings in international affairs have also been extensive since the 1930s, and in the 1950s the University began programs that focused on Latin American and Soviet and East European Studies. The creation of the Institute for International Studies in 1968 brought these interdisciplinary area programs together under the coordination of Government and International Studies. Notre Dame now has area programs in Latin American Studies, Soviet and East European Studies, West European Studies, African Studies, Asian Studies, and Middle Eastern Studies. The department also works closely with the Helen Kellogg Institute for International Studies. Guillermo O'Donnell, the academic director of the Institute and a noted authority on Latin American affairs, is the Helen Kellogg Professor of International Studies. O'Donnell, a native of Argentina who has been a faculty member at several colleges in this country and abroad, holds a joint appointment in the Departments of Government and International Studies and Sociology.

Although the majority of undergraduate majors specialize in American government and politics and over half of the graduate students have concentrations in international relations, the department's commitment to and accomplishment in political theory remain strong. Fred R. Dallmayr, a political theorist with major interests in contemporary political theory, the theory of social science, and modern political thought, has been the Packey J. Dee Professor of Government and International Studies since 1978. In recent years two Notre Dame doctoral recipients have won the American Political Science Association's Leo Straus Award for the finest dissertation in political theory, and one other received honorable mention for that award.

The study of economics at Notre Dame is rooted in the standard theoretical and mathematical techniques of economic analysis. Developing from this foundation, however, are other dimensions that make the Department of Economics distinctive among most other American universities. In their teaching and research, faculty members consider the quantitative data of economic conditions and problems, but they also probe beyond this analysis to address questions of ethics and values surrounding these conditions and problems. While many professional economists look at their discipline as being value-free, the approach at Notre Dame is that values pervade decisions about economic matters and they deserve inquiry.

Historically, economics has been one of the most popular majors within the College, with undergraduates receiving a broad, traditional education in economics. During the 1970s, the graduate program was restructured to emphasize three areas of specialization—economic development, labor economics and industrial relations, and public sector economics. These areas were selected because they confront the most challenging questions deriving from the intersection of values with economics.

Of the three concentrations, Notre Dame's work in developmental economics is particularly notable. Faculty members and graduate students

*PERI ARNOLD*
*Dept. of Government*

*Notre Dame is a place of large ambitions for reconciling quite different goals. It seeks distinction as a research university while remaining a fine undergraduate college. It wants to be open to diverse ideas and thinkers while retaining its Roman Catholic identity. The tensions resulting from these sometimes conflicting ambitions can be enraging. However, these large ambitions also make Notre Dame an enormously exciting university.*

interested in issues related to development analyze causes of poverty and injustice and formulate new economic policies to help people in urban centers, depressed regions, and underdeveloped countries. For many years the University has had close ties with individuals and institutions in Central and South America, and these ties have resulted in academic concerns about Latin American affairs. Economists at Notre Dame devote a considerable amount of their work to developmental issues in Latin America, employing a variety of methodologies in their research. In addition to statistical data, members of the Economics Department also rely on interviews and comparative case studies as part of their scholarship. The involvement of the Helen Kellogg Institute for International Studies in the intellectual life of the University is a significant factor in the teaching and research about developmental economics. Alejandro Foxley, one of Latin America's most respected economists, holds the Helen Kellogg Professorship of International Development. Another member of the Institute, Denis Goulet, is the William and Dorothy O'Neil Professor of Education for Justice and a specialist in the ethics of development. Rev. Ernest Bartell, C.S.C., the Executive Director of the Institute, is also a professor of Economics, whose major interests include education and economic development. The University's work in international economics was enhanced in 1985 with the establishment of the Dr. William M. Scholl Professorship in International Economics.

Notre Dame's involvement in the area of economic development became a central concern in the 1960s, when the Catholic Church began to advocate the need for academic study of the human problems associated with such situations as population growth and resource scarcity. Until this time, the Church had been more interested in labor-industrial relations and the economic issues raised in the workplace following the Industrial Revolution. This area continues to be a focus for an extensive amount of teaching and research. In addition, the Department of Economics, in conjunction with the Law School, annually sponsors a Union-Management Conference that involves the participation of hundreds of people in labor and business.

Notre Dame's Department of Sociology received national recognition in the 1960s for research carried out by its faculty in population analysis and ethnic studies. The population

*MAUREEN T. HALLINAN*
*Dept. of Sociology*

studies were conducted within the Institute for the Study of Population and Social Change of the Center for the Study of Man in Contemporary Society, and they were influential in focusing attention on the issues related to family size, interaction, and planning, especially for Catholics. Several books were published and numerous conferences convened to explore the subject. Ethnic studies, notably about the Chicano and Black experiences in the United States, continue to be a central concern for the department. Teaching and research about Mexican Americans has been especially active and distinctive, leading to (among other accomplishments) an important series of books in Chicano Studies published by the Notre Dame Press. In addition, through the efforts of sociologists, the University has been successful in securing over seventy fellowships from the U.S. Department of Education to support Mexican-American graduate students at Notre Dame. The University's reputation in Chicano studies is a significant factor in attracting these students northward.

Four areas of concentration—social theory,

50 The College of Arts and Letters

The College of Arts and Letters 51

marriage and the family, comparative ethnic studies, and sociology of religion—define much of the teaching and research within the department today. In recent years, there has been greater emphasis placed on studying the various aspects of family life in contemporary society. Joan Aldous, a specialist in the socialization process within families and family policy, became the William R. Kenan, Jr. Professor of Sociology in 1978. Maureen T. Hallinan, a sociologist whose research involves the analysis of children's friendships and the effects of instructional grouping upon student friendships and academic achievement, assumed the William P. and Hazel B. White Chair in Arts and Letters in 1984.

Much of the scholarship about the family and children is empirical, quantitatively collected survey data and analysis. This methodological approach, which is dominant in the discipline today, also pervades the work being done by specialists of the sociology of religion. A current major project involves the study of American Catholicism as part of Notre Dame's interdisciplinary Study of Catholic Parish Life. The work in sociological theory, however, emphasizes humanistic concerns of cultural interpretation rather than quantitative assessments. This perspective, which is rare in contemporary American sociology, is more philosophical in its orientation, broadening the methodological and substantive diversity of the department.

From the 1920s until 1981, the study of anthropology took place within the Department of Sociology or, as it was later designated, the Department of Sociology and Anthropology. In 1981 Notre Dame established an autonomous Department of Anthropology. Teaching and research about the discipline, referred to as the most humanistic of sciences and the most scientific of humanities, focuses primarily on the cultures of the people living in North and South America and in the Mediterranean Middle East. The department, in fact, was instrumental in creating an area studies program about the Middle East, in bringing a Fulbright scholar to the University, and in increasing the holdings of the library in Middle Eastern materials.

Professors in Anthropology are particularly interested in urban modernization, the development of Third World cultures, medical practices in different societies, the psychological composition of peoples of varying cultural settings, and the meaning of religious beliefs and practices to men and women around the world. Though relatively new and small (seven faculty members), the department has a reputation for being one of the strongest within Arts and Letters. There are plans to begin a graduate program in Anthropology in the future.

Notre Dame was the last major Catholic university in the United States to establish a Department of Psychology. Until 1965, when the department began, concern for psychology was

---

*THOMAS WHITMAN*
Dept. of Psychology

*Many have questioned whether it is possible for Notre Dame or any university to achieve real excellence in research and scholarship without diminishing the quality of instruction provided to students. The more appropriate question is under what conditions can excellence in both enterprises be achieved. The answer is at the same time simple and complex: hiring faculty who are teacher-scholars; establishing reasonable teaching loads; and providing support and incentives for sustaining excellence in both domains.*

limited to the interest of some faculty members in Philosophy and Theology. With the founding of the department and the creation of a graduate program in 1969, Notre Dame moved away from the theoretical consideration of psychology. Quantitative, empirical methodology became the dominant approach. This work, however, is conducted in an environment that stresses the importance of helping humanity, especially those who are troubled. The scientific means lead to ends that can be viewed as humanistic.

The Psychology Department is responsible for securing more grant funds than any other department in Arts and Letters. These funds support several different kinds of teaching and research. One area of continuing distinction is counseling. The graduate program in counseling—the University offers a master's in psychological counseling and a doctorate in counseling psychology—is recognized nationally as one of the best in its field. The curriculum for the doctorate is accredited by the American Psychological Association. Students receive professional training by working with people seeking help from the University Counseling Center.

During the past decade, the Psychology Department has become known nationally for its concentration in development and aging. Specializations within this area include cognitive development, mental retardation, and aging. The teaching and scholarship in mental retardation are notable because most universities do not have specialty areas in mental retardation as part of their psychology departments. Notre Dame's program involves both academic research about, and professional experience in, dealing with and remediating retarded behavior. Work in the field of aging began in the 1970s, and the University now has created a Center for Gerontological Education, Research and Services. In addition to conducting an extensive number of research studies, this is the only program in the country to offer training toward advanced degrees and postdoctoral work in gerontological counseling.

Two other programs within Psychology focus on experimental studies. One emphasizes learning and motivation, sensation and perception, and social psychology, while the other considers individual and family development. The second program is conducted jointly with the Department of Sociology, and there are plans to involve faculty members from other departments—Economics, Government and International Studies, and

*MOIRA MARTI GEOFFRION*
*Dept. of Art, Art History and Design*

*Over the past decade the intellectual and creative environment at Notre Dame has blossomed at an energizing and stimulating pace. The visual arts at Notre Dame reflect a new standard of excellence as we make steady progress towards the creation of a campus environment sensitive to artistic expression. We have a long journey before us in our efforts to build a campus culture of depth in visual expression, but we are well on our way towards the recognition that art is not for art's sake alone but for life's sake.*

Theology—in its work. A goal of the College is an integrated, multidisciplinary program about the individual and the family that is unique among American universities.

Beginning in the 1970s and continuing in the 1980s, the fine arts have become the focus of new attention and commitment at Notre Dame. Since the nineteenth century, the arts have played a role in the development of the University, with classes in music and art among the earliest offerings. In-

deed, from 1924 until 1931, a School of Fine Arts existed on the campus, and during the 1920s Music enjoyed the reputation of being one of the most distinguished departments at Notre Dame. The achievements of Professor John Becker as a composer and the memorable performances of the choir of Sacred Heart Church contributed to the stature of the Music Department. Today, however, there are more dimensions to the University's work in the fine arts. There is greater emphasis on combining the humanistic concerns—the aspects of theory, history, and aesthetic understanding—with actual performances or studio shows. This emphasis has meant more attention to instruction and scholarship *about* the arts and more recitals, exhibitions, and performances *of* the arts. The opportunities to understand and to enjoy the arts have been substantially enhanced through the creation of new facilities for students, faculty members, and the public. The Patrick F. Crowley Music Hall was dedicated in 1976, and it provides classrooms, practice rooms, recital and rehearsal halls. The Snite Museum, considered by most art authorities as one of the top five university museums in America, was completed in 1980. Besides its permanent collection of over 12,000 works and the many special exhibitions it sponsors, the Snite Museum houses the Annenberg Auditorium, which is used several times each week for lectures and symposia about the arts, for musical recitals, and for the showing of the many film series conducted by the Department of Communication and Theatre. During 1983 and 1984, the Old Chemistry Hall was completely renovated to provide additional studio space and facilities for faculty and student artists. The building was renamed the Edna and Leo Riley Hall of Art and Design in honor of a major gift from Allan, William, and Gene Riley, all Notre Dame alumni, in memory of their parents. Washington Hall, the campus site since 1881 for dramatic productions, musical performances, poetry readings, and many other activities, was modernized in the early 1980s, expanding the possibilities for theatre and other arts at Notre Dame. These buildings symbolize the new commitment and abiding presence of the fine arts in the cultural life of the University.

In addition to the undergraduate curriculum in theatre and film-video production offered by the Department of Communication and Theatre, Notre Dame also has bachelor's and master's degree programs in Art, Art History, and Design and Music. The Department of Art, Art History, and Design offers two professional degrees—the Bachelor of Fine Arts and the Master of Fine Arts—as well as B.A. and M.A. degrees in art history or studio art. The department has eight areas of concentration: art history, ceramics, fibers, industrial design, painting, photography, printmaking, and sculpture. Many of the classes in art history and in studio work are popular as undergraduate electives. Approximately a thousand non-majors study the traditions of art or create their own works each semester.

The opening of the Snite Museum has had a significant impact on advancing art education and generating greater awareness of the plastic and creative arts. One of only 184 of the nearly 5,000 museums of any type that seek accreditation by the American Association of Museums, the Snite Museum is known for its collections in European religious art, in nineteenth-century French sketches and drawings, in European photography of the nineteenth century, and in American artworks of the pre-Columbian period. A special gallery is devoted to the display of several masterpieces of Ivan Mestrovic, the Yugoslavian artist and sculptor who served on the Notre Dame faculty from 1955 until his death in 1962. The study of exhibits at the Snite Museum is integrated into several art classes, and the additional galleries of O'Shaugnessy Hall, connected to the Snite Museum, provide advanced students and faculty members with an appropriate professional setting for their individual shows and joint exhibitions.

Although there is considerable activity in all facets of art, with the Snite Museum as the focal point, the majority of majors and graduate students specialize in industrial design. This concentration, which combines the study of art history with courses about the designing of products, means of transportation, and advertisements, emphasizes technical knowledge and visual sensitivity. The Notre Dame program is one of only twenty-eight programs accredited by the Industrial Design Society of America. Since Notre Dame began to offer classes in industrial design in 1955, graduates have been especially successful in their work for American and foreign automakers.

The study and practice of religious art and music have long been continuing concerns at Notre Dame. Today the Department of Music enjoys national prominence for its work in sacred and liturgical music. The University, in fact, is one of the few schools in the United States to offer a Master of Music in Music and Liturgy. This interdisciplinary program combines instruction in the history, theory, and performance of sacred music with the study of liturgy in the Department of Theology.

Notre Dame's commitment to enhancing Christian worship with music extends beyond formal course offerings to the training of undergraduates and graduate students to participate in liturgical activities that take place in Sacred Heart

56  The College of Arts and Letters

Church and the dormitory chapels across campus. Members of the Chapel Choir and the Folk Ensemble perform at Masses throughout the year, and many students return to their home parishes to help foster the use of appropriate sacred music into worship at their churches.

The Music Department offers undergraduate majors concentrations in music history, theory, performance, as well as a bachelor degree that combines coursework in all three areas. On the graduate level the department offers the Master of Music (in Music and Liturgy, in Performance and Literature, and in Band and Literature) and a Master of Arts (in Historical Musicology, in

LAURA KLUGHERZ
Dept. of Music

Music Theory, and in Liturgical Music). It is also possible to pursue advanced studies in music of the Middle Ages by seeking a Doctor of Philosophy degree in Medieval Studies, an interdisciplinary program conducted in cooperation with the Medieval Institute.

These programs are just one dimension of the Music Department. Faculty members in Music are also responsible for the instrumental and vocal instruction for several other ensemble groups, including the Band, the oldest university band in the United States; the Glee Club, which tours throughout North America and Europe regularly; the Chamber Orchestra, which offers concerts each semester, and the University Chorale, which performs locally and on tour. These organizations and the other ensembles broaden musical education and appreciation at Notre Dame, and they involve approximately four hundred students from departments other than music.

In addition to their involvement with the ensemble groups, professors of Music combine scholarly publication in theory and history with

CARL L. STAM
Dept. of Music

*In studying great choral music, a conductor is continually in touch with the musical and liturgical history of the Christian Church. Thorough musical analysis reveals only a part of the full aesthetic value of composition. At Notre Dame, one makes no excuses for exploring matters of faith, for making them part of the performance process.*

concert and recital performances. Several faculty members compose their own works, and these compositions are played on campus as well as elsewhere in America and abroad. Like the various art exhibitions and dramatic productions, the numerous musical performances contribute to Notre Dame's cultural vitality.

Besides the fifteen departments of Arts and Letters, there are several programs, institutes, and centers related to the College that bolster and broaden its teaching and research. Since 1978, for example, the College has sponsored a two-semester, sophomore-level "Core Course" that is called "Ideas, Values, and Images." This interdepartmental class, which is taught in approximately thirty seminar sections by senior faculty members of the College, introduces students to formative ideas and writings, providing an opportunity to consider fundamental human problems and values. Participants in the "Core Course" share a common syllabus of readings, lectures, and films, and they focus on such concepts as "Nature," "God," "Society," and "The Individual." The "Core Course" is the only substance-specific class required of Arts and Letters majors. First-year students at the University take part in the "Freshman Seminar Program" and the "Humanities Seminar," which are administered by the English Department and taught by the faculty of the College.

Arts and Letters undergraduates do not only have the chance of majoring in one of the fifteen departments; the College also provides special programs that allow students to receive intensive training in a second area for a double major or a joint degree. These programs include:

—The Black Studies Program for students interested in the Black American experience and the interrelation between the African and American experiences.

—The Arts and Letters Program for Administrators, which is a combined program with the College of Business Administration for students intending to pursue careers in business.

—The Computer Applications Programs for students wanting to learn about computer languages and the applications of computer technology in their disciplines.

—The Arts and Letters Preprofessional Program, which combines the study of the humanities and social sciences with the study of the natural sciences for those who want to go to medical or dental schools.

—The Arts and Letters–Engineering Program, a five-year course of studies that enables students to receive bachelor's degrees in both Arts and Letters and Engineering.

In recent years, the College has inaugurated a series of concentrations in areas of long-standing concern in Arts and Letters. Integrative and interdisciplinary study of "Philosophy, Politics, and Economics," "Individual and Family Development," and "Peace Studies" adds dimension to a student's major.

Institutes and centers play a major role in the intellectual life of the University. Although instruction is an aspect of each institute and center, research and publication are the dominant concerns of the scholars affiliated with these interdepartmental entities.

The oldest institute—the Medieval Institute—was established in 1946, and its focus is the study of Christian civilization of the Middle Ages. Modeled on the work of the Pontifical Institute of the University of Toronto, the Medieval Institute developed out of a program on medieval studies inaugurated by Notre Dame in 1933. Today the Institute offers a comprehensive curriculum and research capability unique among American universities.

Undergraduates, for example, can pursue a sequence of classes leading to the equivalent of a major in Medieval Civilization. In addition, the University awards master's and doctoral degrees in medieval studies. The Institute has a core faculty of its own, and professors from nine departments in Arts and Letters contribute to the undergraduate and graduate degree programs.

The Institute's library, a collection of more than 50,000 books, pamphlets, journals, drawings, and photographic materials, is a significant research center that is used by scholars from this country and abroad. The library has extensive holdings in medieval philosophy and theology. The Astrik L. Gabriel History of Universities Collection, with its primary and secondary materials about medieval education, is unrivaled among research institutions throughout the world. The collection was assembled and named for Canon Astrik L. Gabriel, who was director of the Medieval Institute from 1953 until 1975. Canon Gabriel, a professor emeritus, is a leading authority on medieval education.

The Frank M. Folsom Ambrosiana Microfilm

and Photographic Collection consists of positive and negative microfilms of the 12,000 medieval and renaissance manuscripts held in the Biblioteca Ambrosiana in Milan. The collection also contains about 50,000 photographs and negatives of miniatures and illuminated initials from the manuscripts as well as 15,000 color slides. In addition, the Mary Davis Drawings Collection includes photographs, negatives, and color slides of the 8,000 drawings in the Ambrosiana. Eighty-seven Renaissance drawings, on loan from the Ambrosiana, were exhibited in 1984 and 1985 at the National Gallery of Art in Washington, D.C., at the Snite Museum at Notre Dame, and at three other major art museums in the United States. The exhibition, with original drawings by Leonardo Da Vinci and Raphael, was sponsored by the Medieval Institute, introducing the work and holdings of the Institute to people in all sections of this country.

Three series of scholarly publications appear under the aegis of the Medieval Institute—*Texts and Studies in the History of Mediaeval Education, Publications in Mediaeval Studies,* and *Folia Ambrosiana.* In addition, the University of Notre Dame Press independently publishes a large selection of titles in medieval studies, enhancing the University's reputation in this area.

The Center for the Study of Man in Contemporary Society was created in 1961 to stimulate research and graduate training in the social sciences and humanities at Notre Dame. Beginning with its founding director, George N. Shuster, former president of Hunter College and special assistant to Father Hesburgh, the University's objective has been to develop a cross-disciplinary center for social scientific research and humane reflection on contemporary problems. Some American universities have institutes for social research and institutes for the study of ethics or public policy issues. However, what since 1984 has been called the Center for the Study of Contemporary Society is unique in merging these various concerns into one entity.

In the 1960s, scholars at the Center did landmark studies about the Catholic parochial school system in the United States and about population trends and problems. The research findings of these projects were influential in affecting the thinking and policy decisions of Church and lay leaders. Publications, such as *Catholic Schools in Action: The Notre Dame Study of Catholic Elementary and Secondary Schools in the United States* and *Family and Fertility,* brought attention to the University in a new and different way. Quantitative social science research had entered the mainstream intellectual life of Notre Dame.

Frequently a project develops out of the research interests of one faculty member. For example, the Center for Gerontological Education, Research, and Services evolved from being the work of one psychology professor into an interdisciplinary undertaking with many components involving several scholars. Other projects involve the participation of faculty members from numerous departments from the beginning. The Notre Dame Study of Catholic Parish Life, for instance, is a joint project with the Institute for Pastoral and Social Ministry, and it draws on the resources of specialists in political science, sociology, history, and theology. The study includes historical research into regional patterns of church development, survey research relating parishioners' views and practices with parish structures and patterns of ministry, and on-site observation of parish liturgies and meetings.

Begun in 1981 and continuing through 1988, the study is based on an analysis of 1,100 parishes and intensive investigation of 36 representative parishes. *The National Catholic Reporter* called the multi-phase project "the most comprehensive, comparative, systematic, interdisciplinary probe of Catholic parishes ever attempted."

The Cushwa Center for the Study of American Catholicism operates under the administrative supervision of the Center for the Study of Contemporary Society. Started in 1976 and permanently established with an endowment in 1980, the Cushwa Center sponsors two series of seminars—an interdisciplinary one on American Catholic Studies and another for historians of American Religion—conferences, and lectures on a regular basis. The Center conducts an annual competition to select the best book-length manuscript in American Catholic studies, and it also publishes the *American Catholic Studies Newsletter,* which helps to keep scholars of American Catholicism across the country up-to-date on research and activities in the field. Travel grants are available from the Center, allowing scholars to come to Notre Dame to use the University's extensive library and archival collection of Catholic Americana. A fellowship program supports graduate students.

The Cushwa Center not only brings scholars to campus or assists scholars interested in studying American Catholicism, it also sponsors research of its own. One project, the Theological Education Study, is a comprehensive history of American Catholic theological education. In addition, the historical phase of research for the Notre Dame Study of Catholic Parish Life is being completed under the direction of the Cushwa Center. Six regional histories of parish life will appear. Although the dominant thrust of the Center's work involves historical considerations, scholars in American Studies, English, sociology, theology, religious studies, and ethnic studies take part in its activities. The multi-disciplinary approach and the research capabilities available through the University make the Cushwa Center the only one of its kind for scholars interested in the development of the Catholic Church in the United States.

The Helen Kellogg Institute for International Studies, which began activities in 1982, is not formally related to the College of Arts and Letters. It is a distinct academic entity with its own advisory council. However, many scholars affiliated with the Institute are social scientists and humanists, particularly political scientists and economists, and they have appointments in departments of Arts and Letters.

The Kellogg Institute grew out of Notre Dame's Committee on International Relations, which began in 1949 and dealt with a wide range of issues and problems: international politics, Soviet policy, East Central Europe, and Latin America. The Kellogg Institute concentrates most of its research, education, and outreach programs on Latin America. The decision to focus on this region flows, in part, from Notre Dame's commitment to human service through scholarship and teaching. Historically, too, the Congregation of the Holy Cross has conducted an active ministry in this area of the world. The Institute's emphasis, however, is not exclusively regional. Rather, Latin America is representative of larger global issues that transcend geographic definition and have broader relevance.

The research agenda of the Kellogg Institute is defined by four related themes with strong links to contemporary life in Latin America. The themes include opportunities of and challenges to democratization, alternative strategies for economic development, popular responses to democratization and to development from members of social movements, the arts, and the media, and the role of religion, especially the Catholic Church, in political and socioeconomic changes. Aspects of these themes are pursued by the academics affiliated with the Institute on either a full-time or visiting basis. Two endowed chairs — the Helen Kellogg Professorship in International Studies, occupied by Guillermo O'Donnell, and the Helen Kellogg Professorship of International Development, held by Alejandro Foxley — enable distinguished scholars to provide a strong, long-term foundation to Institute activities. In addition Notre Dame faculty members and experts from elsewhere, especially Latin American institutions, are invited to be fellows of the Institute. While in residence on campus, these academics pursue their individual research projects and take part in seminars with other fellows, Notre Dame faculty, and students. In addition, fellows frequently teach courses and help organize workshops and conferences. Approximately twenty-five fellows are affiliated with the Institute for varying lengths of time during a year. The Institute also publishes a series of *Working Papers*, written by members of the staff, fellows, and invited participants in seminars, workshops, and conferences.

Besides the activities carried out at the University, the Kellogg Institute collaborates with Latin American centers noted for scholarly achievement. By coordinating activities with institutions in Brazil, Argentina, and Chile, the Institute has created a unique "network" to advance the study of development and democratization. Continuing interchange of faculty and students in both directions is an integral element of the Institute's work.

The Kellogg Institute is located in Decio Faculty Hall, a three-building complex adjacent to O'Shaugnessy Hall, the home since 1952 for most of the teaching and administration related to Arts and Letters. The dedication of Decio Faculty Hall, which provides offices for 240 faculty members and includes several seminar and conference rooms, a faculty lounge, and secretarial facilities, took place in 1984, a few months after the establishment of the Institute for Scholarship in the Liberal Arts. Both events were significant in the history of Notre Dame. The new facilities and resources were the centerpiece of a commitment to strengthen teaching and research in the humanities, the social sciences, and the fine arts. That commitment will affect not only the oldest college but the University as a whole in the years to come.

60  *The College of Arts and Letters*

*The College of Arts and Letters* 61

PROFILE

DEAN MICHAEL J. LOUX

COLLEGE OF ARTS AND LETTERS

A FEW MONTHS after Michael J. Loux was named Dean of the College of Arts and Letters in 1983, he announced the establishment of the Institute for Scholarship in the Liberal Arts. In the eyes of many people at Notre Dame, creating the Institute—an ambitious undertaking to support and advance research and teaching—signaled the coming of age for the oldest College in the University. In the opinion of Dean Loux, the founding of the Institute was "a necessary step for Notre Dame to take in our becoming a major university."

Loux, who became the O'Shaughnessy Dean of Arts and Letters in 1985 when the deanship was endowed, brings to his administrative position concern for the heritage of the College along with the commitment to enhance scholarly activity throughout the fifteen departments that make up Arts and Letters. Noting that "excellence in undergraduate teaching is the history of this place," he adds, "but we're a College that has to become better as an institution in scholarship, research, and professional visibility. Our mandate is to improve in these areas without weakening our foundation of strong teaching."

When Loux talks about combining teaching and research, he, in part, draws on his own academic experience. A faculty member in the Philosophy Department since he received his doctorate from the University of Chicago in 1968, he has won both the Charles A. Sheedy Award for Excellence in Teaching and the Thomas Madden Freshman Teaching Award. His scholarly work in metaphysics, Greek philosophy, and the philosophy of language has resulted in the publication of his seven books, including *Ockham's Theory of Terms, Substance and Attribute,* and *The Possible and the Actual: Readings in the Metaphysics of Modality,* and numerous articles. Loux sees no dichotomy between teaching and scholarship: "I don't buy the dilemma of the great teacher who doesn't write. There may be a few, but I'm of the view that your best teachers are going to be your most creative scholars and your most creative scholars are going to be your best teachers. I have always prided myself on being an excellent teacher and being a good scholar, and I have viewed both qualities as necessary for being a productive member of the faculty."

In describing the College as it exists today, Loux discusses "the radical diversities in the departments." He observes: "There are the social and behavioral sciences. They're very different, however much we lump them together. There's a world of difference between Psychology and the other four departments [Anthropology, Economics, Government and International Studies, and Sociology], and a world of difference between Sociology and Economics. Plus we have the fine arts, and in those departments [Art, Art History and Design, Communication and Theatre, and Music] we have the distinction between the humanists, on the one hand, and studio and performing artists, on the other. Then, of course, we have seven departments in the humanities [American Studies, English, History, Modern and Classical Languages, Philosophy, Program of Liberal Studies, and Theology]."

Loux admits that some inevitable tensions arise from having the humanities, the social sciences, and the fine arts together in a single college. Teaching methods, research techniques, professional activities vary. Discussions about qualitative or quantitative approaches occur. Despite such concerns, the dean sees a definite character to Arts and Letters that helps to unify the College and to animate the University.

"We have a specific concept of liberal arts," Loux says. "We can speak in neutralist terms where the phrase 'liberal arts' does not turn out to be synonymous with humanities. We view this concept as a mandate that everybody here—whether chemical engineer, accountant, or biochemist—has a firm grounding in philosophy, theology, history, social science, fine arts, and literature. Every undergraduate has to take requirements in these areas, and these requirements lead to a well-balanced liberal arts core."

In addition to providing a solid foundation in the liberal arts, the College, according to Loux, "is where the Catholic character of the University most clearly exhibits itself." The dean explains that the religious dimension affects the appointment of faculty members, the search for senior scholars for endowed chairs, and the subjects taken up in classes and explored in research projects to a greater degree than in the other colleges. "In both our teaching and research, certain kinds of specialties have been highlighted," Loux says. "In the social sciences, we focus very heavily on development issues affecting the Third World, particularly Latin America. In Philosophy, we do philosophy of religion, traditional metaphysics, and the history of philosophy. Theology stresses systematic theology, liturgy, and scripture. History deals very heavily with the history of Christianity and the American Catholic church. In Sociology there's the emphasis on the sociology of religion, and in Psychology we stress counseling and developmental psychology. I'm not suggesting that anyone sat down with a master plan and said: 'What is a Catholic university going to stress?' No, it's been historical evolution, but that historical evolution has been guided by the ideals of what we are, and it has shaped those ideals. The ideals and mandate shape the choices, and the choices give substance to the ideals."

Concern for the Catholic character of Notre Dame creates connections among the diverse elements of the College. Loux also perceives a distinctive spirit pervading Arts and Letters. He finds faculty members to be critical of programs and policies related to their departments, the College, and the University as a whole. This critical spirit, however, is different from the fault-finding Loux has experienced at other universities. "The criticism here is constructive in a way that it isn't at other places," he observes. "There's a university and collegiate morale here. There is a sense that we're all doing something pretty much the same across the board. We're all part of an enterprise. That critical spirit and appraisal that you want from your humanists, social scientists, and artists are moderated and rendered constructive by the unique spirit of Notre Dame. That spirit comes from our tradition; it comes from our mandate as a Catholic university, and it comes from the tensions that result from that. It comes, in part, from that great debate: How can a university be great and Catholic?"

In recent years suggestions of administrators and of faculty members have led to innovative programs on the undergraduate level. Loux lists the establishment of the London semester abroad opportunity, the Core Course required of all majors in the College, and the combined programs with the Colleges of Science, Engineering, and Business Administration as "significant responses to what many people in the 1970s saw as 'the dying liberal arts.' We helped save ourselves as a College with all of them."

The Institute for Scholarship in the Liberal Arts is another and more elaborate innovation to enhance the work of the College. Although it offers faculty members grants to develop new and imaginative courses, the Institute's primary objective involves the support of research projects. The Institute helps professors to seek grants from public agencies and private foundations, and one year after it was established twenty-nine members of Arts and Letters faculty—one tenth of the entire faculty—received major grants and fellowships. The Institute also sponsors several programs of its own to advance scholarship. For example, faculty members are now able to apply to the Institute for research leaves, for summer research grants, for course reductions to allow additional research time, and for travel grants to conduct research away from campus.

"We had to have a system of support for helping research in the context of a place that was trying to lift itself up by its own bootstraps," explains Loux. "In an emerging university like ours, where you have escalating standards, you have to give the support so that people, in fact, can meet those standards or have a reasonable hope of doing so. The Institute is the way of insuring that." The dean says that a $10 million endowment will help to underwrite the Institute.

Developing a faculty that shares the goal of Notre Dame becoming a major university is, in Loux's opinion, his principal responsibility. "I have to oversee the curriculum and its programs, to insure faculty morale—but the main thing is to build the faculty. That means to improve the faculty that's here, to maximize the chances of excellence on the part of the junior faculty, to make sure every appointment is outstanding, and to find out who are the best senior people we can get." Loux thinks the recent success of filling endowed chairs will have significant long-term impact on strengthening the College, its teaching, particularly on the graduate level, and its research.

Seeking improvement throughout the College defines Loux's attitude and approach. As he looks toward the future, all aspects of Arts and Letters, including his own position, receive his scrutiny. "The first thing I ever said to the department chairmen in 1983 was that the aim of our work is to insure that the College will progress to the point where the people who replace us ought to be much better than we are. We should be building a place that is constantly improving. I would hope that the person who comes into this office will be a better scholar and a better dean than I am. If that person isn't, then we haven't succeeded in building a college."

*John Poirier of the Physics Department doing research at the Fermi National Accelerator Laboratory*

# The College of Science

WHEN NOTRE DAME CELEBRATED its "Centennial of Science" in 1965, scientists from around the world came to the campus as the University reviewed its past and charted its future. During the previous hundred years, Notre Dame had been the site of several achievements in scientific research and education. These milestones—like discovering the basic formula for synthetic rubber, doing pioneer work in germfree animal research, and creating the world's most advanced university-based facility for radiation research—brought more than recognition. They provided both a foundation and a direction for the development of the College of Science as it is today.

Notre Dame's early commitment to teaching and research in science can be traced in large measure to the work and example of two Holy Cross priests, Father John Zahm and Father Julius Nieuwland. Father Zahm, who joined the faculty in 1873, was primarily responsible for making the serious study of science part of the University's curriculum in the late nineteenth century. He helped design and oversaw the construction of Science Hall, which opened in 1884 and now exists as La Fortune Student Center. The Science Hall was significant because it marked the first time the campus had a separate building for classrooms and laboratories for its divisions of biology, chemistry, mathematics, and physics. The sciences were no longer crammed into two structures attached to the old church on campus. Father Zahm had the facilities necessary for the more rigorous academic work he believed students and faculty should do.

Zahm, who wanted Notre Dame to become, in his words, "the intellectual center of the American West," nurtured the growth of science by advocating increased support for these disciplines and by serving as a model researcher and scholar. The author of numerous scientific publications, he published four books between 1893 and 1896, including *Evolution and Dogma* and *Scientific Theory and Catholic Doctrine*. As a teacher and lecturer, Zahm influenced a generation of students and gained a reputation for being "a builder of scholars."

One of the students Zahm influenced but never formally taught was Julius Nieuwland, who graduated from Notre Dame with a bachelor's degree in 1899. After his ordination and the completion of his doctorate in chemistry at Catholic University, he returned to Notre Dame in 1904 to teach botany, his minor in graduate school. In 1909, he founded *The American Midland Naturalist*, a journal about plant life of the Midwest. This academic quarterly, which is now a "general biological journal," has grown in significance since it first appeared, and it currently circulates widely in this country and abroad.

Although he became well known as a botanist and served as editor of *The American Midland Naturalist* for some twenty-five years, Father Nieuwland received considerably more recognition from the scientific community for his work in chemistry. Beginning in 1918, when he became chairman of the Department of Chemistry, he focused most of his research time on chemical experiments. His work in the 1920s on the catalytic polymerization of acetylene led to the basic patents in the manufacture of neoprene, the first general purpose synthetic rubber ever invented. This discovery was of critical importance during the Second World War, when the Axis powers controlled ninety percent of the rubber plantations in the world. Today neoprene is used in tires, hoses, mattresses, cushions, life rafts, and many other products, and it generates $400 million in sales for E.I. DuPont de Nemours and Company. DuPont, the developer of neoprene, engaged Father Nieuwland as a consultant while this synthetic rubber was being perfected. The fees and royalties purchased library books about chemistry for the University and helped support the construction of Nieuwland Science Hall, which was completed in 1952, sixteen years after the death of the priest-scientist.

Father Nieuwland earned international acclaim for his discoveries and how they were applied. Guiding him, however, was the principle that new knowledge rather than any practical application should be the objective of scientific research conducted at a university. Writing in the *Notre Dame Alumnus* in the 1920s, he said: "The discovery of something absolutely new is the objective of research, and though apparently not very important for the time being, each new truth may become useful in the future." This emphasis on basic research took root, and Notre Dame also became known as the place that fostered serious, innovative research and teaching in science. With guidance from figures like Zahm and Nieuwland, the University had the foundation for a College of Science that would grow and develop as the scientific disciplines became more significant, sophisticated, and specialized in post-Depression America.

The campus-wide administrative reorganization of 1920 created seven departments in the College of Science: agriculture, botany, chemistry, mathematics, pharmacy, physics, and zoology. Two of the original departments, agriculture and pharmacy, were discontinued in the 1930s, and botany and zoology merged to form the Department of Biology in 1925. Today six departments exist:

Biological Sciences
Chemistry
Earth Sciences
Mathematics
Physics
Pre-Professional Studies

In the recent past, the College of Science has had the fewest number of majors of the four Colleges awarding undergraduate degrees. Graduate students, however, are another matter. Science ranks second behind Arts and Letters in granting of master's degrees and doctorates. Graduate instruction and research leading to the master of science and the doctorate are available in biological sciences, chemistry, and physics. Doctoral programs exist in mathematics and in two interdisciplinary fields of "Chemical Physics" and "Biochemistry, Biophysics, and Molecular Biology."

Although Father Nieuwland's numerous discoveries were primarily responsible for bringing Notre Dame's work in chemistry to the attention of the scientific community and the public at large, the University's teaching and research in the discipline date back to the mid-1800s. Laboratory experiments conducted at that time were among the first ever attempted at an American university. The first doctorate in chemistry was conferred in 1912, and a few years later Chemistry Hall became the first building on campus devoted to a single science.

Given the influence of Father Nieuwland, the Department of Chemistry first concentrated on developing a program in organic chemistry. This period yielded significant studies in acetylene chemistry, liquid ammonia, and boron trifluoride. Starting in 1930, the department began to expand its areas of inquiry, and physical chemistry became a focus. Notre Dame's landmark work in radiation chemistry, which was initiated in the 1940s, is an important component of the physical chemistry program. As the department evolved and became more diverse, inorganic chemistry and biochemistry were added as areas of concentration. Today the four subdisciplines of organic chemistry, physical chemistry, inorganic chemistry, and biochemistry comprise graduate specialty programs. In addition, interdepartmental and interdisciplinary programs in chemical physics and in biochemistry, biophysics, and molecular biology exist. On the undergraduate level, three programs are offered—one in chemistry as a career, another in biochemistry, and a third which combines the study of chemistry with a sequence of courses in other scientific disciplines, like physics, earth sciences, and environmental studies.

Although the department is of moderate size —approximately 25 faculty members, 65 graduate students, 25 postdoctoral fellows, and 75 undergraduate majors—Notre Dame was recently rated fourteenth in the nation for being able to attract financial support for chemical research. A

*J. KERRY THOMAS*
*Dept. of Chemistry*

*Notre Dame is a unique environment in that it provides an excellent education for its students, research opportunities for its faculty, and a commitment to values which benefits the entire community.*

*XAVIER CREARY*
*Dept. of Chemistry*

*The primary objectives of a University are the transfer of knowledge between faculty and students (teaching) and the expansion of those bodies of knowledge (research). These two fundamental aspects of university life can complement and inspire each other. The reaffirmation of the fundamental importance of research at Notre Dame has helped to insure that faculty remain provocative, enthusiastic, and current in their teaching as well.*

high percentage of this support comes from the Office of Basic Energy Sciences of the Department of Energy for operating the Notre Dame Radiation Laboratory, which is discussed later in this chapter. Of late, however, the University's work in biochemistry has been receiving increased levels of outside support. Teaching and research in biochemistry began in the 1960s with a grant from the National Science Foundation. Today this area of chemistry attracts over a third of all graduate students, and it is the most popular concentration for undergraduates. A considerable extent of the biochemical research being carried out at Notre Dame addresses health related problems like the formation and the dissolution of blood clots and the processes of blood coagulation. Francis J. Castellino, whose research contributions to understanding the structure, function, and activation properties of proteins involved in blood coagulation and fibrinolysis have earned international recognition, is the Kleiderer/Pezold Professor of Biochemistry. Since 1979 Castellino has also served as the Dean of the College of Science.

The Department of Chemistry also has other endowed professorships. Anthony M. Trozzolo, an organic chemist who specializes in photochemistry, is the Charles L. Huisking Professor of Chemistry, and J. Kerry Thomas, noted for developing techniques now widely used in physical chemistry, occupies the Julius A. Nieuwland Professorship of Science. These chaired professors, their colleagues, and students use research facilities and instrumentation available in Stepan Chemistry Hall, which was dedicated in 1982, Nieuwland Science Hall, and the Radiation Laboratory. The laboratories and equipment make state-of-the-art basic research in chemistry possible. The department also annually sponsors two lecture series—the Nieuwland Lectures and the Reilly Lectures—which bring several distinguished chemists from the United States and abroad to the campus for week-long visits that include formal presentations of papers as well as informal interaction with students and faculty.

Through the influence of Father Zahm, Notre Dame increased its offerings in physics in the 1870s, the decade this discipline entered the curriculum of the University's fledgling "Scientific Course." Prior to 1934, however, the Department of Physics existed primarily as a service department. Faculty members taught engineering and pre-medical students the basics of physics, but did little to cultivate majors, to offer graduate courses, or to engage in research. During the 1930s, the department changed its approach and began to emphasize a distinct research program and graduate education.

Nuclear physics became the dominant concern, and the University built the first Van de Graaf accelerator to be located in the Midwest. It was used to study the interaction of electrons and gamma rays with nuclei. The first disintegration of a nucleus by electrons was accomplished at Notre Dame in 1939, and some of the earliest work on metastable levels in nuclei was done at this time.

Shortly before World War II began, the University completed work on an enclosed and pressurized accelerator. This more sophisticated accelerator was used by scientists working on the Manhattan Project for studies in radiation damage. The work of Notre Dame's nuclear physicists and the presence of the advanced equipment helped to make the University a center for radiation research in the United States.

After the war, the Department of Physics grew and diversified. By instituting programs in three experimental areas—nuclear, surface, and polymer—as well as a concentration in theoretical physics, the department became more comprehensive and attractive to graduate students. Today, with a faculty of approximately 30, Notre Dame continues to support teaching and research in nuclear and theoretical physics. Three other areas of focus are atomic physics, elementary particle or high energy physics, and solid-state/low temperature or condensed matter physics. All of the central areas of interest in contemporary physics are represented in the department, and it is also involved in an interdisciplinary program in chemical physics. Although a large majority of physics undergraduates select the "career program" and go on to graduate school, they also have the opportunity to take part in four other bachelor degree programs: physics in medicine, applied physics, physics with chemistry, and physics with earth sciences.

Historically, Notre Dame's work in nuclear physics has helped to advance modern physics, bringing considerable recognition to the department. The University has helped to support this basic research on the composition of matter by constructing the Nuclear Structure Laboratory on campus. This facility, Notre Dame's oldest laboratory, is one of only nine government-designated and university-based accelerator laboratories in the United States. The lab runs experiments which (among other things) measure atomic masses, study the structure of heavy nuclei and the way they spin, and investigate the reactions of heavy ions, by using two accelerators, one operating at eight million volts and the other at two million volts.

As new theories of nuclear structure incorporate considerations of quarks and gluons (the elementary constituents of matter), the studies of

*NEAL M. CASON*
Dept. of Physics

*Basic research in the Department of Physics has increased enormously in both depth and in breadth over the past two decades. The excitement generated by this work permeates the lives of our faculty and graduate students, and invites our undergraduates to participate in the process of discovery.*

Notre Dame's researchers in nuclear physics and elementary particle or high energy physics have become more closely related. Many experiments in elementary particle physics are conducted at the Fermi National Accelerator Laboratory and at the Brookhaven National Laboratory. Researchers from Notre Dame frequently join with physicists from other universities in studying such topics as the properties of quarks and gluons and the particles they comprise. After experiments are performed off-campus, the data they yield are analyzed at Notre Dame.

Atomic physicists at Notre Dame also use the Nuclear Structure Laboratory and other facilities, like the Argonne National Laboratory, as they study the structure and decay characteristics of few-electron atoms and ions. This research advances the theoretical understanding of atoms at their most fundamental level.

The department's program in solid-state/low-temperature or condensed matter physics has experimental areas in superconductivity, rare-earth magnetism, and x-ray absorption studies of condensed-matter systems. This program was enhanced in 1983 through the appointment of John D. Dow, a specialist in theoretical solid-state physics, to the Frank M. Freimann Professorship of Physics. In 1984 Notre Dame researchers organized the first International Conference on Superlattices, Microstructures, and Microdevices. As silicon chips reach their limits of transistor capacity, other semiconductors are becoming necessary. Superlattices are man-made crystals that will increase the power and capacity of computers in the 1990s. Development of these ultra-high-speed computers will help scientists to pinpoint tumors in cancer patients, to predict storms and tornado movements, and to map stars in distant galaxies. Jacek K. Furdyna, former director of Purdue University's Materials Research Laboratory and a leading figure in the design and development of new semiconductor materials, was appointed to the Aurora and Tom Marquez University Professorship in 1986. The endowed chair was established for a specialist in computer technology and information theory.

The teaching of mathematics at Notre Dame dates back to the founding of the University in 1842. Father Sorin incorporated the study of arithmetic and elementary collegiate mathematics into the original curriculum. Until the late 1930s, however, the status of the Department of Mathematics was similar to that of the Department of Physics. Both departments served the University, particularly the College of Engineering, but as freestanding disciplines they lacked strength and diversity. In mathematics, this situation began to change in 1937 with the arrival of Karl Menger, a noted mathematician in this country and abroad. As chairman, Menger designed a department that not only provided the necessary service courses but also included a graduate program and a serious concern for research and scholarly publishing. What Menger started took root and led to the development of a department that has received widespread recognition within the mathematics community. Six members of the current faculty have received the prestigious Sloan Fellowships for Basic Research, and there has been a marked increase in recent years in the number of research grants from the National Science Foundation awarded to Notre Dame mathematicians.

Given the moderate size of the Department of Mathematics (a faculty of 35), there are specific areas of concentration on the graduate level rather than teaching and research programs in all of the subdisciplines. The focus is on pure mathematics —the math of original ideas—and several of its facets: algebra, complex analysis, differential equations, differential geometry, logic, number theory, algebraic geometry, and topology. The Rev. Howard J. Kenna Professorship of Mathematics, which honors a former member of the department who became Provincial of the Congregation of the Holy Cross, is occupied by Timothy O'Meara, a mathematician of international reputation, whose areas of specialty include algebra, the theory of numbers, and arithmetic properties of classical groups. His work in developing the isomorphism theory of linear groups is widely recognized as significant to research and teaching about modern algebra. O'Meara has also served as Provost of the University since 1978. The endowment from the Kenna Chair helps to support visiting algebraists and to sponsor a series of lectures that brings noted mathematicians to the campus each year. Some of these lectures are published by the University of Notre Dame Press in its series entitled *Notre Dame Mathematical Lectures.*

Internationally, the stature of the department benefits considerably from the scholarly contributions of Wilhelm Stoll, a faculty member at Notre Dame since 1960. Stoll is widely known for his research in complex analysis and value distribution theory. Mathematicians doing research about complex variables deal with problems that arise in extending the techniques of calculus and analytical geometry to spaces defined in terms of complex numbers. Several noted mathematicians (from Germany, France, Hungary, Japan, China, and the United States) participated in a seminar at Notre Dame in 1984 to honor Stoll for his work in complex analysis. During this seminar, the University established an endowment for the acquisition of mathematical books in Stoll's name.

In addition to having a strong faculty of junior and senior members, the standing of the department benefits from the teaching and research of visiting professors who regularly come to Notre Dame from universities overseas. Mathematics has one of the University's most active programs for visiting scholars. This program helps to establish relationships internationally, with one result being that Notre Dame mathematicians, in turn, are frequently invited to be visiting professors at universities abroad.

While the number of graduate students in mathematics has remained constant (at between 32 and 35) during recent years, undergraduate majors have doubled. This sharp increase is principally due to the popularity of the bachelor's program that combines the study of mathematics with computer science. Undergraduates are also able to pursue other joint programs—such as math and social science, engineering, education, and life science—as well as an "honors" and a "career" major.

The Department of Biological Sciences, which was formed in 1985, results from the merger of two departments: biology and microbiology. Establishment of the combined department brings together related teaching and research programs that share common interests and goals. The new department continues to have distinct specialty areas; however, it now offers faculty and students, especially those pursuing graduate degrees, greater diversity and more possibility for interdisciplinary inquiry. Having a single department dissolves the boundaries between such subfields as ecology, physiology, and cell biology and fosters more comprehensive study of the life sciences—from the molecular to the organismal levels. What was formerly known as the Department of Biology came into being during the academic year of 1925-1926. The creation of this department united Notre Dame's work in botany, zoology, anatomy, cytology, and bacteriology, which had begun in the nineteenth century. Rev. Alexander M. Kirsch, C.S.C., directed the study of the natural sciences from 1874 to 1918, and he was instrumental in building the foundation for the subsequent Department of Biology. Before the turn of the century, Father Kirsch founded the Laboratory of Cellular Biology, the first such laboratory in the United States, and he became widely known for his lectures and publications on cytology.

Father Nieuwland, of course, made significant contributions to botany. Besides being the founder and first editor of *The American Midland Naturalist*, he published nearly one hundred botanical papers, accumulated a large library of rare botanical books printed prior to 1753, and collected thousands of plant specimens. Father Nieuwland was also responsible for bringing the noted botanist Edward Lee Greene to Notre Dame in 1914. When Greene died, he left his botanical library of over 3,500 volumes and his herbarium to the University. Today the Notre Dame Memorial Library houses the books of Nieuwland and Greene, and the collection—of both historical and scientific value—is consulted by botanists from this country and abroad. The Nieuwland and Greene Herbaria on campus contain approximately 250,000 plant specimens.

The former Department of Microbiology, the second academic unit involved in the creation of the Department of Biological Sciences, developed primarily out of the work carried out at Notre Dame's LOBUND Laboratory, which is described later. Drawing on the teaching and research ca-

*STEPHEN R. CARPENTER*
Dept. of Biological Sciences

*Creative researchers bring the excitement of discovery into the classroom, and interactions with bright students sharpen our thinking about research problems. Our strongest assets are our undergraduates and our research.*

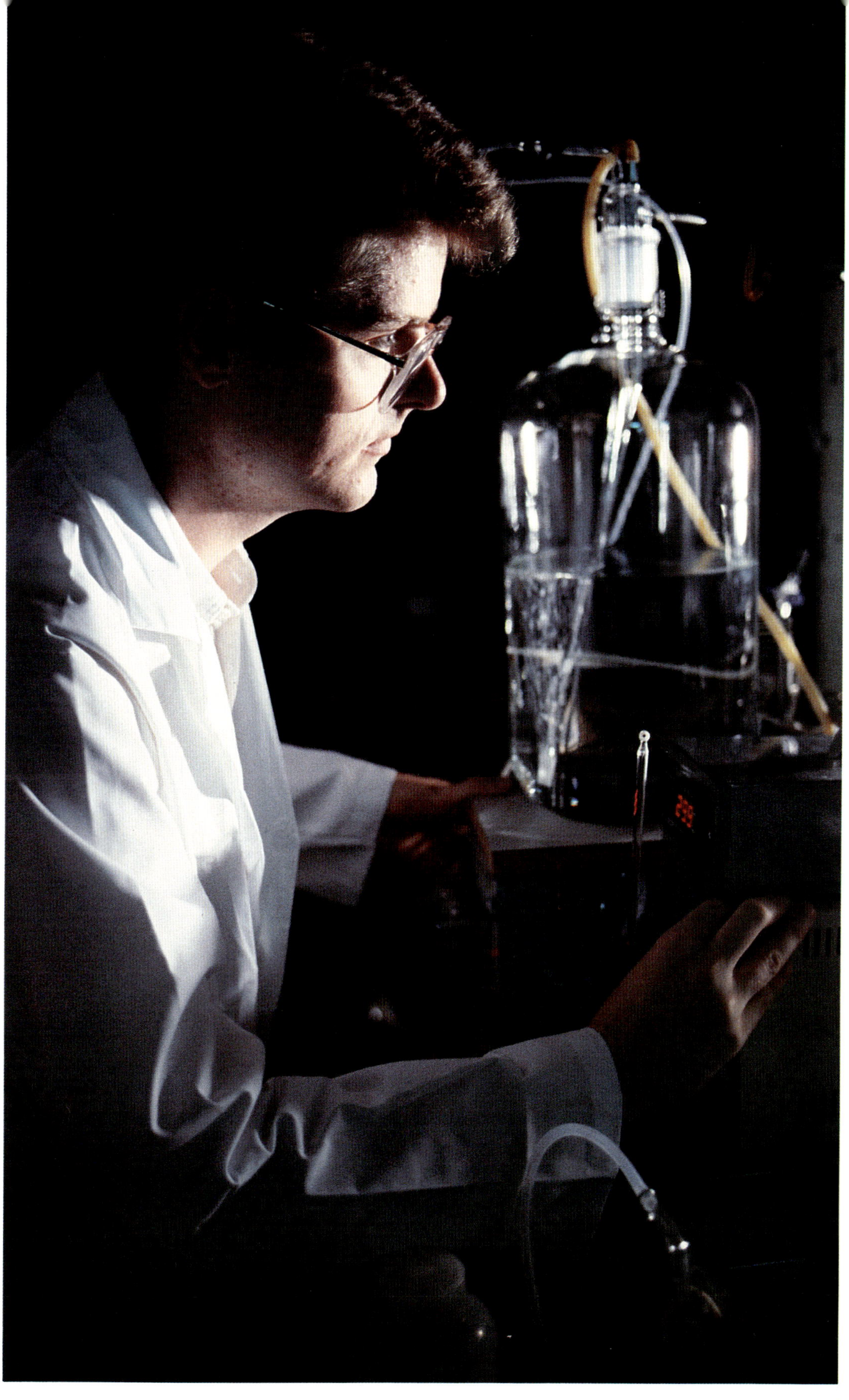

pabilities of scientists associated with LOBUND, the University established a graduate program in microbiology in 1966. An undergraduate major was inaugurated in 1975. As the department grew, it broadened its focus beyond germfree research or gnotobiotics to include a concentration in molecular biology, the subdiscipline responsible for so many recent scientific discoveries, like recombinant DNA research or genetic engineering.

The areas of specialization are not rigidly defined in the Department of Biological Sciences. In addition to the LOBUND-related research involving germfree animal life technology and its applications, special programs exist in aquatic biology, computers in biology, parasitology, and vector biology. The possibilities for projects in aquatic biology are enhanced from doing work at the University's 8,000-acre Environmental Research Center, which is located in the Upper Peninsula of Michigan and Wisconsin. The heavily wooded, private facility contains more than 20 lakes and has a wide range of habitats for ecological, limnological, and entomological research. The Center, one of the few of its kind for any university, includes laboratory and living facilities.

Integrating the use of computers into teaching and research in the biological sciences has become a distinctive element of the department, and Notre Dame is recognized as a leader in this field. Biologists use computers to create ecological simulation models, to make inventories of plants, insects, or animals, to do numerical taxonomy, to provide environmental data management and assessment, and to complete other procedures. The University maintains BIOBUND, a data and literature bank with a special emphasis on the plants, animals, and environment of Indiana, and MODABUND, a computerized file of over 30,000 literature references to mosquitoes.

Given the pioneering nature of the University's work in biocomputing, faculty members conduct instructional programs for professors from other universities and colleges about incorporating computers into their teaching and research. Beginning in 1981, week-long courses have taken place on campus and at other sites across the country. In addition to these pedagogical efforts, several of the leading publications about biocomputing and using biocomputing techniques have been written by Notre Dame professors.

The Vector Biology Laboratory that operates within the department was founded in 1957, and it now enjoys an international reputation for its specialized research about mosquitoes. The program focuses on the genetics, physiology, and ecology of *Aedes* mosquitoes, and the multidisciplinary undertaking involves arbovirology, parasitology, biochemistry, pheromones, formal genetics, population dynamics, cytogenetics, ultrastructure, and genetic control. The laboratory has received outside funding from the National Institutes of Health and other agencies. The grants from NIH, in fact, constitute the longest continuous support of a research project by NIH.

For several years after it was established, the laboratory directed much of its work to studying the mosquito responsible for transmitting yellow fever (*Aedes aegypti*). From 1970 until 1977 after years of laboratory research, scientists from Notre Dame led the mosquito biology unit of the International Centre for Insect Physiology and Ecology in Mombasa, Kenya. This project in Africa and related efforts in India produced significant scientific and public health-related results, particularly in the genetic control of mosquitoes.

In 1975 an encephalitis epidemic in the United States began to shift the focus of the Vector Biology Laboratory. "We were running around putting out fires all over the world, when all of a sudden it became apparent that the biggest fire of all was raging right here at home," says George B. Craig, the George and Winifred Clark Professor of Biology and the director of the laboratory. Encephalitis, the serious and often fatal disease characterized by inflammation of the brain, is transmitted by *Aedes* mosquitoes. The principal object of study is the treehole mosquito (*Aedes triseriatus*), the primary cause of encephalitis in the midwestern United States. Control of this mosquito is nearly impossible at present. Insecticides cannot be applied to reach treeholes or discarded car tires, two most common breeding sites. No vaccine exists. According to Craig, who was elected to the National Academy of Sciences in 1983 for his numerous contributions to vector biology, "We are trying to find some genetic 'Achilles' heel to exploit to control the disease. With a proper understanding of factors affecting transmission, someday we may be able to use genetic techniques to replace vectors with noninfecting strains of *Aedes triseriatus*."

Besides this project, the Vector Biology Laboratory serves as the World Health Organization International Reference Centre for *Aedes* mosquitoes, maintaining over 180 genetic strains and 52 species, which it supplies to other laboratories throughout the world. The Laboratory for Arbovirus Research and Surveillance also operates within the Vector Biology Laboratory. As a result of Notre Dame's concentration in this area, the laboratory is responsible for training more predoctoral and postdoctoral vector biologists than any other laboratory nationally or internationally.

The teaching and research programs of the Department of Biological Sciences are carried out in the Paul V. Galvin Life Science Center, which was dedicated in 1972. An expansion of research projects necessitated the construction of the Frank M. Freimann Research Facility, which was completed in 1985. This new research facility is adjacent to the Galvin Life Science Center.

Courses in geology and mineralogy at Notre Dame date back to 1863–64, and Science Hall, built 20 years later, featured an extensive collection of geological specimens as part of its museum. In 1948 the University enlarged its work in this discipline by formally establishing a Department of Geology. Twenty-four years later the department's name was changed to the Department of Earth Sciences, a decision reflecting the increasing diversity within the area. As it is currently organized, the Department of Earth Sciences encompasses the study of geology, geochemistry, geophysics, hydrology, oceanography, and meteorology.

Exclusively an undergraduate department, the majors in Earth Sciences participate in one of eight different programs. Although the majority of students follow the program for the professional geologist, others specialize in geochemistry, marine geology, geophysics, paleobiology, geology and hydrology, and earth sciences with mathematics and computing science. A five-year combined program in geology and civil engineering also exists. Almost three-quarters of the graduates in Earth Sciences pursue graduate degrees at other universities, and the highest percentage of these people work in the petroleum industry.

The research interests of the earth scientists at Notre Dame cover such topics as paleontology of the Western United States and the effects of weathering and pollution on buildings and monuments. Some of the publications emanating from the department involve collaboration between faculty members and advanced undergraduate students. In addition to its undergraduate teaching programs and the advanced research projects, Earth Sciences also conducts special summer institutes to help minority high school students learn about geology. These programs, which are funded by several oil companies, enable youths from the Chicago area to make field trips to Montana to study geological formations.

The Department of Preprofessional Studies is one of only 10 interdisciplinary undergraduate programs in the United States designed exclusively to prepare students for medical and dental school and for related professions. At most other universities, students specialize in a specific area of science, like biology, prior to graduation. At Notre Dame, students in Preprofessional Studies are able to take a variety of courses in the sciences —biology, chemistry, mathematics, and physics— as well as several electives within the College of Science and the University. Given the diversity of the curriculum and the involvement of so many disciplines, the work of the department is primarily administrative in nature.

Preprofessional Studies has existed as a separate academic unit since 1961. Its program of premedical studies has been accredited by the American Medical Association, and graduates of the department have earned a high (80 percent) rate of acceptance to medical and dental schools. Besides a diverse scientific education, most of these graduates take with them experience of working in a hospital. Students participate in three different hospital volunteer programs in the South Bend area.

In addition to the Department of Preprofessional Studies, Notre Dame conducts the South Bend Center for Medical Education. The Center, one of seven in the Indiana University Medical School system, offers the first two years of medical education to potential graduates of the I.U. Medical School. The Center also participates in programs that lead to graduate degrees from Notre Dame in biomedically oriented areas, such as human anatomy, human physiology, and neuroscience. Regular Notre Dame faculty members contribute to the teaching and research carried out by the Center.

Besides the six academic departments, two University institutes—LOBUND (an acronym for Laboratories of Bacteriology at the University of Notre Dame) and the Radiation Laboratory—are affiliated with the College of Science. Although each institute operates autonomously from the departments to which it is related, many of the scientists who work at these laboratories offer classes as well as conduct research.

Since its founding in 1935, LOBUND has received international recognition as the premier laboratory for germfree research. James A. Reyniers, a bacteriologist at Notre Dame for many years, was a pioneer in developing and utilizing germfree animals and in designing and building sterile, germfree environments and enclosures. The work of Reyniers and his associates contributed significantly to the establishment of gnotobiotics (germfree research) as a serious and valuable subdiscipline of science. During the early years of LOBUND, Reyniers was particularly influential in creating the germfree animal model (rats, mice, chickens, and others) for use in experiments to study health conditions and problems like cancer, heart disease, virus infection, and tooth decay.

The longest operating facility of its kind in the world, LOBUND today continues to be responsible for defining the norms and methodologies of germfree research. Generations of animals and the most sophisticated technology enable the scientists at LOBUND to develop and work with model systems where the diseases affecting the animals have counterparts in humans. The rats and mice are isolated from any hazards from the outside, and researchers concentrate on the causes and effects involved in specific health problems. Work done at LOBUND, for example, revealed that cancer was *not* caused by a virus, a theory that had wide acceptance before the early 1960s. The scientists at Notre Dame showed that animals without any viruses or contact with viruses could still contract cancer. Living in a world without germs was no defense against the disease.

LOBUND is a multi-disciplinary institute that involves the participation of specialists from several scientific areas: microbiology (virology, bacteriology, physiology, immunology), pathology, oncology, nutrition, biochemistry, radiation biology, and epidemiology. Current research interests include cancer, heart diseases, dental decay, ecology, nutrition, virology, cell membranes, transplantation immunology, congenital diseases, and experimental surgery. Studying the interrelationship of aging, diet, and cancer has become a central undertaking at LOBUND. Recent research findings showed that a high-fat diet yields an elevated incidence of breast and intestinal cancer in animals. In another study, the lifespan of experimental animals was markedly extended by reducing and regulating their diet. These animals, too, had no evidence of disease.

Discovering new techniques for cross-species transplants has also become a subject of inquiry during recent years. In 1984 scientists at LOBUND successfully transferred bone-marrow cells from mice to rats to create rats that produce mouse blood. All of the rats involved in the study survived the marrow transplants for at least three hundred days, and they produced the normal levels of red and white blood cells. Ultimately, these experiments and others related to it could improve the methods of transplanting tissues from one species to another.

All of the research carried out at LOBUND does not involve germfree animals. There are other aspects to the work of the laboratory. The germfree plastic bubble that was home to the 12-year-old Houston boy, David, until his death in 1984 was designed and constructed by Notre Dame researchers. The boy, who was born without a functioning immune system, was the oldest survivor of this genetic defect, and he required a germfree environment to live. Sterile enclosures developed at LOBUND have also been used in surgery, chemotherapy, radiotherapy, in the treatment of burn victims as well as in the American space program.

The work of LOBUND is conducted in the Galvin Life Science Center and in the Reyniers Germfree Life Building, a building on the northern edge of the campus where much of the early germfree research was carried out. Funding for the many different projects of LOBUND come from several sources. The University has also created an endowment to benefit the institute. In 1985 the Coleman Foundation, Inc., of Chicago established the Coleman Chair in Life Sciences at Notre Dame. This endowed professorship, the first in the world in germfree research, is reserved for the director of LOBUND. Morris Pollard, whose studies of cancer, the relationship between diet and longevity, and the effects of environmental pollutants have received international recognition, is the first occupant of the Coleman Chair. He has directed LOBUND since 1961.

In future years LOBUND will continue to refine the techniques of germfree research and to explore new possibilities of such studies. The tools of modern molecular biology will play a key role in the scientific work that is conducted at LOBUND.

The Radiation Laboratory, the other institute affiliated with the College of Science, is a facility owned by the United States Department of Energy but operated by Notre Dame. The Radiation Lab is continuing—and dramatically expanding—the University's early work in learning what effects radiation has on matter and how radiation can be used to study unusual reactants involved in attempts to design future energy sources. The construction of the 65,000-square-foot facility, which was completed in 1963 under the auspices of the Atomic Energy Commission, was in many ways the culmination of ground-breaking efforts in radiation research carried out by faculty members in the Departments of Physics and Chemistry that dated back to their involvement in the Manhattan Project in the 1940s. Following World War II, Notre Dame scientists sustained and broadened their inquiry in this area.

Today the Radiation Laboratory is regarded as the foremost research center of its type in the world. Its work is interdisciplinary in nature, encompassing the efforts of chemists, physicists, biologists, and engineers. During its early years, the lab's studies focused on in-depth comprehension of the radiation process itself. The emphasis now is on what radiation processes can do, with a special concern for understanding the various processes that follow the absorption of ionizing and ultraviolet radiation. The research emanating from the Radiation Laboratory—an average of one hundred academic papers annually—is basic rather than applied. Scientific publications, instead of products, result from the experiments that are conducted. Some of the studies, however, have led to information that has provided more sophisticated understanding of the radiation treatment of cancer and the storage of solar energy.

Professor Robert H. Schuler, who occupies the Henkels Chair in Radiation Chemistry at the University, is the Director of the Radiation Laboratory. Schuler is an internationally recognized authority on radiation chemistry. The staff of the Radiation Laboratory is made up of members of the teaching and research faculty of the University as well as professional specialists, research associates, and advanced students working in collaboration with research advisors. Approximately 90 to 100 people are affiliated with the lab, the majority of whom hold doctoral degrees in science or engineering. A high percentage of the work done at the Radiation Laboratory is collaborative, scientists from the United States and abroad coming to Notre Dame to do research. In a typical year, representatives from 30 different external institutions—for example, the University of Texas, Vanderbilt University, Indiana University, University of Paris, the Royal Institution (England), University of Tokyo, Weizmann Institute of Science (Israel), and Indian Institute of Technology—carried out projects using the lab's facilities. Thus far specialists in radiation from over 50 countries have completed experiments at the University. The numerous requests from outsiders to come to the Radiation Laboratory reflect the international reputation the institute enjoys.

The laboratory has an extensive array of sophisticated equipment. Four electron accelerators, including a 10-million-electron-volt linear accelerator, are housed in underground vaults adjacent to the main laboratory building. Studies with visible and ultraviolet light are carried out by using different types of optical sources. The lab has several lasers capable of producing large light pulses in microseconds. Analytical facilities include various types of spectrophotometers, electron-spin-resonance spectrometers, spectrofluorimeters, gas and liquid chromatographs, a differential scanning calorimeter, and light-scattering and radiochemical apparatus. Many of the instruments are linked to minicomputers and to the University's central computer.

Besides being the catalyst for numerous experiments and publications, the laboratory is also the site of the Radiation Chemistry Data Center, a resource facility that is jointly sponsored by the Department of Energy and the Office of Standard Reference Data of the National Bureau of Standards. The Center provides data and information to radiation chemists and other scientists in this country and overseas.

Since the 1970s, the College of Science has experienced significant growth. New areas of modern scientific inquiry have become integral to the life of the College. New buildings as well as sophisticated laboratory facilities and contemporary equipment have enhanced research and teaching across the disciplines. These advances and additions, however, exist in an intellectual environment that has changed little during the past half-century. Father Nieuwland's insistence on discovering "something absolutely new" that leads to "new truth" serves as a fundamental principle for the thinking and activities in science at the University. The commitment to "new truth" that is communicated through published research and classroom instruction has helped guide the College for several decades, and it will continue to be a hallmark of future scientific undertakings at Notre Dame.

PROFILE

DEAN FRANCIS J. CASTELLINO

COLLEGE OF SCIENCE

WHEN DEAN FRANCIS J. CASTELLINO looks at the College of Science, he sees both continuity and change. According to Castellino, the effective combination of teaching and research has been a constant of the College and its allied institutes for the past forty to fifty years. Since the 1970s, however, he notes that there has been a new approach in choosing the scientific areas to study. Strategic selection of subjects by departmental faculty and College and University administrators has replaced serendipitous growth areas of earlier times.

Castellino, who was named dean in 1979, views the College of Science as being in a different stage of development from the other Colleges at Notre Dame—Arts and Letters, Engineering, and Business Administration. In their cases, trying to attain balance between teaching and research on a college-wide basis has occurred more recently, and there is a formative quality to the work being conducted in several departments. "In the College of Science, we reached maturation with the attitude of research and teaching a long time ago," says Castellino, who besides being dean is the Kleiderer-Pezold Professor of Biochemistry. "We are not evolving this attitude any longer. We've had here, for four to five decades, certain individuals who were outstanding researchers and outstanding teachers at the same time. To say now that we want more research is not necessary for this College. We have been in the teaching-research mode for years. We now must concentrate on being successful in these ventures and not sacrificing one component for the sake of the other."

Castellino believes that the accomplishments of Notre Dame scientists many years ago in at least four areas were instrumental in making the University known within the scientific community and in establishing the proper balance between research and teaching. He singles out the work leading to the discovery of neoprene, the study of the effects of radiation on matter, the nuclear physics program, and the pioneering efforts in germfree research as activities that helped create the foundation on which the contemporary College builds. Castellino sees parallels among the past accomplishments. "I don't think Notre Dame was necessarily looking to make a major splash in research when Father Nieuwland was working on the acetylene chemistry that led to discovery of neoprene," the dean observes. (Rev. Julius Nieuwland, C.S.C., helped to discover neoprene, the first high-quality synthetic rubber, by conducting chemical experiments in the 1920s.) "We just happened to have a good scientist who was here for a very specific reason. I also don't believe Notre Dame ever consciously tried to have a major radiation laboratory, but we had some good people who did their jobs quite well. The same can be said about the nuclear physics program that began prior to the Second World War and the germfree research that dates back to the 1930s. These things that made us what we are were mainly chance. It was serendipity. We just had good people around who wanted to be here and who were quite successful in their professions."

Today, though, the development of the College of Science is more methodical. As Castellino explains, "During the period after 1970, there was greater recognition of what quality should be, and I think at that point, quality was more or less planned within the College. Today we're certainly carefully considering each area that we want to get into. The best example is our recent plunge into molecular biology. That was planned. Our program in solid-state physics was planned. We had the resources, so we could begin these areas. Everything we do today is subjected to serious scrutiny, as to what science is hot and what science is not going to cool off. We do not move into faddish areas as soon as the pendulum swings in Washington, but we also cannot ignore the signals as to what kinds of research are fundable, interesting to the professional and lay communities, and what is in the public interest. Delicate balances are present, and your judgments had

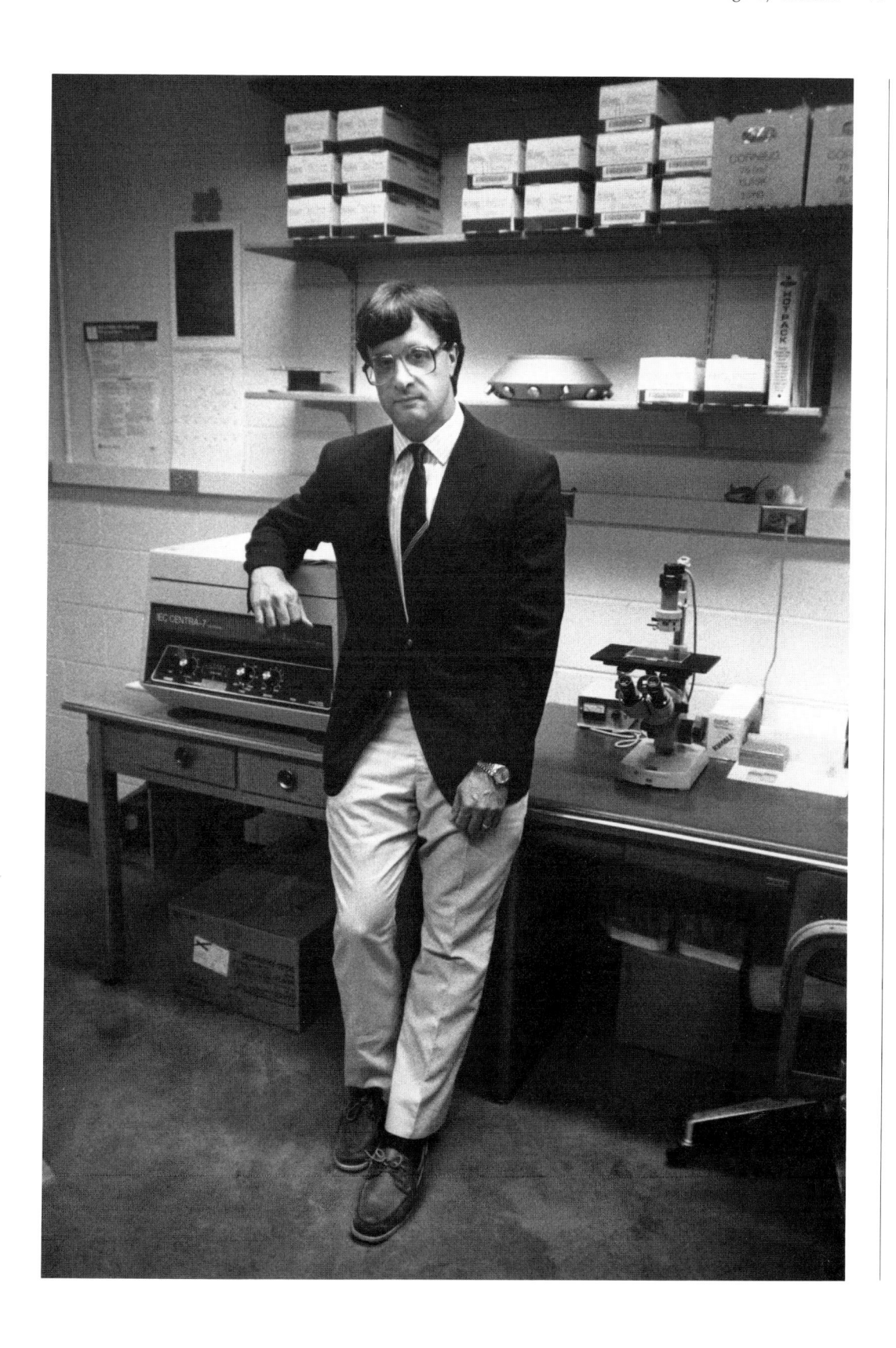

The College of Science 79

better be correct, or else you have expensive problems on your hands."

In planning new programs and directing existing ones, Castellino emphasizes that the size of the College and the availability of financial resources are significant factors in defining the work of Notre Dame scientists. "We can't cover all of the bases," the dean admits. "We're too small. That's why we plan specific areas. In fact, the way I like to think about every department is not as, say, a Physics Department or a Mathematics Department, but as the kinds of physics and mathematics that we do. There's a lot we're not involved in, and obviously, we make no impact in those areas. But, within the departments, we are competitive in every area upon which we focus. Our scope is limited, but our intensity is not. We're not missing the necessary areas, but there are aspects of those areas that, had we more money, we might really want to participate in."

Although limitations result from the size of the College, Castellino also sees benefits from "the smallness of the place." There is strength without numbers. As he explains: "It's virtually impossible to do something really good here and be ignored. For example, I think it's possible for a faculty member in the College of Science to say: 'Notre Dame is different for me being here in the following ways.' To enumerate those ways: Anybody who has done something significant can see that the place has changed because of him or her. It's also extremely easy for an idea to be implemented at Notre Dame, and I think the faculty understands this. It is easy to communicate with any echelon of structure in the University. We're small enough and communicative enough and give the faculty quite a large say in what we do. Therefore, they feel they can see their accomplishments tangibly. That's very distinctive. In many places, especially the larger universities, you can do or say something and never see it recognized or implemented. At Notre Dame, individuals can change the College of Science."

According to Castellino, another element that helps to foster change and to lead to accomplishments is a spirit of cooperation that pervades the College and the University. He believes that some of this spirit can be traced to the Catholic nature of Notre Dame and to the types of people that are attracted to this kind of university. The dean admits that "you can't really do Catholic science"; however, he perceives an intangible benefit that develops from Notre Dame's religious character. This intangible affects not only faculty members in certain ways, but it also influences undergraduate and graduate students. Unlike schools elsewhere with which he is familiar, Castellino finds students in the College of Science more interested in exploring the moral and ethical implications of what they're learning in the classroom and doing in a laboratory.

Historically, the Catholicity of Notre Dame has been a significant factor in recruiting and keeping professors of science, according to Castellino. "There are people who are here because they have a firm desire to be at a Catholic university," he observes. "I would say that's one reason why we don't have as much turnover of faculty." In recent yeras, however, the dean detects a tempering of religious motivation. "Unfortunately, I don't think that the Catholic nature is as big an overall concern to the younger faculty as it was earlier, in the sense that this facet pervades their lives. Many of them are here simply because they find it an outstanding place to develop their careers. While I am nervous about the implications, it is nonetheless, a big compliment to the College and the University. I'm not saying that the Catholicity of Notre Dame is not important to the young faculty. Many, in fact, come because of it—but that, alone, would not keep them here, as was the case with previous generations of faculty. As you evolve into an outstanding university, you're going to get people who are present only because this is a stimulating place to be. In that sense we should not be overly disturbed, but we need to be extremely careful that we do not swing to the other side and, in fact, lose our identity. I think we just have to do the best we can and now try to attract people who want a healthy blend of both worlds."

In the scholarly realm, Castellino emphasizes that to improve the College you must maintain and, indeed, strengthen the connections between teaching and research. "I think it's very important to interweave teaching and research in science, because I believe people performing research do stay current and can teach more effectively than people who don't do research or participate in scholarship. I view research and scholarship in science as major components of teaching. These activities are so related that I don't even like to talk about them separately."

Castellino's own academic career reflects the interweaving of research with teaching as well as a commitment to remain at the forefront of his discipline. He joined the Notre Dame faculty in 1970, following two years of postdoctoral work at Duke University. During the 1960s, he earned a bachelor's degree in chemistry from the University of Scranton and his master's and Ph.D. degrees in biochemistry from the University of Iowa. A specialist in protein chemistry and blood coagulation, Castellino has focused his study for the past several years on the structure, function, and activation mechanisms of the proteins used in the human body for forming and dissolving blood clots. This basic research, which has the ultimate objective of solving several problems that arise when clotting occurs either too rapidly or not quickly enough, has received considerable recognition in the scientific and medical communities. Castellino and his research team of faculty members, postdoctoral fellows, and graduate students receive grant support from such agencies as the National Institutes of Health, the National Science Foundation, the American Heart Association, and the Indiana Heart Association. As a result of his research accomplishments, Castellino has been elected a member of the American Society of Biological Chemists, the International Society for Thrombosis and Hemostasis, and elected a fellow of the New York Academy of Sciences.

Even with his duties as dean, Castellino continues to be active as a scientist. He has had to reduce some of his teaching load, but he conducts his own research and works with graduate students and postdoctoral fellows a portion of each day. "I know what impact I've had on the University and in my field, and I'm happy with what I've accomplished," Castellino says. "My research program is still very strong, but whether it could have been better, were I not dean, or whether it would be poorer, is hard to say. It's not obvious that either would be the case. Being a dean gives you a lot of other things to think about, and that may actually help your own research. The way I view it, if I had to walk away from this job tomorrow, I could do something I'm very happy with—that's being a professor of chemistry. When an administrator is serving in such a capacity because there are no other options available to that person, then you really have a problem on your hands."

During his tenure as dean, Castellino points to "the whole refocusing, direction, and modernization of life sciences" as the most notable accomplishment. The new state-of-the-art facility for animal research is the culmination of these efforts. He also cites the establishment of the solid-state program in physics, the enhanced reputation of the Mathematics Department, and the construction of Stepan Chemistry Hall to maintain the long-time strength of the Chemistry Department as significant factors in advancing science at Notre Dame. On the teaching side, all of these advances have been incorporated into an outstanding curriculum for the student, and his exposure to the top professors. Looking back, he notes; "Beginning in the late '70s, we had a big spurt of hiring and development which has lasted until this time. I think now we have to give the younger people a chance to settle in, to do their work, and to establish themselves. There will probably be another substantial growth phase in the 1990s."

According to Castellino, money will play a decisive role in the future of research in the College. "Research in science is exceedingly expensive, and the financial obstacles to success are enormous. The monetary picture determines whether or not you're going to be a research university. Whether faculty come and go, whether we have endowed chairs, and who comes to fill them—all of this is very important. But it's all so tied into the finances and what the University is tangibly doing to underpin research. Grants are getting a lot smaller, which means fewer universities will be doing major science. Is this University going to be able to put in the missing resources? If not, we're probably going to lose out big, very big. If the financial resources are there and Notre Dame's commitment to science remains strong, we'll be one of the survivors, because the talent is already in place."

# The College of Engineering

THE UNITED STATES experienced a technology rush during the last three decades of the nineteenth century. New inventions and discoveries propelled advances in transportation, communication, industrialization, agriculture, and domestic life. Beginning in 1873, with the establishment of a formal course of study in engineering, Notre Dame participated in what historians call "the age of energy." Notre Dame was not only the first Catholic university to offer a degree in engineering, it was also the site of several significant discoveries that contributed to the growth of modern technology.

Albert Zahm, the younger brother of Rev. John Zahm, performed many of his pioneering experiments in aeronautics on the campus during the 1880s and early 1890s. As a Notre Dame junior in 1882, he built what some scholars consider to be the first wind tunnel in the United States for comparing the lift and drag of aeronautical models. Several years later, while on the faculty at the Catholic University in Washington, D.C., he constructed the first large wind tunnel in the world. The development of wind tunnels, however, was just one of Zahm's concerns. As a professor at Notre Dame, and a pioneer in aviation, he designed an air-worthy helicopter and a man-carrying glider. The launching pad for Zahm's glider flights was the roof of Science Hall, which is now LaFortune Student Center. At one point in conducting his experiments he tried, without success, to get a balloonist to release the gliders from higher altitudes over the campus.

Besides these discoveries, Zahm wrote several academic papers that explained how to design and to fly an airplane. His paper, "Stability of Aeroplanes and Flying Machines," which was presented at the First International Aeronautics Congress in Chicago in 1893, described the requirements for equilibrium and stable flight of an aircraft for the first time in America. Zahm's work was influential during the early days of flight, and it also began a tradition for future research projects in engineering at Notre Dame which continues today.

In the field of electrical engineering the University first drew national recognition in the 1890s with the experiments of Jerome J. Green, a professor from 1895 until 1914 at Notre Dame. Influenced by the inventions of Marconi and others in Europe, Green developed wireless communication instruments as soon as he arrived. By transmitting a message between two campus halls in 1895, Green became the first American to send a wireless message. Four years later and with more sophisticated equipment, Green sent a message from St. Mary's College to Notre Dame. Several reporters from Chicago newspapers witnessed this experiment, which resulted in considerable acclaim for Green and the University.

The research activities of Zahm and Green helped to spur interest in engineering at Notre

Dame. At the University and elsewhere, however, the marked growth in engineering education developed largely in response to the technological needs of society. As specialty areas—like aeronautics or electrical engineering—became more central to the lives and livelihoods of people, these areas grew into distinct disciplines with their own departments and academic associations. Today the College of Engineering includes five departments—Aerospace and Mechanical, Chemical, Civil, Electrical and Computer Engineering, and Materials Science and Engineering—and the School of Architecture, the first architectural program of a Catholic university in the United States. Each of the departments has bachelor's, master's, and doctoral programs. The School of Architecture offers a Bachelor of Architecture, a five-year course of study, and a Master of Architecture, which began in 1985.

Although the 1970s did not sustain the post-Sputnik growth period of the late 1950s and 1960s, the faculty members in the College today are facing what educators call a "crisis in engineering." The need for people to contribute to the evolution of the Computer Age, the Space Age, and the other technological advances is now so acute that undergraduate enrollments have reached their maximum numbers. For example, Electrical Engineering, which had 127 undergraduate majors in 1975, had 402 majors (sophomores through seniors) ten years later, making it one of the largest majors for undergraduates in the entire University. The crisis has affected graduate education, too. With well-paying positions readily available upon graduation, fewer bachelor degree recipients are willing to pursue advanced degrees in engineering, resulting in a smaller number of potential faculty members (with doctorates and other qualifications). This means hiring new professors has become more of a challenge for the College

*Department of Electrical & Computer Engineering*

and throughout engineering education in America. The situation of an abundance of undergraduates and keen competition for graduate students and prospective faculty members comes at a time when the University is striving to bolster its commitment to advanced research in engineering. Trying to achieve the appropriate balance between teaching demands and research time is a frequently discussed concern among College administrators and professors.

Civil engineering at Notre Dame dates back to 1873 when it became the first discipline to enter the engineering curriculum. Closely connected to the science program during its early years, the Civil Engineering Department emphasized drawing and applied mathematics. As a former district supervisor of public roads, Father Edward Sorin, the University's founder, knew that post–Civil War America needed skilled people to design and oversee the building of new roadways and railroad routes. When the demand for this type of expertise grew, Notre Dame enlarged its

ization are bioengineering, water resources, environmental engineering, and structures and mechanics. Besides the Master of Science in Civil Engineering, Notre Dame offers a Master of Science in Environmental Engineering and a Master of Science in Bioengineering. The graduate program in bioengineering is interdisciplinary in nature and involves not only work in several departments in the College of Engineering but also several courses in the Departments of Biological Sciences and Chemistry in the College of Science. A dominant interest of bioengineers at Notre Dame is the microbial management and disposal of waste materials.

Started in 1962, the environmental engineering program in its initial stages concentrated on issues related to water supply, wastewater treatment, and water pollution control. During recent years, additional topics, like sedimentation and stratigraphy, environmental chemistry, subsurface hydrology, and hazardous waste management, have received attention and research support. Currently, there are major undertakings in the numerical simulation of hydrologic problems and in the use of field studies to investigate the flow of groundwater.

A notable project being carried out by environmental engineers in the department is the development of the sequencing batch reactor, which can be used to treat domestic and industrial wastes. Instead of treating wastewater in different stages and tanks, a sequencing batch reactor completes the treatment process more efficiently and more economically in a single tank. The conceptual work, the computer modeling, and the "test-tube" studies took place at Notre Dame, with funding support from the National Science Foundation and the U.S. Environmental Protection Agency. Pilot testing of the sequencing batch reactors has occurred at municipal and industrial waste treatment sites. As additional reactors are designed and constructed in this country and abroad, research to make this technology more sophisticated and beneficial will continue. In 1983, the University sponsored a symposium about the use of genetically engineered organisms in the treatment process of the sequencing batch reactor. Like nearly all of the scholarly activities conducted in the College, this project combines basic research—the discovery of new knowledge—with practical, technical applications. The emphasis, though, is on the conceptual or theoretical aspects of the inquiry.

curriculum, expanding a two-year program that encompassed the junior and senior years into a four-year course of study.

Today the faculty of the Civil Engineering Department conducts classes and does research in the fundamental areas of the discipline: structural analysis and design, hydraulics and hydrology, water supply and wastewater disposal, materials of construction, soil mechanics and foundations, and transportation engineering. The principal areas of sustained inquiry and graduate special-

*WILLIAM G. GRAY*
Dept. of Civil Engineering

*Research is not a luxury to be engaged in by the faculty in lieu of preparing lectures or meeting with students. The dual emphasis at Notre Dame on teaching and research ensures that the faculty will be current and bring the spirit of independent inquiry to the classroom.*

The structural engineering program emphasizes structural analysis, structural design, and soil-structure interaction. Using soil as a building material is just one of the research interests within the department. A specific concern with long-term safety and economic benefits involves the design of culvert bridges that combine large steel plates and soil as a structural component. These culvert bridges could ultimately replace the much more costly traditional deck bridges built of reinforced concrete or steel. A goal of this project is the development of design guidelines outlining culvert bridge construction for state highway departments across the country. Structural engineers are also investigating how random vibrations affect the design of buildings and other structures in regions where earthquakes and other such natural disturbances occur. This work involves numerical simulation and modeling.

The department has one endowed chair, the Massman Professorship of Civil Engineering. Future plans include the establishment of a program to assist and educate people in developing nations, especially in Latin America, where problems in civil engineering are so critical.

A program in mechanical engineering entered the Notre Dame curriculum in 1886. Although the course of study in the early years was primarily limited to mathematics, machine drawing, and shop practice, the aeronautical experiments of Albert Zahm, technically a professor of mathematics, had close links to the Mechanical Engineering Department. When flight technology became a dominant concern, the University created a Department of Aeronautical Engineering in 1935. The combined department—Aerospace and Mechanical Engineering—was established in 1969, and it has the largest faculty (26) in the College. Undergraduate and graduate students today can earn degrees in either discipline. Current areas of specialization in aerospace engineering include aerodynamics, flight dynamics, propulsion, wind tunnel testing, aerospace structures, and aerospace design. Research and teaching concerns in mechanical engineering are fluid mechanics, solid and continuum mechanics, thermodynamics, heat and mass transfer, combustion, systems and control, design, dynamics, and robotics.

Wind tunnel research is the most sustained individual area of inquiry within the College of Engineering. Zahm's invention was but the beginning. When Professor F. N. M. Brown came to Notre Dame in 1935 to found the Aeronautical Engineering Department, he brought with him a desire to investigate flow visualization by using smoke in wind tunnels. From 1935 until his retirement from the faculty in 1969, Brown designed and experimented with two- and three-dimensional smoke tunnels. He was the first researcher to develop a large, three-dimensional research smoke tunnel capable of speeds up to 67 meters per second. He also devised a moveable smoke rake and a kerosene smoke generator to produce large quantities of smoke, which helped him to take the first three-dimensional photographs of smoke flows. Engineering historians credit Brown with most of the advances in smoke-visualization techniques, and his work (frequently conducted with Robert Eikenberry, now a Professor Emeritus) has made possible the study of several complex problems in aerodynamics.

An expansion of Brown's efforts occurred on the Notre Dame campus in 1959, when one of his colleagues, Vincent Goddard, built the first supersonic smoke visualization wind tunnel. There are currently three supersonic smoke visualization wind tunnels and two low-speed smoke visualization tunnels in the Aerospace Laboratory, the only facility with such resources in the world. Several faculty members continue to do research to improve the design and usage of these tunnels. One such project involves creating different inlets for wind tunnels, allowing for more sophisticated experiments. Other projects address the influence of wind shears on aircraft and the performance of airfoils at low Reynolds numbers. Calculating what these airfoils will do develops from the desire to improve the low speed performance of aircraft and to design more advanced remotely piloted vehicles, jet engine fan blades, and propellers at high altitudes.

For some forty years, aerodynamic research has been conducted in a building that was used by the military during the Second World War to train officers at Notre Dame. In 1985, the University announced plans for a new Aerospace Laboratory. Features of the proposed facility—a new high velocity subsonic wind tunnel, an underground chamber to accumulate the exhaust from supersonic tunnels, and completely controlled lighting to photograph air flows—would enhance research possibilities in this area. Moreover, there would be more space for the existing wind tunnels and for the equipment, such as lasers and computers, that are needed to conduct experiments.

"The significance of Brown's experiments in smoke visualization and other measurements involving the use of wind tunnels have become recognized as landmark studies in aerodynamic research," notes Thomas J. Mueller, a Professor of Aerospace and Mechanical Engineering and the Director of Engineering Research and Graduate Studies in the College. "The equipment and techniques he developed made Notre Dame the acknowledged leader in research of this kind, and the University in recent years has continued to strengthen its aerodynamic program. Our work today has applications not only in the design of various kinds of aircraft but also in the design of automotive vehicles, trains, and even tall buildings."

In addition to its work in aerodynamics, the Department of Aerospace and Mechanical Engineering has received international recognition for its research in the thermal sciences. One specialty of this group of faculty members involves the transfer of heat under different conditions and circumstances. Much of this inquiry in heat transfer is theoretical and mathematical. It is basic research without immediate application. Some projects, however, combine fundamental and experimental research, and they have specific technological benefits as goals. For several years, for example, Notre Dame engineers have been studying the characteristics of fire and smoke in enclosed areas, like homes, apartment houses, hotels, office buildings, and airplanes. Computer models predict how fire and smoke might spread, and these calculations receive laboratory testing. The objective of UNDSAFE—University of Notre Dame Smoke and Fire in Enclosures—is the development of a computerized system that will immediately simulate what will happen if a fire is not extinguished in a specific enclosure. The system will also provide information about escape routes and fire-fighting strategies. A safety system of this kind could be included in the architectural design of the building or airplane, saving lives and reducing structural damage.

Several facets of the UNDSAFE program have been conducted by K. T. Yang, who was appointed to the Viola D. Hank Professorship of Engineering in 1985. Yang, a member of the Notre Dame faculty since 1955, has received international recognition for his contributions to the understanding of heat transfer. Some fifty of his research projects have been supported with federal funds.

A related component of the thermal sciences research—with distinctly different goals from UNDSAFE—concerns the study of heat transfer in ovens. By investigating different ways to enhance the flow of hot air, engineers hope to be able to design a more efficient oven. Much of the work with heat transfer has the potential of improving safety. Another project involving Aerospace and Mechanical Engineering, as well as other departments of the College, has similar intentions. Researchers are conducting experiments that will lead to the fracture and removal of ice from roads and rail systems. Notre Dame professors are responsible for doing the basic research into the physics of ice formation and for proposing the mechanical possibilities, like laser beams or microwaves, that might be used to control ice and improve transportation safety. Begun with funding from the Urban Mass Transportation Administration, the project is a cooperative effort with industry, and the technology already developed has been used in the transit systems of Chicago, Boston, and Lansing, Michigan.

A new area of inquiry in the Department of Aerospace and Mechanical Engineering is robotics. As the use of robots in industry and elsewhere has become a technological fact rather than a science fiction fantasy, engineers have had to design the various components and auxiliary equipment these machines require. A robotics laboratory was established in the College in 1985, and the teaching and research related to it emphasize how to analyze the functions of robots and how to improve the design of robots. Faculty members and students who work in the special lab are able to use five educational robots, a robotic arm equipped with a vision system, and computers that control what the robots do. Future plans include the acquisition of even more sophisticated equipment and an interdisciplinary project involving professors and students in the Department of Electrical Engineering.

Experimental and practical courses in electrical engineering were first offered at Notre Dame in 1891 as part of the mechanical engineering curriculum. Edison's invention of the incandescent lamp in 1879 had profound effects on American culture and society. Engineers throughout the country sought ways to use electrical power. At Notre Dame a Dynamo Room, complete with large-scale batteries, direct and alternating Edison and Thomas Houston dynamos and motors, and other apparatus, was set up in the basement of Science Hall. Besides serving as a laboratory for students, this facility also generated electricity for the campus. As a result of the Dynamo Room, the University became one of the first schools in the world to provide electrical illumination of its principal buildings and grounds. Growth within the field of electrical engineering prompted Notre Dame to establish a separate and distinct Department of Electrical Engineering in 1895. In 1986 the name of the department was changed to the Department of Electrical and Computer Engineering to reflect the current trends in the discipline.

The last years of the nineteenth century and the first decades of the current century created a foundation for understanding the phenomenon of electricity. Today, with advances in high technology receiving so much attention and affecting our lives on a daily basis, the computer has become a central focus of inquiry in electrical engineering. Notre Dame currently has a graduate specialty area in computers, and the University offers a Computer Engineering Sequence in addition to its regular bachelor's degree program in electrical engineering. Discovering more sophisticated ways of using personal computers and studying the interactions between small, personal computers and large, mainframe computers are two primary concerns of engineers in the department. Notre Dame also recently established a computer-aided design laboratory that allows faculty members and students to design any type of electrical or electronic circuit by using the computer with its sophisticated graphics capabilities.

Besides computers and microprocessors, other

*K. T. YANG*
*Dept. of Aerospace & Mechanical Engineering*

*While educating our students and developing them into whole persons must remain our primary duty, we must continue to shoulder our responsibilities in solving many of the problems of our society and the world through creative thinking and innovative research.*

mote control mechanisms on rockets. Devising more efficient means of controlling jet engines is one practical application of this work. One specific project, funded by the National Aeronautics and Space Administration (NASA), has as its objective the control of jet engines by digital computers. This technology, which would markedly change aviation and make the work of future pilots easier, will require extensive testing before the theories are translated into practice.

Some of this country's leading figures in control systems are members of the department's faculty, including Michael K. Sain, the Frank M. Freimann Professor of Electrical Engineering. A faculty member at Notre Dame since 1965, he assumed the Freimann Professorship in 1983. Sain is recognized throughout his discipline for the algebraic techniques he uses to devise control sys-

ANTHONY N. MICHEL
Dept. of Electrical Engineering

*Volatile changes brought about by technology and science result in controversies regarding fundamental human values. It is essential that our mission include the preparation of technologically literate leaders who will bring a moral viewpoint to decisions of consequence into the next century.*

areas of research include systems theory, control systems, electromagnetics, automata and coding theory, communications systems, and solid-state materials. For the past several years, the department has received most of its recognition and research support for its numerous activities in systems theory and control systems. A primary interest of several faculty members involves the theory and design of linear multivariable control systems. Much of this work is abstract and highly mathematical. The applications, however, are far-reaching, and they encompass everything from relatively simple control systems (like a thermostat on a furnace or an air-conditioner) to the complex automatic pilot systems on airplanes or re-

RICHARD KWOR
Dept. of Electrical Engineering

*The dual emphasis on teaching and research has profoundly changed Notre Dame during the past fifteen years.*

tems and also for the engineering applications he designs for systems. In combining algebraic abstractions with practical applications, he is a rarity in his profession. Sain along with five other professors in the department—one-fourth of the faculty—have the distinction of being Fellows of the Institute of Electrical and Electronics Engineers. In 1984, the Institute honored Sain and Professor Anthony Michel with two of the Centennial Medals it awarded to prominent engineers to mark its hundredth anniversary.

The Department of Electrical and Computer Engineering also has an ongoing and growing program in solid-state materials, devices, and electromagnetics. One project, conducted as part of the College's interdisciplinary research into techniques for deicing transit systems, involves the theoretical modeling and experimental design of radio frequency technology that can be effectively used on ice-covered power rails of transit lines. Another area of study, with considerable potential significance, focuses on developing more reliable integrated circuits and chips for the next generation of computers. If the goal of this work is achieved, the speed, cost, reliability, and size of computer circuitry will improve.

Expansion in the mass manufacture of products that occurred during the early 1900s created a demand for engineers who were able to solve the chemical problems related to this new area of growth. Although the course "Principles of Chemical Engineering" did not enter the curriculum until 1921, Notre Dame formally established a chemical engineering program in 1909. In its first decade, the program was primarily composed of classes in chemistry, mechanical engineering, drawing, and shop training. However, as the work of the chemical engineer became more sophisticated and central to twentieth-century life, the Department of Chemical Engineering enlarged its own classroom activities and developed a research agenda. Today the doctoral program of the department ranks in the top twenty among all doctoral programs in Chemical Engineering in the United States, according to a 1982 report issued by the National Academy Press. The graduate program ranked sixth nationally in both the number of research publications and in program improvement during the previous five years. Roger A. Schmitz, who is the Keating-Crawford Professor of Chemical Engineering as well as the McCloskey Dean of Engineering, was elected to the prestigious National Academy of Engineering in 1984. Schmitz and Professor James J. Carberry, a Notre Dame faculty member since 1961, have each received the R. H. Wilhelm Award from the American Institute of Chemical Engineers for research contributions to advance their discipline.

Ongoing research activities in the department address a majority of fundamental concerns in the discipline: bioseparations, chemical reaction engineering, energy conversion, kinetics and catalysis, modeling, simulation and realtime computing, phase equilibria, process dynamics and control, statistical mechanics, thermodynamics, and transport phenomena. The teaching and research being carried out in catalysis and chemical reaction engineering is a particular area of distinction.

The study of catalysis involves inquiry into the modifications of the rates of chemical reaction by substances (catalysts), which do not become consumed in the process. Although most chemical reactions occur on their own, few reactions occur quickly enough to be valuable in industry or production. As a result, the majority of reactions require the involvement of catalysts. Unlike departments of Chemical Engineering elsewhere, researchers at Notre Dame investigate all of the aspects of catalysis—the composition of catalysts, the reactivity, the selectivity, and the stability. Most of this theoretical and experimental research is fundamental in nature. It is new knowledge covering the spectrum of catalysis. Numerous applications follow, however. For example, chemical engineers at Notre Dame have recently worked on a computer model for a more sophisticated catalytic converter for automobiles. The goal of this project, conducted in cooperation with the Department of Energy and Ford Motor Company, was the development of a converter that allowed minimum pollution emissions and maximum fuel efficiency. Additional research endeavors seek to improve chemical reactions that play roles in energy conversion and pollution control.

Although the largest number of Chemical Engineering professors specialize in catalysis and chemical reaction engineering, other members of the relatively small faculty of nine people concentrate on thermodynamics, phase equilibria, separation processes, process control, transport phenomena, and fluid mechanics. In 1973 the department created the Solar Laboratory for Thermal Applications. Researchers affiliated with this laboratory have continuously collected data for over a decade, resulting in a predictive equation

*E. E. WOLF*
*Dept. of Chemical Engineering*

*Research leads the faculty to the frontiers of knowledge. At the same time the University's dedication to the teaching of values provides the student with the appropriate balance between their professional and spiritual formation.*

about solar radiation. Related activities of this project include studies of solar collector technology, solar desalination, and solar distillation of alcohol.

Besides the teaching and research conducted by the department, Chemical Engineering annually sponsors the Reilly Lectureship series, perhaps the oldest endowed lectureship in chemical engineering in the United States. The series brings noted researchers to the campus for formal lectures and informal discussions with students and faculty.

A gift from a civil engineering alumnus, John F. Cushing, in 1930 allowed the construction of Cushing Hall of Engineering. Explaining the motivation for his gift, Cushing articulated a defining —and abiding—characteristic of the College's approach to engineering education: "I conceive that an engineer must be a man with a conscience in his profession. The gravest of all natural responsibilities are borne by him. He will be responsible for human safety and human lives. The engineer must know how to do it, and have the strength of character to do it right. I find at Notre Dame a technical training that ranks with the best and a training in character foundation nowhere excelled." When Cushing Hall opened in 1933, it brought together in a single building for the first time all of the engineering departments.

Occupying some of these then-modern facilities were the faculty and students of a new program—the Department of Metallurgy, which was created during the 1932–33 academic year. Subsequently renamed the Department of Metallurgical Engineering and Materials Science and now known as the Department of Materials Science and Engineering, this discipline was one of the last to enter the curriculum, but it was the first to establish a doctoral program. This advancement in graduate education took place in 1941, the same year when the Department of Mining Engineering was disbanded after a thirty-three-year existence. The majority of doctoral programs in the College were instituted in the early 1960s.

Throughout its history, Materials Science and Engineering has consistently received outside recognition in both teaching and research. The undergraduate program, for example, was recently ranked among the top twenty in the nation. One faculty member is a Fellow of the American Society for Metals. Another, George Kuczynski, a professor emeritus, is a recipient of the Frenkel Prize, the highest award of the International Institute for the Science of Sintering. Kuczynski helped to establish the basic theory of sintering, which involves heating a mass of fine metal particles at a temperature below their melting point to weld them together. The Kuczynski Medal is awarded quadrennially by the International Institute for the Science of Sintering to the author of the best paper published in the journal *Physics of Sintering*.

In its teaching and research activities, the department concentrates on developing understanding about why materials act as they do and how to control and improve material behavior. Specific areas of inquiry include corrosion, abrasive and erosive wear, sintering, electrical contact materi-

*School of Architecture*

als, amorphous materials, magnetic materials, surface analytical studies, and applications of computers in metallurgical education. During the past several years, much of the attention of the department has been directed to basic research investigating the corrosion of materials and wear-related phenomena. However, as this aspect of engineering has felt the impact of and attraction to developments in advanced, high technology, there has been more concern for exploring the properties of surfaces in their various stages and conditions.

One objective of this surface science research is the discovery of materials that will perform the same functions as precious metals when those metals are used in industry, like electronic components (computers, televisions, telephone, and radios). A specific project involves finding a substitute for gold in the electrical contacts now found in electronic instruments. The gold is highly conductive and resistant to corrosion — but, of course, terribly expensive. A new ceramic material is being tested as a possible replacement for gold. Developing new metallic, ceramic, and plastic surfaces will, ultimately, help to save scarce (and costly) strategic materials.

Historians trace Notre Dame's initial instruction in architectural design to a drawing class offered in 1858, fifteen years before civil engineering entered the curriculum. Until the University-wide reorganization of 1920, the program in architecture operated autonomously. A bachelor of science degree in architecture was introduced in 1898, and a College of Architecture was established in 1906. Classified as a department for many years, Architecture was redesignated a School of Architecture in 1983. This change, in part, was made to reflect the substantial differences between the degree programs of architecture and those of the five engineering departments in the College of Engineering. Notre Dame is one of only three Catholic universities in the United States to offer undergraduate and graduate degree programs in architecture. Its professional degree program is one of ninety-one nationwide recognized by the National Architectural Accrediting Board. Until 1965, no other university in Indiana taught architecture.

Given its moderate size—approximately 215 students and fourteen faculty members—the School of Architecture offers a balanced professional degree program at the undergraduate level and a graduate program with an emphasis on design. Rooted in the tradition of the Beaux-Arts competition days, architectural design is the principal area of concentration. This work is supplemented by focused activity in the areas of history/ environment/behavior, technology, and practice. The programs are enhanced by studying two cities that are the sites of enduring architectural achievements—Rome and Chicago. In 1969, the University initiated its course of architectural studies in Rome. A required component of the five-year bachelor's curriculum, these studies abroad enable students to engage in close analysis of buildings and other structures of historical significance and influence. As a result, a student's own creative project is informed by and rooted in classic and modern expressions of architectural design. Notre Dame is one of the few schools, if not the only professional program, in America that has a mandatory course of studies abroad for its undergraduate students.

Similar to the study experience in Rome, the School of Architecture is developing a comparable course of study in Chicago. These studies center on the city and suburbs and the works of Louis Sullivan, Dankmar Adler, Frank Lloyd Wright, Ludwig Mies van der Rohe, C. F. Murphy, and the other great architects who have made Chicago a laboratory for architectural study. As the noted architect John H. Burgee has observed, "Chicago *is* the history of architecture in this country." A 1956 graduate of Notre Dame, Burgee is a member of the University's Visitors in Architecture program, a formal lecture and advanced design review series that brings distinguished professionals to the campus.

The School's recognized strength is its design program, and faculty members have won several national and statewide design competitions in past years. For example, the published architec-

*STEVEN W. HURTT*
Dept. of Architecture

*Notre Dame is full of promise. Nothing is easy here, but you can feel and see the striving for something better. Dissatisfaction and conflict exist because we are seeking to make Notre Dame a more ideal place.*

tural and urban design of community facilities and housing for Roosevelt Island, New York, received a national first prize award. The design included plans for one thousand units of low, moderate, and high income dwellings. The architectural design of a small complex of living-working units in the "New American House" competition was honored with a national merit award. The teaching and research of the Architecture faculty focus on such specific areas as architecture and urbanism, visual studies, architectural restoration, historical and theoretical studies, ecclesiastical architecture, and space perception. Much of the faculty research is creative in nature, leading to the analysis, design, and visual presentation of buildings and structures for small towns and urban settings.

The campus facilities of the School of Architecture are located in a three-story building, which previously served as the main library of the University. This building houses studios, classrooms, offices, and the Architecture Library and Architecture Slide Library. The School's facility in Rome—with a studio, classrooms, lecture and seminar rooms, a library, and offices—was recently renovated. Located in the heart of the city, the Center was dedicated in 1986.

Cushing Hall, for many years the home of the College of Engineering, continues to provide necessary classroom, laboratory, and office space. A suite of offices in Cushing serve as the headquarters of the National Consortium for Graduate Degrees for Minorities in Engineering, Inc. Established in 1976, this nonprofit corporation involving 48 universities and over 50 industrial and governmental employers provides American Indians, Black Americans, Mexican Americans, and Puerto Ricans with opportunities for summer employment and with graduate fellowships. Joseph C. Hogan, the former dean of the College of Engineering, and Rev. Theodore M. Hesburgh, C.S.C., president of Notre Dame, were instrumental in founding this national consortium. One hundred minority students, sponsored by the consortium, received graduate degrees in 1986.

Most of the teaching and research of the engineering departments, however, now take place in the Fitzpatrick Hall of Engineering. Adjoining Cushing Hall, it was dedicated in 1979, and encompasses 155,000 square feet with five levels of classrooms, offices, laboratories, shops, and computing centers. Besides housing the College's own library, Fitzpatrick has a sophisticated computer graphics facility that allows students and faculty members in all departments to work in three-dimensions on whatever object they are designing. This computer-aided design capability increases the speed, accuracy, and ease of the engineer's work.

Having the extensive and modern facilities of Fitzpatrick Hall, as well as the other instrumentation in other buildings, helps to foster the College-wide commitment to advanced research that has existed since the 1960s. In 1960 the College received about $100,000 in external support for research and educational programs. By 1967, the research agenda flourished—outside support was in excess of $500,000, and the University was awarded a prestigious "Project Themis" grant by the Department of Defense in recognition of excellence and potential. In the 1980s the College has been receiving over $2.5 million per year to underwrite research and instructional projects.

Although the pioneering accomplishments of people like Zahm, Green, and Brown provide both a heritage and a foundation, the essence of engineering is present and future discovery. With technical knowledge growing more quickly than at any time in history, the College has a double, and demanding, responsibility of contributing to that new knowledge and of preparing young engineers and architects to make their own contributions.

PROFILE

DEAN ROGER A. SCHMITZ

COLLEGE OF ENGINEERING

ROGER A. SCHMITZ has spent much of his life analyzing reactions. When he was elected to the National Academy of Engineering in 1984, he was honored for his accomplishments in engineering aspects of chemical reactions. Today, when Schmitz speaks about the College of Engineering that he leads as the Matthew H. McCloskey Dean, he stresses how certain aspects of the College and University produce reactions in the teaching and research carried out in engineering at Notre Dame.

"I don't think there's anything very different about the way we teach engineering subjects, either undergraduate or graduate, or about our research," says Schmitz. "Our programs are similar to those at many other places. The differences here are mainly consequences of the nature and size of the University. Students are usually taught in small classes, so there is a close faculty-student relationship at both the graduate and the undergraduate levels. Another aspect of the size is that we are not large enough to be able to offer all of the specialties. Some engineering colleges have ten or twelve departments; we have five engineering departments in addition to the School of Architecture."

Schmitz sees both positive and negative features to the size of his College, with its 95 faculty members, 200 graduate students, and 1700 undergraduates. Besides the benefits of a small student-faculty ratio he believes "a strong spirit of cooperation" pervades the College and animates its work. "The faculty here feels more a part of the College and, in fact, of the University as a whole than is the case at many engineering colleges. The same is true for undergraduate students. Our students take the majority of their courses outside of our College. I think we're well-integrated into the academic community. In addition, interdisciplinary teaching and research activities are easily fostered here because faculty are acquainted with each other and don't have boundaries and buildings separating departments."

Schmitz, however, is aware that the moderate size of the College has its drawbacks. "In some respects we don't have enough breadth, and it is difficult for us to produce a sufficient quantity of research and Ph.D. students to make a real impact in the world of research and graduate education. We are determined to improve in that regard, but we will have to make our impact with quality, not quantity. We will have to be very selective and exercise good judgment regarding the specialty areas we select and the type of faculty we hire. It is important that every faculty member in our College be an outstanding teacher and researcher. We can't afford slackers."

In seeking professors for the College, Schmitz is particularly interested in men and women who are capable of being effective in both the classroom and in research. "For the modern engineering educator, teaching and research go hand in hand. Outstanding teachers must keep their course materials up-to-date, and this requires constant awareness of the latest developments. Those best at maintaining such awareness and at bringing the excitement of new knowledge to students are, naturally, those contributing to the development of that new knowledge through research. The tie between teaching and research in our College is further enhanced by the fact that nearly all of our research activities are closely tied to the direction of the thesis and dissertation work of graduate students."

Besides the significance of size on the College, Schmitz believes the Catholic character of the University creates " a special connection of people to this place." The reaction he perceives occurs externally, but its consequences affect several aspects of teaching and research. "The Catholicity doesn't come into our programs directly, but I think the Catholicity tends to bring us together. Many of the faculty are themselves Catholic, while other members share the University's values. As a whole, they relate strongly to the University and its overall mission. There is certainly a different spirit at Notre Dame—sort of an inspiration that causes faculty to do more—to do better. I know that some faculty would say that they wouldn't have the emotional involvement at another university that they have here. Here they're willing to sacrifice. They stayed here through periods when our salaries were low and they could have gone to other places. They are willing to take on extra loads and extra assignments because they really believe in the place. They feel it's a place worth building, preserving, and making outstanding, and they're proud of it."

Schmitz admits that it's not easy to describe the spirit that pervades the College. But he's often reminded of its existence. "Professors who visit here from other universities often say that they would like to see a similar spirit at their school. There aren't many places where faculty feel that a life devoted to the university and what it stands for is a life well spent. Many faculty feel that way about Notre Dame."

Schmitz joined the faculty as the Keating-Crawford Professor of Chemical Engineering and Chairman of the Department of Chemical Engineering after serving from 1962 until 1979 as a professor at the University of Illinois. During his tenure at Illinois, Schmitz received a Guggenheim Fellowship in 1968–1969 to do research about the dynamics and control of chemically reacting systems. The publications that resulted from this work won for him the Allan P. Colburn Award of the American Institute of Chemical Engineers in 1970. Schmitz, who has a doctorate from the University of Minnesota, received the University of Illinois Campus Award for Excellence in Undergraduate Teaching in 1975 and the George Westinghouse Award of the American Society for Engineering Education in 1977 for "excellence and innovation" in teaching. In 1981, the year he assumed the deanship at Notre Dame, he received the R. H. Wilhelm Award from the American Institute of Chemical Engineers for his theoretical and experimental work in chemical reactor stability and dynamics, and kinetic oscillations.

Explaining his decision to leave the University of Illinois, his undergraduate alma mater, Schmitz says, "I had always been interested in, and attracted to, Notre Dame. I thought that engineering had great potential here, and I simply seized the opportunity to come and contribute."

Schmitz's efforts, however, have been hampered by the widely discussed national "crisis in engineering education" that started in the 1970s and continued into the 1980s. The nationwide crisis—with its surging undergraduate enrollments, its shortage of new engineering professors and doctoral students, and the problems associated with obsolete equipment in instructional and research laboratories—has eased somewhat, but it still exists. Electrical and computer engineering are areas particularly affected, according to Schmitz. One year, he explains, the number of undergraduate students rose to record numbers, while the number of new Ph.D.'s qualified for faculty positions actually decreased in some fields. "In recent years it has been difficult for us just to keep pace with demands for necessities much less make substantial gains."

The crisis notwithstanding, the dean sees progress within the College. "We take pride in our teaching, and on the whole it's very good," he states. "The research is outstanding in some spots, while still developing in others. Probably in most respects we'd have to say our research is still in a developing mode, with plenty of potential for improvement."

According to Schmitz, fields of established strength can be found in all departments, and he adds: "In all cases I could point to a few individuals who really got things going. Eventually I hope the quality will stretch across every specialization."

For the College to continue to improve, Schmitz believes it's necessary to attract established and promising professors, to offer attractive appointments and opportunities for exciting research for graduate students, and to provide and maintain a full complement of modern laboratory and research services. A principal priority involves the recruiting of senior teacher-scholars for endowed chairs that exist in the College. Comments Schmitz, "Our best hope for making major gains in the short run is to get some really outstanding people into chaired positions."

Schmitz hopes that some of the future chairholders will be instrumental in establishing formal interdisciplinary programs in the College of Engineering and, in some cases, jointly with the College of Science. As an example, a center for materials research, particularly microelectronic materials, would involve specialists in chemical, electrical, and materials engineering as well as physicists and chemists. Other possibilities include programs in bioengineering, automation (robotics), applied mathematics, and hazardous waste management. In each case, Schmitz foresees the endeavor as primarily helping to advance the research and graduate education components of the College and University.

Although Schmitz continues to teach graduate students and to conduct research, most of his efforts are devoted to strengthening the College of Engineering and to improving technological resources throughout the campus. In 1985, he was also appointed Special Assistant to the Provost for Computing, a position that makes him responsible for all computer support to instruction, research, and administration. Devoting about twenty percent of his time to this job, Schmitz leads a University-wide undertaking to improve all facets of computing at Notre Dame. The Computing Center and the Office of Information Systems report to him.

Schmitz notes that during the past decade computers have become increasingly significant in teaching, research, and administration. "What in the past was a machine used just for computations and calculations—and therefore used by accountants, scientists, and engineers—now goes much, much further. Now it is an information-processing technology, which includes word-processing and all sorts of communication. Today it extends to everybody. Arts and Letters students need access to computers nearly as much as students in other Colleges, and faculty in all of the Colleges and the Law School use them more extensively."

Schmitz says that Notre Dame was at the forefront of technological developments in computing during the 1960s and early 1970s. "In those years," he remarks, "you could buy a single machine—the latest, biggest computer—and you were at the leading edge of computing." As the technology expanded to encompass new hardware (like minicomputers and personal computers), more highly sophisticated programs, and possibilities of networks between computers of various sizes, Notre Dame was slow to become involved. Schmitz says, "In some respects, we practically stood still through the late 1970s and early 1980s just when computing developments were taking place more rapidly than ever world-wide. As a consequence, we found ourselves about ten years behind, which is a serious gap in computing capabilities. Fortunately, we've made some gains in recent years, and I am confident that there will be many more substantial gains in the near future."

Schmitz currently directs a task force of faculty members and administrators that is developing a strategic plan for the use of computers across the University. "We're studying the entire picture—the academic side, the administrative side, library automation, campus networking, and everything else associated with computing at Notre Dame," explains Schmitz. "We're putting together a description of what we think computing should be here, now and in the foreseeable future. We're also developing an implementation plan, showing how the total picture should be developed over a period of three to five years, and what sort of funding it will require. There's no question it will require the commitment of large sums of money."

Schmitz realizes that what needs to be accomplished "to get us to where computing should be at a major university nowadays" will be an ambitious project that will ultimately have consequences in the lives of most people at Notre Dame. The magnitude of the undertaking notwithstanding, he sees the work as necessary to recover the past and to prepare for the future. "We want to get this campus right up to the forefront, where it will provide the latest in proven technology for faculty, students, administrators, and the support staff."

Schmitz believes that providing access to students, faculty, administrators, and others is a key factor to having a successful university-wide computing system. A principal component to achieving complete access is the creation of networks that link computers together—whether they be personal computers, minicomputers, or the mainframe computer in the Computing Center that has the largest capacity, speed, and sophistication. Schmitz says that a local network connecting all of the computers in the College of Engineering already exists, and he predicts that in a few years there will be several other local networks as well as an all-campus network. "Building that whole picture is difficult," admits Schmitz. "Strategic planning is crucial."

Like other members of the engineering profession, Roger Schmitz approaches all of his work as the setter of goals and the solver of problems, and he keeps looking toward the future. He sees his reponsibilities as Special Assistant to the Provost for Computing as important to the University in the years ahead, but he devotes his greatest amount of time and energy to guiding his College to what he hopes will be a new level of accomplishment and stature. As he says: "I believe that our faculty share the vision of an engineering college at Notre Dame which attracts outstanding scholars to its faculty—scholars who in turn attract the world's best graduate students to engage in important and exciting research endeavors, who join enthusiastically in teaching undergraduate and graduate students, and whose character and contributions are aligned with the mission of the University. If the vision becomes reality, our College will surely be among the top few engineering colleges in the country. We're not there yet, but we have a good start, and we have the potential. The dean has the responsibility not only to articulate the vision, but to make decisions and set priorities which are consistent with it—that will turn the vision into reality."

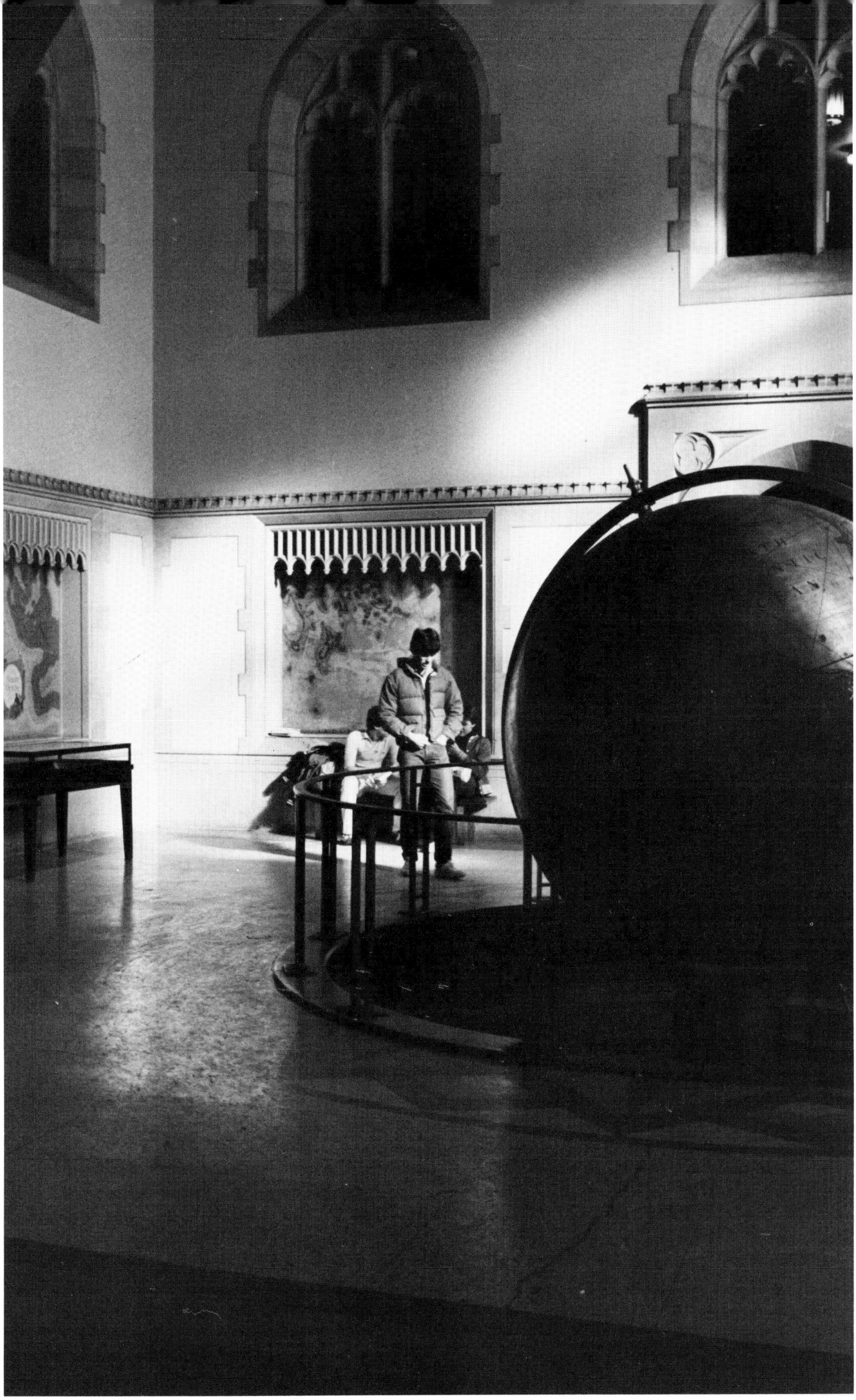

# The College of Business Administration

THE BEGINNING was far from auspicious. In an effort to improve the education of prospective businessmen being graduated from Notre Dame, the University created a Department of Commerce as part of the College of Arts and Letters in 1913–14. The first course in commerce offered in the fall of 1913 enrolled six students, a number smaller than many of the typing, bookkeeping, and other commercial classes that had composed a rudimentary business curriculum at Notre Dame during the nineteenth century. But the lack of interest in the substantive study of commerce was temporary. During the next four years, student support grew, and the University responded by developing a diverse set of classes that approached business from several perspectives. An early focus of attention was international trade and foreign commerce. In 1917, Notre Dame became the first university in the United States to offer a four-year course of studies in foreign commerce.

Guiding the development of business education at the University was Rev. John F. O'Hara, a young Holy Cross priest, whose previous experience included service in the American embassy at Montevideo, Uruguay, cattle-driving in Argentina, and study at the Wharton School of Finance and Commerce. Given his personal interest in South America and what he saw as the religious unity between Notre Dame and the countries of South America, Father O'Hara envisioned numerous possibilities for educating young men to become involved in commerce, especially foreign commerce. Central to his work in building the new department was his idea that ethical business conduct would promote a cordial relationship of "good neighborliness" between the United States and South America.

Under Father O'Hara's leadership, the study of commerce mushroomed. In 1921, eight years after its six-student beginning, the College of Commerce (which, by then, had thirteen faculty members) was formally created for the almost four hundred students enrolled in the program. As the dean from 1921 until his resignation in 1925, Father O'Hara oversaw a curriculum of eighty-five classes in the Departments of Accounting, Marketing Science, Transportation, Finance, and Foreign Trade. By 1925, the youngest University College had become as large as the oldest, the College of Arts and Letters.

Father O'Hara, who served as President of Notre Dame from 1934 until 1939 and was Cardinal Archbishop of Philadelphia when he died in 1960, was succeeded as dean by James E. McCarthy. McCarthy, who like O'Hara had worked in South America, served as dean for thirty years, from 1925 until 1955. During his tenure, one of the longest of any dean in the history of the University, the College continued to expand.

In 1930, when College enrollment was nearing a thousand students, Edward Nash Hurley, the chairman of the United States Shipping Board, made a contribution to Notre Dame to underwrite the costs for building what he envisioned as "the College of Foreign and Domestic Commerce." In announcing his gift, Hurley said: "The University of Notre Dame is rendering a valuable service to American industry by educating young men in its School of Foreign and Domestic Commerce, particularly because the University features the great importance of foreign trade to the future industrial development of our country." The Hurley building, which continues to be a major facility of the College, emphasizes the interests in international commerce. Trade maps of the seven continents decorate the walls at the entrance, and an eight-foot revolving aluminum globe depicting the world's major trading routes occupies the middle of the foyer. Outside, perched atop the tower above the main door, is a copper, three-masted clipper ship in full sail.

The Hurley gift of 1930 provided a necessary academic building for the College. However, the passage of the Hawley-Smoot Tariff Act in 1930, which resulted in a sharp decline of foreign trade, significantly altered the intellectual course of the College. With fewer people needed in international trade, Notre Dame did less with its foreign commerce programs. Greater attention was paid to preparing students to work at home for American corporations.

Notable changes in business education at Notre Dame began to occur in 1951 with the arrival of Professor James W. Culliton from the Harvard Graduate School of Business Administration. An innovator who was encouraged to propose improvements to the undergraduate curriculum to make it more rigorous, Culliton designed what was called the Program for Administrators (PFA). This experimental program emphasized instruction in the processes of administration and management rather than specialization in a particular facet of business. Several components of the Program for Administrators became the basis for a thorough revision of the College's curriculum that took place in the 1950s. Culliton served as dean from 1955 until 1962, when President John Kennedy appointed him to be a member of the U.S. Tariff Commission.

The formative years of the College established lines of continuity that extend to the present. Father O'Hara's belief in the connection between business practices and religious values remains an abiding concern, so, too, is the willingness to explore the dimensions of international commerce. Seeking an appropriate balance between business courses and offerings from Arts and Letters and Science is still a fundamental objective in the undergraduate curriculum. These continuities, however, operate within a College that, in many ways, is vastly different from the one Father O'Hara founded and McCarthy directed for three decades. Besides the strengthened undergraduate curriculum, there now exists a commitment to graduate education, to serious scholarly research, and to executive development that enriches the College and deepens its work. From the roots of the early years, the College of Business Administration (the name was formally changed in 1961) currently has four departments—Accountancy, Finance and Business Economics, Management, and Marketing. In addition to undergraduate degree programs in each of these fields, the College offers the Master of Business Administration (MBA) and administers the Master of Science in Administration (MSA) program. In recent years the College has also established a Center for Research in Business, a Center for Research in Banking, and a Center for Ethics and Religious Values in Business.

The structure of the undergraduate degree programs in the College of Business Administration shares several similarities with the bachelor's programs in the three other Colleges. The structure, however, has distinct differences, too. Majors are required to study the basic principles of the four fields of business (accounting, finance, management, and marketing) and other foundation courses in business before concentrating on a specific area during junior and senior years. By

DAVID N. RICCHIUTE
Dept. of Accountancy

taking such classes as "Principles of Accounting," "Business Finance," "Principles of Management," "Principles of Marketing," "Statistics in Business," and "Computers in Business," students have an integrated foundation for common understanding that helps them to see the inter-connections between the various aspects of contemporary business. This structure, which also exists within the Master of Business Administration programs, enhances the potential graduate's ability to adapt to changing needs and to analyze the business problems. Another feature of the undergraduate curriculum that makes it different from most programs at other universities is the opportunity and encouragement to take elective courses from departments outside of the College. This latitude, along with requirements in theology, philosophy, and other arts and science courses, provides an education that has breadth as well as a professional orientation. In a recent University of Virginia survey of business school deans and corporate executives, the undergraduate program at Notre Dame ranked among the ten best in the nation.

The Department of Accountancy has the largest number of undergraduate majors of the University's thirty-four academic departments. There are currently more than five hundred majors, and there are predictions that the number will approach six hundred during the next few years. Approximately half of the students receiving the Bachelor of Business Administration select accounting as their area of concentration. In turn, about two-thirds of the accounting graduates go to work in public accounting, the majority with the "Big Eight" firms. The remainder enter industry and private business at the management level.

In addition to being popular, the Department of Accountancy has achieved a national reputation for excellence. The most recent national poll of professors conducted by *Public Accounting Report* ranks the undergraduate accounting program seventh in the United States. Leading the survey are Illinois, Texas, Michigan, Southern California, Ohio State, and Brigham Young. Trailing Notre Dame are such schools as Wisconsin, Wharton, California-Berkeley, and Virginia.

Historically, Accountancy has been highly regarded, and graduates have been sought by the leading firms. A decade ago, for example, twenty-six percent of the Notre Dame students who took the CPA examination passed all four parts of the exam on the first effort. The national average at the time was seven percent. In recent years, there has been increased emphasis on scholarly research, which is presented at national conferences and published in journals, and on graduate education. Specific areas of research interest include financial and managerial accounting, auditing, taxation, accounting systems, and accounting for not-for-profit organizations. Several accounting firms make gifts to the University to support grants and fellowships for faculty research. Arthur Andersen & Co. has pledged to endow a professorship in Accountancy. This will be the department's second chair. The first is the Vincent and Rose Lizzadro Professorship in Accountancy, which was established in 1985.

To strengthen and to add diversity to the accounting program for master's degree candidates, the department recently introduced a concentration in taxation. This concentration is designed to prepare MBA graduates for the growing complexities of federal tax legislation, and it covers such subjects as "Taxation of Corporations and Shareholders," "Partnerships and Tax Shelters," and "Estate and Gift Taxes." The sequence also requires students to complete a tax course offered by the Law School.

Another tax-related project conducted by the department assists low income residents of the local area in the preparation of their federal and state tax forms. Started in 1972, the tax assistance program involves the work of seniors in Accountancy, faculty members, and local certified public accountants. Approximately two thousand taxpayers a year take advantage of this complimentary service.

Although accounting is the choice of most undergraduate business majors, the largest percentage of graduate students specialize in finance. Courses in the Department of Finance and Business Economics explore (among other topics) "Portfolio Management and Investment Strategy," "Commercial Bank Management," and "International Financial Management." On the undergraduate level, students with a concentration in Finance and Business Economics have the opportunity to select from six sequences of courses in preparing for a career or for graduate school. The sequences include corporate finance, investments, financial institutions, insurance management, pre-law preparation, and business economics. Just under half of the undergraduate students concentrate in finance work for banks or other financial institutions.

The faculty of the department is made up of specialists in both finance, the study of how institutions raise and use funds, and business economics, the applications of economic theories to solve corporate and organizational problems. Research interests of professors in Finance and Business Economics are diverse. Recent publications have focused on such subjects as securities markets, corporate financing and investing decisions, financial institutions, managerial economics, monetary economics, and finance for not-for-profit institutions. The teaching and research of the department is enhanced by two endowed professorships. The C. R. Smith Professorship of Business Administration was inaugurated in 1975, the first such endowed position within the College. Lee A. Tavis, a specialist in international finance who has done pioneering research on the impact of multinational corporations on the development of Third World countries, occupies the Smith Chair. The Bernard J. Hank Professorship of Business Administration was formally established in 1981, when Frank K. Reilly joined the faculty. Reilly, who has also served as dean of the Col-

104  *The College of Business Administration*

The College of Business Administration 105

lege since 1981, is noted for his research about securities markets, investments, and portfolio management.

To enhance the teaching and research of the Finance Department, the faculty and students take part in two annual events that bring leading figures from the financial community to campus. The Finance Forum, which is sponsored by the Finance Club and dates back to 1959, allows students and faculty to hear and interact with prominent executives during a two-day period each spring. The Financial Institutions Series, started in 1981, takes place each fall. The speakers in this series address the numerous changes taking place

*(REV.) E. WILLIAM BEAUCHAMP, C.S.C.*
*Dept. of Management*

*The faculty challenge our students in the classroom to think, to question, to learn, and to be aware of their responsibility for the world they will inherit. When our students graduate, I hope they are prepared, not to know all the answers, but to know the questions that must be asked.*

NANCY CARTER
Dept. of Management

*I am convinced that the creative tension which evolves from attempting excellence in teaching and research simultaneously impels us to go beyond what we thought personally possible.*

ROBERT P. VECCHIO
Dept. of Management

*Notre Dame is now entering an era where faculty excellence in both scholarship and teaching is expected and rewarded.*

agement," "Government, Business, and Society," "Organization and Administrative Problems," and "Corporate Strategy and Planning."

The Department of Management has two distinct areas of concentration. Organization Behavior/Human Resource Management addresses such subjects as theories of leadership, labor relations, personnel administration, business law, and business ethics. The other concentration is the computer-based specialty of Management Information Systems. A recent addition to the curriculum, Management Information Systems recognize the importance of computers to contemporary corporations. Although computers are used widely throughout the College, the Department of Management is responsible for most of the instruction in computer use.

The diversity within the department leads to a wide range of research interests among the faculty. Some of the more significant scholarly contributions have focused on organizational behavior, management information systems, business ethics, and personnel administration. Three endowed chairs—the Franklin D. Schurz Professor-

in the financial services sector of the economy.

The Department of Management has the largest number of faculty members and offers the greatest number of classes of any of the four departments in the College of Business Administration. The department is large because many of its courses are fundamental to understanding the different dimensions of business and to preparing a person to become an effective manager. Given their significance, several courses in Management are requirements for all undergraduate students in the College. These include "Principles of Management," "Statistics in Business," "Computers in Business," and either "Legal Environment of Business" or "Business Law." On the master's level, the following courses make up the management foundation: "Computers and Management Information Systems," "Statistics," "Organizational Behavior," "Management Science," "Operations Manship of Management, the Arthur F. and Mary J. O'Neil Professorship of Business, and the Ray Siegfried Professorship of Business to advance the study of entrepreneurship—are located within the department and strengthen its work. Robert P. Vecchio, a specialist in personnel and organizational behavior, was appointed to the Schurz Professorship in 1986. He joined the Notre Dame faculty in 1976.

While the study of marketing has always been an integral part of the curriculum of the College, the Department of Marketing was not formally created until 1947. The new department replaced the academic unit that had helped to launch business education at Notre Dame, the Department of Foreign Commerce. Since the late 1940s, classes and research about international business have been diffused throughout the College's four departments.

The undergraduate curriculum of the Department of Marketing allows students to select a specific area of specialization from five possibilities: Retailing and Distribution Management, Industrial Marketing, Mass Communications and Advertising, Sales and Sales Management, and International Marketing. In recent years the sequence of classes about Sales and Sales Management has been the most popular choice of students, reflecting a trend that is occurring in business education across the country.

The scholarly research of faculty members encompasses several aspects of marketing. Generally, however, it focuses on subjects related to consumer decision-making, channels of distribution, the ethical and social dimensions of marketing, and corporate marketing strategy. The diversity of research interests contributes to the breadth of the department. In the future, however, there will be greater effort on developing a specific focus of attention to which several faculty members can contribute. The appointment of recognized scholars to the Aloysius and Eleanor Nathe Chair in Marketing Strategy and the Howard J. Korth Professorship of Marketing are steps toward this objective.

In the history of the College of Business Administration, 1967 and 1968 stand out as landmark years. In 1967, the Master's in Business Administration Program was inaugurated after five years of planning and research by Dean Thomas Murphy and Associate Dean John Malone. In 1968, a $1 million gift from Ramona Hayes Healy

---

*(REV.) DAVID T. TYSON, C.S.C.*
Dept. of Management

Notre Dame has become confident in its Catholicity. The inquiry for truth and fidelity to a tradition are not at odds in our understanding of our mission. In fact, their combination insures our contribution to American higher education as we approach the twenty-first century.

and her husband, John F. Healy, a 1930 Notre Dame alumnus, allowed for the construction of the Hayes-Healy Center, which adjoins the original academic building of the College. The Hayes-Healy Center includes lecture, conference, and seminar rooms; extensive computer facilities; an organizational behavior laboratory, and offices for faculty members and administrators.

The enrollment in the MBA program has grown dramatically since 1967. During its first few years, approximately 150 students were involved. Today over 300 students participate.

Although the graduate program as a whole is built on a foundation of courses in management, finance, accounting, and marketing, there are three distinct avenues leading to the degree. Students without an undergraduate business degree pursue a two-year, four-semester curriculum. Alternatively, students who already have a bachelor's degree in business are able to take part in a one year program that encompasses a summer session of intensive review and two semesters of work during the regular academic year. Finally, the Executive MBA Program is designed for experienced managers who work full-time. These executives take classes one full day each week during a two-year period.

The graduate curriculum combines theoretical instruction in such disciplines as accounting, economics, the behavioral sciences, mathematics, statistics, and law with practical situational analysis of actual cases in business. Two distinctive features of the program are its emphasis on examining ethical and moral issues and their implications for business management, and its accent on international dimensions of business. Considering questions of values and the social responsibilities of corporations is an abiding concern that has its origins in the religious, morally sensitive character of the University. One required course, "Government, Business, Society," has as a principal focus the ethical dimensions of business decisions and practices. Moral considerations pervade discussions in other classes as well.

Students in the MBA program obtain global perspectives about business operations through "International Business," a required course. In addition, the College conducts a semester of study in London as an option for second-year students in the regular MBA Program. Begun in 1977, and the first of its kind in American business education, the London MBA Program enables its participants to explore international business from

*MICHAEL J. ETZEL*
*Dept. of Marketing*

*I find the sense of loyalty and pride at Notre Dame delightfully refreshing in an increasingly cynical world.*

the vantage point of one of the world's leading financial centers. Classes are taught by a member of Notre Dame's faculty, who serves as Resident Director, and by several professors from various universities in England. Supplementing the formal curriculum are fieldwork with British companies, tours of financial institutions in London, and interaction with the London offices of international investment firms and multinational corporations. Similar to the concern for ethics and values, this project in international business on the graduate level continues an historic component of the College that can be traced to its founding.

A relatively new aspect of graduate business education at Notre Dame is the Executive MBA Program, which was inaugurated in 1982. The first such program in Northern Indiana, the Execu-

The College of Business Administration 109

tive MBA exists for experienced administrators who desire a professional degree in management while still retaining their executive positions. A total of eighty men and women from Indiana, Michigan, Illinois, and Ohio annually participate in the two-year program. The curriculum is similar to the regular MBA Program, but builds on the extensive and varied work experience of the participants.

To respond to the need for life-long learning by business executives, the College of Business Administration conducts numerous non-credit educational programs through its Executive Development Center, established in 1983. The Center enables executives to renew and up-date their knowledge and skills by sponsoring a variety of programs—from individual evening dinner meetings for area business leaders to the three-week "Executive Development Program" that brings mid-career managers from across the country to campus during the summer. The "Executive Development Program" explores a wide range of topics but also emphasizes some unique areas, like using the microcomputer in management, doing business abroad, understanding the role of women in the corporation, and fostering sensitivity to the ethical implications of decisions. Other Executive Seminars are more specialized, such as "Basic Accounting and Finance for Small Businesses," "Credit Analysis," "Bond Analysis and Portfolio Management," "Negotiating and Doing Business with the Japanese," and "Psychology of Selling." Some of the Center's programs are designed for specific corporations, associations, and organizations. For example, the National Association of Broadcasters sponsors a two-week management development seminar for fifty senior executives at Notre Dame. In the future, the Center plans to telecast some of its conferences to major cities throughout the country. This system of "teleconferencing" proceedings will allow the participation of executives who are unable to travel to the campus.

In addition to the Master of Business Administration degree, the College administers a Master of Science in Administration (MSA). This program, which began in 1954, was created to train people involved in the administration of not-for-profit institutions, such as schools, churches, hospitals, religious communities, nursing homes, and welfare agencies. Recognized as a pioneering project and one of the few such graduate undertakings in the United States, the MSA Program is conducted almost exclusively during the summer. Priests, sisters, and brothers make up almost half of the participants, and, historically, the administration of church-related organizations and institutions has been a primary focus. In recent years, there has been greater emphasis placed on such areas as the administration of health care facilities and social service agencies.

Work for the Master of Science in Administration typically entails three summers of study. In addition, students can take part in various one-week workshops without pursuing the graduate degree. Workshop topics include "Marketing for Not-for-Profit Organizations," "The Role of the Treasurer in the Religious Community," and "Balancing the Healing Mission with Business Ethics." Approximately 350 people participate in the workshops each year, while there are about 175 enrolled in the MSA Program.

To conform to the University-wide standards that have taken hold at Notre Dame since the 1970s, advanced scholarship has become a primary activity for faculty members in Business Administration. Research and publication have taken place throughout the history of the College. For example, several influential textbooks —such as E. Jerome McCarthy's *Basic Marketing: A Managerial Approach*, Raymond P. Kent's two volumes *Money and Banking* and *Corporate Financial Management*, and L. Edgar Crane's *Marketing Communication*—were written by Notre Dame professors during the 1950s and 1960s. More recently, though, the emphasis on achieving balance between effective teaching and sound scholarship has dramatically affected work within the College of Business Administration. New and different criteria for evaluating faculty members now exist.

In an effort to foster scholarly productivity and visibility, the College created a Center for Research in Business in 1983. Drawing on the recognized strengths of the four departments, and the faculty members with endowed professorships, the center focuses on specific areas for investigation, such as "Accounting and Taxation," "Corporate Strategy and Planning," "Financial Markets and Institutions," "Industrial and Consumer Marketing," "Management for Not-for-Profit Organizations," and "Multinational Management." Because its purpose is to foster and support research throughout the College, the Center has many dimensions. It awards research grants and assistantships, sponsors research seminars and publications, and acquires research materials and support services and facilities.

The first major publication produced by the Center was the "National Working Paper Index," which appeared in 1984. This annual bibliography of working papers in business research completed at universities across the country is distributed to approximately one hundred scholarly institutions in America. A future activity of the Center involves the establishment of post-doctoral research fellowships. The recipients of these fellowships will work directly with professors holding endowed chairs in the College.

Two centers that have links to the Center for Research in Business but also possess autonomous status are the Center for Ethics and Religious Values in Business and the Center for Research in Banking. The Center for Ethics and Religious Values in Business evolved from the University's Joint Committee of Business, Theology, and Philosophy, which was formed in 1976 to encourage dialogue between business executives and scholars in the humanities. A grant from General Electric Company formally established the Center in 1981.

Through biennial symposia, research, and publications, the Center addresses issues related to religious thinking and the business world. Three subjects considered by participants at national conferences convened at Notre Dame have been "The Judeo-Christian Vision and the Modern Corporation," "Co-Creation: A Religious Vision of Corporate Power" (about Pope John Paul II's encyclical "On Human Work"), and "Catholic Social Teaching and the U.S. Economy." The third conference, which took place in December of 1983, involved the presentation of a series of working papers from varying viewpoints that were used by the American Catholic bishops in writing their pastoral letter on the economy. Each symposium results in the publication of a book that brings together the papers of the conference speakers.

The Center's emphasis on religious and moral values makes it different from the majority of business ethics programs elsewhere. According to Rev. Oliver Williams, C.S.C., co-director of the Center and a faculty member in the Department of Management, "Traditional ethics reaches moral values through human reason. But many people who are Christian want to discuss how their religious values enter the work life. The two perspectives actually compliment each other." Co-director John Houck, Professor of Management, believes that the work of the Center requires strict balance between religious idealism and business realism: "Religious thinking has difficulty with concepts like competition, so important to the business world. Our role is to show that the two can be compatible."

In 1985 the College of Business Administration established the Center for Research in Banking with initial funding from a group of twenty Indiana banks. To broaden its perspective and increase its funding the Center subsequently added a number of sponsors from throughout the country. Faculty members connected with the Center work on studies of relevance to bankers in dealing with the constantly changing financial services environment.

There are two sets of research. The first is directed research that involves topics suggested by the Advisory Board of the Center, which in-

*(REV.) OLIVER F. WILLIAMS, C.S.C.*
*Dept. of Management*

*With a growing number of Catholics in major leadership positions in corporate America and government, Catholics have truly come of age in the United States. The traditional American passion for justice can be widened and deepened with the social and political wisdom of the Catholic tradition. Our exciting task is to provide intellectual leadership to meet this challenge.*

cludes sponsors of the Center and faculty representatives from all departments of the College. Topics investigated include: "The Likely Impact of Regional Interstate Banking Laws" and "An Analysis of the Adequacy of State and Federal Depositor Insurance." In addition, the Center supports faculty initiated research of interest to financial institutions. Examples include "The Use of Financial Futures to Hedge Bank Portfolios," "The Scheduling and Evaluation of Bank Tellers," and "Bond Duration and Portfolio Immunization." The research is subsequently discussed during two annual seminars conducted for Center sponsors. The Center also supports a lecture series that brings academics from other universities and representatives of the banking industry to campus for formal presentations and informal discussions with students, faculty, and sponsors of the Center. This lecture series is one of several organized by the College to promote continuing relationships between the University and other academic institutions and business institutions across the country.

In addition to the research centers, the College has been involved in an interdisciplinary project that probes the impact of multinational corporations on developing countries. Considering the moral dimensions of doing business in Latin America, Asia, and Africa is a central concern of the Program, but there are other components to its work. The program has a seven-step process that encompasses several years of annual workshops, specialized field research, and international conferences and seminars to review the research and to discuss recommendations.

Lee Tavis, the C. R. Smith Professor of Business Administration and director of the Program, notes that multinational corporations are influential agents of change with the power to help or to hurt people in developing countries. "The key question becomes: How can they responsibly wield that power?" Tavis says. "In financial management if you can't quantify something, it doesn't exist. We're finding ways to quantify developmental responsibility. For the first time executives will be able to evaluate their local managers on this dimension of corporate life."

The Program began its work in 1978 by focusing on "Multinational Managers and Poverty in the Third World." A grant from the Rockefeller Foundation in 1984 and support from fourteen multinational corporations enabled the Program to establish two additional task forces of academics, multinational executives, religious leaders, and governmental officials on "Multinational Corporations and Host Government Regulatory Participation" and "Multinational Corporate Involvement with Religious Groups." A distinctive feature of the Program and its task forces is the combined participation of representatives from the relevant sectors of society, which leads to research and recommendations rooted in scholarly analysis and the actual experience of corporations involved in the Third World.

During its first fifty years, the College of Business Administration concentrated on developing an undergraduate curriculum that joined technical competence in business with a concern for humanistic and religious values. That heritage continues today, and during the past two decades scholarly research, graduate education, and executive development have also become vital components in the life of the College. These new dimensions add intellectual depth to the College, broaden its academic commitment, and strengthen its foundation for future growth and achievement.

*LEE A. TAVIS*
*Dept. of Finance and Business Economics*

PROFILE

DEAN FRANK K. REILLY

COLLEGE OF BUSINESS ADMINISTRATION

WHEN FRANK K. REILLY RETURNED to Notre Dame in 1981, he found the College of Business Administration that he had been asked to direct as dean in a state of transition. Since his student days in the late 1950s, when undergraduate education was the overriding concern, the College had significantly broadened its mission. A graduate program leading to a Master's in Business Administration and a greater commitment to research and scholarly publication had become integral elements in the life of the College. Reilly sees the expansion and improvement of the instructional programs and the research opportunities as fundamental in completing the transition from the past and in "building a College that has a strong national reputation."

During the past few years, the College has taken several strides toward the goals Reilly and others envision for the future. The bachelor's program in business currently enjoys a ranking in the top ten in the United States. The MBA curriculum has become more rigorous, and the program has been enlarged. More faculty members and students than ever before are involved in graduate education in business, with the establishment of the Executive MBA Program in 1982 an important factor in the increase. A year later, the Executive Development Center, which sponsors numerous non-credit programs for executives in various fields, was instituted. Research within the College has been enhanced through the creation of the Center for Research in Business in 1983 and the Center for Research in Banking in 1985.

Reilly believes that "the development of a research environment" is crucial in strengthening the College as a whole. "The research is in its formative stages, but that is what's going to give our College its national reputation," he explains. "We're building a base for excellence in research, but to take that next step to get into the 'Big Leagues' we need to develop our research centers. Before the 1970s, our research was rather limited. In the '70s we initiated a research program and probably were in the 'C' League. In the '80s we have moved to the 'B' League. To take that next step to the 'A' League, we need our research centers to be fully operational. You need that support and the resources that allow the faculty to produce at a top level, and to attract and retain the very best faculty, especially when you don't have a Ph.D. program."

Besides increasing faculty productivity and making Notre Dame more attractive to promising and established teacher-scholars, Reilly thinks the new concentration on research has fostered a stronger sense of collegiality within the College and helped improve teaching on both the undergraduate and graduate levels. "There has always been collegiality on a social level," he remarks, "but in the past few years that collegiality has begun to pervade the teaching and research environment. This bond between scholars is enhanced through research seminars and research presentations, where the faculty present research and talk about it. Currently there is an enormous amount of joint research within the College—somewhere between 80 and 90 percent of our research is joint research."

The collegiality Reilly describes is different from the atmosphere of some business schools of his acquaintance. "In certain cases people become very competitive and protective about their research. I can think of examples where the faculty won't talk about their research because they are worried that a colleague is going to steal the idea. That is definitely not the environment at Notre Dame. People are intellectually stimulated and they may disagree, but they discuss the differences in a constructive manner that encourages and helps their colleagues." Reilly feels that the collegiality within the research environment is linked to a spirit of caring that pervades the University and the desire to make Notre Dame an outstanding University.

Reilly contends that there is a definite relationship between the concentration on research and what's happening in the classrooms of the College of Business Administration. "I'm absolutely convinced that the research emphasis has made our faculty better teachers. Because of their research, they're better informed and more at the leading edge of their fields. As a result, our students are getting a better education. Good research and good teaching are *complementary,* not competitive."

Helping create balance between teaching and research is a principal challenge facing Reilly as dean. He and other University officials know that both activities must be combined effectively to have a business school with a national reputation. In Reilly's own case, teaching and research are the foundation of his academic life. When he accepted the deanship in 1981, he also assumed the Bernard J. Hank Professorship of Business Administration. Despite his administrative responsibilities, Reilly continues to teach on a regular basis—a graduate course each year about investments, as well as numerous presentations to programs of the Executive Development Center. He has also continued to publish books and articles. Since coming to Notre Dame, he has completed revised editions of two of his books, *Investment Analysis and Portfolio Management* and *Investments*, has contributed to several handbooks, and written numerous articles and conference papers. The book *Investments*, which appeared in its second edition in 1986, is the leading textbook in its field and has been adopted for classes at nearly three hundred schools across the country. His *Investment Analysis* book is a required text for the Chartered Financial Analyst exam.

Reilly, who received his bachelor's in business administration from Notre Dame in 1957, his MBA from Northwestern University, and his doctorate from the University of Chicago in 1968, was a professor of business at the University of Kansas, the University of Wyoming, and the University of Illinois until 1981. While at Illinois, he received both the Outstanding Educator Award and the Outstanding Graduate Teaching Award. Before beginning his academic career, Reilly was a senior security analyst and a trader of stocks and bonds for several years. He has maintained his professional affiliations as a Chartered Financial Analyst (CFA) and is active in the Institute of CFAs. His involvement with academic associations is reflected in the fact that he is past president of the Financial Management Association, the Midwest Business Administration Association, and the Eastern Finance Association.

As the College develops new programs and a new environment, Reilly thinks it is important to keep such changes in perspective. He doesn't want them to be at odds with the tradition of business education at Notre Dame and its distinctive characteristics. The dean wants to strengthen the two areas of inquiry that have existed since the College was established in 1921. "A concern with ethical factors involved in business decisions and our heavy emphasis on the international dimensions of business make us unique," Reilly notes. "A course in ethics is required in the graduate programs and strongly encouraged for undergraduates. Beyond these requirements, the concern for ethics pervades all of our courses. Our concern for international business is more widespread than at other schools, and we have had a longer standing interest in the subject. Many schools are just getting involved."

Reilly hopes that the College's Center for Ethics and Religious Values in Business will receive additional financial support so it can expand its activities. "This is an area where we are not only unique but also strong," he says. "We have an opportunity to become a major force in the area." The establishment of the Ray W. and Kenneth G. Herrick Chair in International Business strengthens the College's work in this area.

Another traditional strength of the College, the undergraduate program, is a source of concern for Reilly in one respect. "We want our students to be liberally educated as well as competent in business matters. Because we recognize the value of a liberal education, we want the students to go out of the College for their free electives. A problem we face is having them take a good, integrated program. Unfortunately, in some cases, they take a hodgepodge of classes. It would be more valuable for them to take several courses in one area to get broad but also deep exposure to the subject. We expect a new advising system to remedy the problem and strengthen our undergraduate program."

Although Reilly looks forward to the day when he will return to full-time teaching and research, he wants to see the College achieve the potential he and others see in it. "I believe that the way I can contribute to the University is to help build an outstanding College of Business Administration. The University cannot become known as a great university unless the College of Business shares in that dream. I think it's important to have all of the colleges strong. You can't emphasize one and neglect other segments because those ignored can offset the outstanding units. Hence, I think it is essential that Notre Dame has a nationally ranked College of Business, and I want to help build that ranking."

*Construction of the new addition to the Law School*

# The Law School

AT THE DEDICATION of the University of Notre Dame's London Law Centre in 1983, Chief Justice Warren E. Burger said: "American law schools for the most part perform very well the task of training in the law and in legal analysis. But a system of legal education that teaches lawyers to think brilliantly yet fails to teach them how to act with civility and according to high professional standards with a commitment to human values has failed to perform its mission." The Chief Justice, however, was not completely critical of legal education. Calling Notre Dame a leader in integrating ethical and moral considerations into teaching and research, he noted that "Notre Dame has a rare opportunity to encourage a reexamination of the moral basis and the jurisprudential assumptions on which our legal system and our legal education are based."

Fostering sensitivity to moral and ethical questions, especially their relationship to all aspects of the law, has been a continuing concern throughout the history of legal education and scholarship at Notre Dame. The Law School, the oldest law school under Catholic auspices in the United States, began in 1869. Providing legal instruction to Notre Dame students was one of Father Edward Sorin's earliest dreams for the school he founded in 1842. Indeed, in the first published catalog issued by the University in 1854, Father Sorin announced his intention of establishing a Department of Law. Four years later, courses in constitutional law appeared in the curriculum. A decade after these classes were offered, the Board of Trustees voted to create a distinct department.

From 1869 until the academic year of 1882–83, a student could earn a bachelor of laws degree by completing two years of course work, by participating in the weekly moot court proceedings, and by writing an essay on a specific legal matter. But in 1882–1883 Notre Dame became the fourth school in the country to institute a three-year program. Adding another year of study allowed more thorough instruction in the law and provided a greater degree of professionalism to the education students received. Notre Dame helped to pioneer the three-year course of legal studies, which subsequently became and continues to this day as the standard length of time to complete degree requirements at law schools throughout the United States.

Another significant occurrence of 1883 was the return to campus of William J. Hoynes, who was named the first dean of law in January of that year. Hoynes, an 1872 law graduate of the University of Michigan, had received a master of arts degree from Notre Dame in 1878. Before accepting the deanship, he had practiced law in Chicago and had been a newspaper editor in New Jersey and in Illinois. Hoynes served as dean from 1883 until 1919 and as a visible (and vigorous) dean emeritus from 1919 until his death in 1933. Although never advancing beyond private in the Union Army during the Civil War, he came to be known as "Colonel" Hoynes throughout his fifty years at Notre Dame. During his long tenure as dean, he significantly improved legal education at the University. In fact, not long after Hoynes took over, the *Chicago Law Journal* reported that "within the past three or four years the Law Department of the University of Notre Dame . . . has taken rank among the very best law schools in the country."

Hoynes taught no fewer than four classes each day and presided over moot court as part of his duties. His legendary teaching, his personal involvement with students, and his concern for the ethical and philosophical aspects of the law were highly influential, and several of his qualities took root in the Law School, and continue to flourish today. In *A Century of Law at Notre Dame*, Rev. Philip S. Moore, C.S.C., provides a telling assessment of Hoynes: "During those fifty years [1883–1933] he not only developed and strengthened what was then called the Law Department, but also became perhaps the best known and best loved professor ever to serve on the faculty of the university. He was at once a strong personality, a master teacher, and a 'character' whose little foibles and vanities charmed colleagues and students alike."

With support from several administrators at Notre Dame, Hoynes made legal education an integral part of University life. He also oversaw and helped to guide the remarkable growth of the law program and its facilities. When Hoynes arrived in 1883, the Administration building was the home of law classrooms and offices. Then, from 1889 until 1918, Law occupied a portion of the first floor of Sorin Hall, where Hoynes himself lived as a "bachelor don" for many years. In 1919, a separate building, the Hoynes College of Law, was dedicated. (It is now the Crowley Hall of Music.) During the 1920s, Law continued to expand, and in 1930 the present law building near the entrance to the campus was completed. Renovations and additions in the 1970s and 1980s have almost tripled the size of the original facility, with both of these recent expansions helping to enlarge the library of the Law School and providing more classroom and office space.

The principal legacy of Colonel Hoynes (besides the humorous anecdotes that abound about him) was the firm foundation for legal studies that he constructed. He emphasized skill and service as being hallmarks of Notre Dame graduates in law. Succeeding deans and professors built on this base to strengthen the Law School, and to make it a more influential force in American legal education.

One of the most important figures to contribute to the development of the Law School was Joseph O'Meara, the dean from 1952 until 1968. O'Meara had as his primary goals academic excellence and professional competence for everyone associated with the Law School. Influenced by the achievements of Ivy League law schools, especially those at Harvard and Yale, O'Meara actively sought promising students from across the country through an extensive scholarship program. In addition to raising the standards of admission, introducing requirements to make the Law School more selective, and designing a more rigorous curriculum, O'Meara enlarged the faculty and hired professors who were expected not only to teach but also to challenge the students to meet high professional standards. O'Meara also supported the coeducation of the Law School, which occurred in 1965–66, seven years before the Notre Dame undergraduate program, and he established the Legal Aid and Defender Association to provide legal service to the poor. In *A Century of Law at Notre Dame*, Father Moore summarizes the accomplishments of O'Meara's tenure as dean: "The aim or purpose of legal instruction at Notre Dame remained substantially the same in the O'Meara era as it had always been, to produce the lawyer well grounded in the fundamentals of law, trained in the essential skills of the practitioner, and deeply imbued with a sense of the moral responsibilities of the members of the legal profession. But this aim or purpose was more consistently insisted upon and expressed in several different ways."

O'Meara's insistence on competence and compassion as fundamental to the work and lives of students and faculty members brought greater recognition to the Law School than it had achieved in its first eighty years. One Ohio Bar Association survey conducted at this time ranked Notre Dame with Harvard, Yale, and Michigan as the best out-of-state schools in preparing students to take the state bar examination. In the realm of scholarship, John T. Noonan, a professor of law at Notre Dame from 1962 until 1969, published *Contraception: A History of its Treatment by the Catholic Theologians and Canonists* in 1965, and it is acknowledged internationally to be the definitive study of its subject. Professor Noonan has recently been appointed as a Judge of the United States Court of Appeals for the Ninth Circuit.

The years since the celebration of the Law School's centenary have been marked by efforts to enrich traditional areas of strength and to launch new programs that enhance Notre Dame's standing in legal education. The long-standing commitment to effective teaching and to a close relationship between students and faculty remains a central feature of the Law School's character. Instead of an intensely competitive experience similar to the one depicted in the popular movie and television series "Paper Chase," most professors and students see the Notre Dame Law School as a collegial endeavor. Professor Joseph Bauer, a graduate of Harvard Law School, who joined the Notre Dame faculty in 1973 and has also taught at the University of Michigan Law School and at the University of North Carolina School of Law, remarks, "One thing that would commend me to Notre Dame is the community. Law School is a less unpleasant experience here. Students know one another and have access to the faculty. It is easier to learn in that environment." Professor Kenneth Ripple adds, "We in the faculty try to be role models. Students are able to see how an integrated life in the law is led. We do clone ourselves here, and the students become our colleagues. When we choose a student body, we're, in effect, choosing our colleagues."

Collegiality or civility exists within the program despite the fact that there has been increased competition in recent years to become a law student at Notre Dame. Anywhere from ten to twelve applicants vie for each place in the first-year class. As the Law School has improved and become more recognized, the quality of potential students has reflected this advancement. Even though the school itself has more than doubled its size in the past two decades (from 180 in 1965 to 505 in 1985), there is now greater depth in the ability and potential of the student body.

The challenge that was successfully faced by Dean Thomas L. Shaffer (1970–1975) was how to maintain the quality of both the student body and the program despite the increase in the number of students. Dean Shaffer first established a principle of critical size. The student body would have to be large enough to justify sufficient faculty positions needed to offer a comprehensive curriculum. On the other hand, Notre Dame should never go beyond the "small law school" category because, as a medium or large law school, it would not be possible to maintain both the atmosphere of collegiality and the concentration on values. Since "small law schools" are generally considered to be those having 550 or fewer students, Notre Dame still remains comfortably within that category.

Dean Shaffer was also determined to maintain some of the essential features of the Notre Dame

*JOSEPH P. BAUER*
Law School

*The Notre Dame Law School is striving to maintain a diverse, concerned, and academically excellent student body, a faculty committed to quality teaching and research, and an environment in which ethical, normative, and moral questions are addressed advertently and without embarrassment.*

atmosphere. Small class size and a low student-faculty ratio were among his goals and the concept of "open door" faculty offices was maintained. The "open door" policy specifies that no faculty member at Notre Dame is permitted to list office hours since students should feel welcome to consult with the faculty at any time except when the teacher is preparing for class. Most importantly, Dean Shaffer began experiments which have resulted in Notre Dame's unique admissions system. Although many law schools base admissions primarily on gradepoint averages and Law School Admissions Test scores, Notre Dame has developed a highly personalized program that looks at many aspects of a student's background. Notre Dame goes beyond the gradepoint average by doing a transcript analysis looking for factors such as progress made during the applicant's undergraduate career and whether the student has challenged himself or herself through difficult electives. Of more importance than the standardized test scores are an applicant's capacity for leadership and a demonstrated concern for exploring value questions and issues. Decisions about admission are based on these latter factors because the legal education Notre Dame students receive continues to combine substantive understanding of the law's practices and procedures with sensitivity to the ethical and human implications of what a lawyer does in professional life. The value orientation of the Law School distinguishes it from most of the other law schools, whether public or private, in the United States. While pursuing moral considerations might be an adjunct activity elsewhere, it is an integral component to the Notre Dame law program.

This commitment, which draws much of its strength from the Catholic character and religious orientation of the University, pervades the teaching, research, and service activities of the Law School. In the classroom, for instance, students are required to take courses on "law and ethics" during three of their six semesters. In addition, a class in jurisprudence is a requirement at Notre Dame, making the Law School one of only two in the country where having background in the philosophy of law is a necessity.

Exploring value questions, however, goes beyond the required courses that revolve principally around such issues. As Professor Fernand N. Dutile observes, "Most of us in all of our classes seize the opportunity to address ethical issues. You have to be alert to it, and the Law School and the University provide that mandate. If you don't do it, you've neglected the professional training a lawyer needs." By combining substantive knowledge and moral sensitivity, the Law School seeks to educate men and women who possess professional competence as well as a partisanship for justice, an ability to respond to human need, and a compassion for their clients, colleagues, and others affected by the legal process.

Another unique feature of Notre Dame Law School is its development in recent years of distinctive teaching and research projects in international and comparative law. The centerpiece of this work is the Concannon Programme of International Law, which supports a Notre Dame London Law Centre as well as scholarly endeavors on international law conducted on campus. Founded in 1968, the Notre Dame London Law Centre is unique in American legal education. It is the only program that offers law study abroad on a year-round basis, including a summer school session. Second-year students are able to enroll in classes traditionally offered in American law schools—courses in such areas as business associations, commercial transactions, evidence, trusts and es-

*TANG T.T. LE*
Law School

tates, and jurisprudence—but these courses are offered on a comparative law basis making comparisons between foreign legal systems and American law. Other courses focus directly on subjects like public international law, common market law, and international regulation of trade and business. European professors compose the majority faculty of the Law Centre, but the presence of a Director from the home campus and other American professors assures that the London student will not fall behind his or her stateside colleague on developments in American law. Hans Van Houtte, the noted international law scholar at Catholic University in Louvain, Belgium, served as the first Distinguished Visiting Concannon Professor and has taught in the London Summer Programme since 1983. In 1981 Professor Van Houtte was a member of the home campus faculty at Notre Dame, teaching and doing research under the auspices of the Concannon Programme of International Law.

At the dedication ceremonies for the London Centre, Father Theodore Hesburgh stated, "It's a marvelous thing for young lawyers to be citizens of the world and to know how law is a force for peace (because it's for justice) and also how it's a force for civilizing the rest of the world." Calling Notre Dame a pioneer in legal education, Chief Justice Burger added, "It's what we need to have a broader gauged profession, and I think Notre Dame is on the way to producing that. I suspect it will be copied by other law schools."

The Notre Dame London experience is more than the enrollment of American students in a foreign law school and is different from an American law program run abroad. It is an international and comparative law program, taught in a foreign centre but designed to be an integral part of a normal American law school curriculum. Students are exposed to law subjects within a foreign environment through a distinguished international faculty, all of this within the framework of a rigorous American law school structure. Students in this program can take advantage of this international environment outside the Centre classroom atmosphere as well as in it. Students can supplement the Centre's curriculum by doing academic work at the University of London, at King's College, and at the School of Oriental and African Studies. Many students enjoy clerking experiences with London law firms or corporate or government offices, and some participate in London legal aid activities. Students also engage in a variety of co-curricular activities. One such activity involves the publication of the *Notre Dame International and Comparative Law Journal.* Started in 1983 to coincide with the formal dedication of the London Law Centre that featured the address of Chief Justice Burger, the *Journal* includes original articles by scholars and students as well as the English translations of significant court cases that have taken place in foreign countries. In some instances, the *Journal* is the only English source to provide the actual decisions that have been rendered in key international cases.

One of the most popular co-curricular activities for Law Centre students is the moot court competition. Oral arguments take place in the Royal Courts of Justice, seat of Britain's highest courts, before American attorneys and, at times, British judges. The moot court proceedings in London are a part of the tradition of Notre Dame students receiving extensive practical experience in legal affairs as part of their education. During the early years of the Law School, moot court was a weekly exercise, and it was conducted to give students (in the words of one catalog) "the opportunity to gain poise, self-command, and quickness of decision." In 1950 intramural and intercollegiate competition became integral to the moot court activities. Today there are three divisions in moot court competition—appellate, trial, and international—as well as the Notre Dame Law School Trial Competition. A highlight of moot court each year is the Moot Court Final Argument, which involves the most successful third-year students in oral argument before a Mock Supreme Court composed of federal and state judges. In recent years several Justices of the United States Supreme Court—Thurgood Marshall, Potter Stewart, William Rehnquist, John Paul Stevens, and Harry Blackmun—have come to campus to judge the winner of the Final Argument.

Since the late 1940s, the Law School has been recognized nationally for its pioneering efforts in trial advocacy. Professor Edward Barrett, who joined the faculty in 1948 and served on it over thirty years, created a "practice court" to acquaint students with actual courtroom procedures. An imaginative teacher who understood the value of "learning by doing," he introduced several techniques in the teaching of trial advocacy that were later adopted at law schools across the country. Now enhancing Notre Dame's work and reputation in this area is the National Institute for Trial

Advocacy, which moved its headquarters to the Law School in 1979.

Directed by Notre Dame Professor James Seckinger, the Institute exists to help develop effective and professionally responsible trial lawyers in the United States. Established in 1970, the Institute annually conducts some twenty programs and workshops at university sites throughout America. Lawyers and law school professors attend these sessions to improve their skills in the courtroom and in the classroom. In its first fifteen years of operation, over seven thousand lawyers and teachers have participated in programs sponsored by the Institute. Besides these formal training activities, the Institute creates educational materials—books, videotapes, and audiotapes—that can be used for the continuing education of lawyers or in law classes. Over a hundred audio-visual tapes and more than thirty publications are available from the Institute. Many of the materials have been developed at Notre Dame by members of the Law School faculty. Commenting on the impact of the Institute, which works closely with the American Bar Association and other professional groups, Professor Seckinger says: "In most law schools, faculty members use

NITA teaching methodologies, and in most cases they also use our materials."

Another dimension to the practical, professional training of law students is the Notre Dame Legal Aid and Defender Association. Combining learning with service, students involved in this program work as interns who help to provide legal assistance to people in need. The client might be an indigent facing a small claims matter, a migrant worker with legal problems, or a prisoner seeking post-conviction remedies in a state or federal court or before a parole or clemency board. By participating in the Legal Aid and Defender Association, which has existed since 1965, second- and third-year students are actually able to make court appearances on behalf of lower income individuals in Indiana and Michigan. In addition, Notre Dame is one of the law schools authorized to provide students the opportunity to prepare legal briefs and to present oral arguments at the appellate level. The students, under the supervision of faculty members, represent indigent clients in the United States Court of Appeals for the Seventh Circuit, which is located in Chicago.

Besides the various courtroom experiences that

are available, the Law School recognizes the significance of clear and cogent writing to the effectiveness of any lawyer. A course in legal writing is a requirement during a student's first semester. However, unlike other schools where a law professor with an interest in writing or drafting offers such a class, Notre Dame is distinctive by having a trained teacher of writing with a doctorate in English as a faculty member. As a result, the emphasis throughout the course remains fixed on effective writing and how to achieve it in preparing legal documents. Advanced students seeking to develop greater expertise in legal writing have the opportunity to work on one of the several publications emanating from the Law School. One of the oldest, university-based legal journals in the United States is *The Notre Dame Law Review*, which is entirely edited by students under the supervision of a faculty advisor. Founded in 1925 as *The Notre Dame Lawyer*, the publication changed its name in 1982. Appearing five times a year, *The Law Review* circulates nationally and includes articles, case notes, and book reviews by students, professors, judges, and practicing attorneys. It is frequently cited in court opinions and by other authors.

The present and future of the Law School lies in taking on new challenges while maintaining traditional strengths. To accomplish this, the present administration has developed a long-range plan that explains the traditional law school mission as: "To be an outstanding teaching Law School, continuing to prepare attorneys who have both competence and compassion and whose decisions are guided by the values and morality which Notre Dame represents." In addition, the Law School has defined a newly intensified mission of: "Through faculty scholarship and institutional projects to be recognized as a leader among institutions making contributions to the development of law, the system of justice, the legal profession, and legal education, concentrating on the unique qualities of the Notre Dame value system." The taking on of the objectives presented by that second mission has not only been accomplished without de-emphasizing the first, but has enhanced the quality of teaching.

In the long-range planning process, the Law School first examined those aspects of its history which gave it a strong teaching reputation. In instances where Notre Dame had been drifting away from its traditional strength, the Law School disregarded the trends of other law schools and returned to former practices. In other areas, action was taken to guarantee continuation of certain basic academic principles at Notre Dame. A rigorous curriculum has been adopted changing the emphasis from mainly elective to heavily required. A traditional grading system has been imposed and is applied in such a way that a student's academic accomplishments are not only properly evaluated but distinguishable from others in the student's class (in contrast to trends toward pass/fail grading and other techniques of grade inflation).

The maintaining of the Law School in the "small school" category has been guaranteed by

*PATRICIA A. O'HARA*
Law School

*The Notre Dame Law School is rooted in a tradition which weds the goal of professional competence with the added dimension of emphasizing the moral questions underlying the law. In a faculty and student body which represent a wide spectrum of religious backgrounds and political views, we do not always agree on the answers to these fundamental questions. We are united, however, in our effort to raise these issues and to make them an integral part of our curriculum and scholarship.*

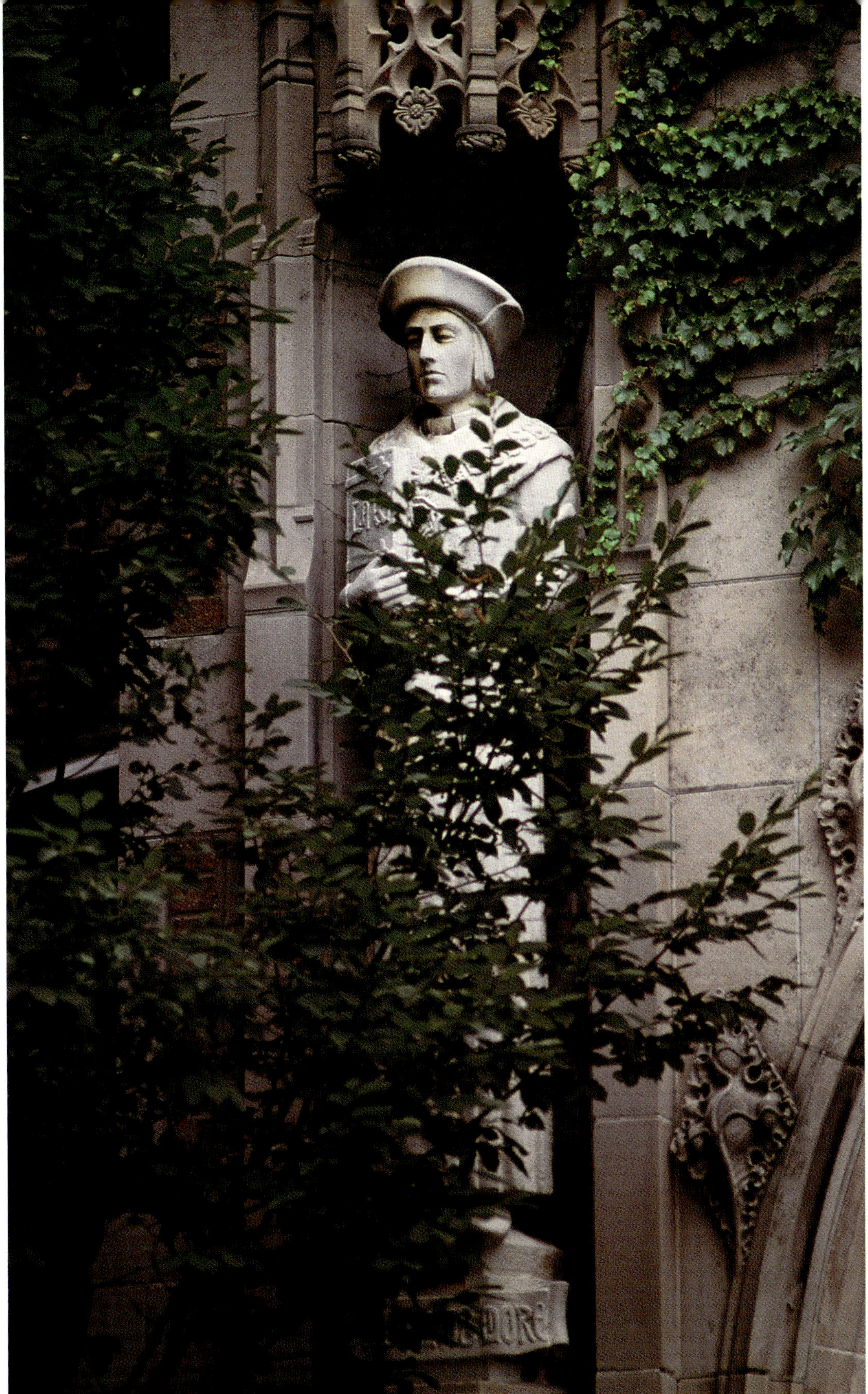

the design of the building additions in 1973 and 1986. Classrooms are arranged so as to accommodate only small classes, and faculty offices are sufficiently large to allow for the after-class discussions between faculty and students which are encouraged by the "open door" policy. Many aspects of the physical plant emphasize the personalized training objectives of the Law School, including one of the most extensive video systems available at a legal institution. This system is used, among other purposes, for replay of student work in client counseling, moot court, and trial advocacy. Faculty have the opportunity to critique student technique on a one-on-one basis.

The experiments of the highly personalized admissions system have now been firmly implanted as an established practice. Notre Dame is perhaps the only major law school where the Dean makes the final decision on every admissions file. This system has worked so well that the administration is satisfied that there is no way of materially improving on the depth of quality of the student body other than by increased financial aid to students. Despite concerns to the contrary, the emphasis in the admissions process on demonstrated leadership and value-orientation has neither lowered the median academic qualifications nor produced students who are so competitive that they cannot work civilly within the unique collegial atmosphere of Notre Dame. Current students are highly competitive against their own standards but rarely feel the need to focus competition on their classmates. Therefore, student study groups, cooperative projects, and a general collegial atmosphere abound.

Making contributions to legal research and literature is not new to the Notre Dame Law School but regarding scholarship with a national impact as a major mission without de-emphasizing the teaching mission requires some major developments in the Law School. The faculty size has been increased, reducing individual classloads and making time available for scholarship. Also, sabbaticals may be provided for those faculty members needing released time to complete a major piece of research. The Summer School sessions have been eliminated allowing the faculty, on an annual basis, a solid block of work time to do research. (The faculty had concluded that the average student was disadvantaged by trying to accelerate his law program through summer studies.) Student research assistants are now assigned to faculty, and faculty are provided scholarship incentives through summer stipends and merit pay increases. Most importantly, the hiring of new faculty is being made not only on the criterion of teaching ability but based on potential for the production of scholarship that has a national impact.

Already the research scholarship plan is paying off in a number of ways. While in the past the faculty as a whole was able to produce only a handful of law review articles in any academic year, now most faculty, especially those recently hired, are producing articles, manuscripts, and books at a rate comparable to that of faculty in the most prestigious law schools. For example, Professor Dutile is finishing his sixth book in a six-year period. Associate Dean Joseph Bauer is co-authoring a major series of treatises on the law of anti-trust. Professor Ripple has published a

*G. ROBERT BLAKEY*
Law School

*Notre Dame is not merely a place where individuals struggle within their own isolated worlds, seeking to clarify their own visions of reality, but a community that shares the deepest values.*

seminal work on constitutional litigation. Teaching materials used by other law schools are being written by current Notre Dame faculty members.

The appointment of recognized scholars to endowed professorships has focused attention on the commitment to make publishing a central concern. Professor Edward J. Murphy, whose book *Studies in Contract Law* is used as a textbook in over forty law schools, is the John N. Matthews Professor of Law. Professor Murphy has recently co-authored *Sales and Credit Transactions Handbook* with Professor Tang Thanh Trai Le, the former Dean of Hue Law School in Vietnam, now a professor at Notre Dame. Professor G. Robert Blakey, the author of three books and one of the country's foremost authorities on organized crime, is the William and Dorothy O'Neill Professor of Law. Besides his scholarly work, Professor Blakey has served as a special attorney in the Justice Department and as the chief counsel to senate and congressional committees. His book, *The Plot to Kill the President*, was written after his service as chief counsel and staff director of the House select committee that investigated the assassinations of President John F. Kennedy and the Reverend Martin Luther King.

As the quality and quantity of research have increased, professors have also become more involved in professional work outside the traditional modes of scholarship that contribute directly to the American legal system. During the past few years, members of the Law faculty have participated in several significant Supreme Court cases. Notre Dame professors have prepared formal briefs on behalf of parties, and they have orally argued cases in front of the high court itself. In addition, faculty members are now more active on governmental and bar association committees. Dean David T. Link has chaired a Section, a Standing Committee, and a Special Presidential Committee of the American Bar Association, and the present and immediate past reporters for the Judicial Conference's Advisory Committee on Appellate Rules are members of the Notre Dame faculty (Professors Ripple and Carol Mooney). Faculty are frequently called on as experts to testify before congressional committees.

"The intellectual life of the law is not limited to academics," notes Professor Kenneth F. Ripple. "Notre Dame understands this, and the Law School has now established its intellectual self-identity, on the campus and off the campus." Professor Ripple, who prior to joining the faculty in 1973 served as special assistant to the Chief Justice of the United States Supreme Court, was appointed by President Ronald Reagan in 1985 as a Judge of the United States Court of Appeals for the Seventh Circuit. The first full time Notre Dame faculty member to receive a federal judgeship, he continues to teach and to conduct research at the Law School.

The examination of the ethical and philosophical implications of the law is a dominant characteristic of the scholarly publications that are either sponsored by the Law School or researched and written by members of the Law faculty. *The American Journal of Jurisprudence*, which from 1956 until 1970 was called the *Natural Law Forum*, is perhaps the only journal in the English language devoted to investigating the principles and applications of the natural law and of legal philosophy. The journal, which promotes the scholarly search for universal standards relevant to the solution of contemporary problems, is the annual publication of the Natural Law Institute, established by the Law School in 1947. In addition to *The American Journal of Jurisprudence*, the Natural Law Institute also sponsors one in-

*KENNETH F. RIPPLE*
Law School

*(REV.) MICHAEL McCAFFERTY, C.S.C.*
Law School

*The Catholic university must not only encourage the development of new knowledge and critical thinking, it must also assist committed men and women in their efforts to deepen and articulate their faith.*

vited lecture on campus each year. Some of the lecturers have included Lon J. Fuller, John Rawls, and Robert Nozick.

In 1984 the first issue of *The Notre Dame Journal of Law, Ethics & Public Policy* appeared. This quarterly publication is unique among legal periodicals because it analyzes legal and public issues from an ethical perspective. Each issue of the *Journal* focuses on a single topic, and scholars, policymakers, and advanced law students from Notre Dame explore the subject from a variety of viewpoints and use differing approaches and methodologies. The inaugural issue on "Law and Morality" featured articles by President Ronald Reagan, Governor Mario Cuomo of New York, Congressman Henry Hyde, Rev. Theodore M. Hesburgh, C.S.C., president of Notre Dame, and Oxford scholars John Finnis and Joseph Raz. Other topics of early issues were "The Line Item Veto," "Liberty as a Value in the Constitution," and "The Role of the U.S. in International Organizations." Describing the objective of the publication, Professor Douglas W. Kmiec wrote in the foreword of the first issue that "the *Journal*'s aim is to draw upon religious teaching and philosophy within the broad spectrum of Judeo-Christian values in order to make practical application of those insights to timely issues of public concern."

The *Notre Dame Journal of Law, Ethics & Public Policy* is published under the auspices of the Thomas J. White Center on Law and Government, which Professor Kmiec directs. The White Center was established at the Law School in 1977. Besides the *Journal*, the White Center sponsors a lecture series that brings prominent men and women from government, academe, and religion to Notre Dame. Such people as Gerald Ford, Gary Hart, Nancy Landon Kassenbaum, Leonard Woodcock, Phyllis Schlafly, Eleanor Smeal, and William Bennett have delivered lectures. In the Fall of 1985 the Center brought Joseph Cardinal Bernardin of Chicago and John Cardinal O'Connor of New York to the University to discuss their views of the relationship between Catholicism and contemporary political and social issues.

Many of the lectures are later revised and published in the *Notre Dame Journal of Law, Ethics & Public Policy*. Much of the editorial work that is done on the *Journal* is completed by second- and third-year law students who are chosen to be White Scholars. Selected on a competitive basis, these scholars take part in the various activities of the Center, and they also conduct research on the ethical implications of public policy questions and topics. This research takes place on campus and during summer internships in Washington, D.C., where the students work in governmental and policy-related agencies. A specific goal for each scholar is the preparation of a publishable article for the *Journal*. The larger objective of the White Center's programs for students is the training of men and women for public service through the combining of a value-oriented legal education with practical governmental experience.

The heart of law school scholarship is the Law School library. The library is the law scholar's laboratory and scholarship can be no better than the library materials available for any particular project. Over the years the Notre Dame Law library has built up an adequate working collection, but it had neither the materials nor the staff to qualify for classification as a quality research library. In other words, although the Notre Dame Law library was sufficient for the teaching mission, faculty had to use other libraries for much of the in-depth scholarship research in which they were engaged.

As part of the planning process the University has recognized that if the Law School is to accomplish its scholarly mission the Law library must be converted into a high quality research facility. This means increasing the depth of the book and microfilm holdings and putting the Law School on the cutting edge of computer research, video disc storage, and other techniques of modern legal research. It also means staffing the Law library with librarians who are themselves lawyers and qualified legal researchers.

Much has been done to begin to convert the Law library to a quality research facility. The Law School has begun the process by recognizing that it already has two special collections that contain works which are unique and can form the nucleus of further library development. One of these collections is the Law School holdings in the field of jurisprudence. Many of these books, including some rare old manuscripts, came to the University through the gift of the Gould Natural Law Library collection. With Notre Dame's special commitment to jurisprudence and the fact that *The American Journal of Jurisprudence* is published at Notre Dame, the Law School plans to build on this special collection.

The library and archive in American civil and international human rights is particularly noteworthy. Maintained by the Center for Civil and Human Rights, which was founded in 1973, the library and archive contain all of the publications of the U.S. Commission on Civil Rights, including the personal papers of Father Hesburgh, who served fifteen years (from 1957 through 1972) as a Commission member. He was Chairman of the Commission from 1969 until he resigned at the end of 1972. Other materials in this unique collection are the publications of several international human rights organizations, the records of President Gerald Ford's Clemency Board about Vietnam-era draft violations and military absence offenses, the trial and appellate court briefs of the Civil Rights Division of the Department of Justice, documents on American Indian law, and information about the status and treatment of refugees around the world.

Besides serving as a rich resource for scholars doing research about domestic, civil, and international human rights, the Center for Civil and Human Rights has sponsored publications, symposia, and lectures. A major study of the Clemency Program that led to President Jimmy Carter's declaration of amnesty was carried out by the Center, and it has conducted conferences on the treatment of the terminally ill and the rights of the parents in the education of children. Such public figures as Earl Warren, Arthur Goldberg, and R. Sargent Shriver have come to campus under the Center's auspices.

The University has made a major commitment to the research library concept. The 1986 building addition is designed mainly to accommodate the expanded collection, new technology, and staff of a research library. A substantial increase in the library's operating budget has been authorized and significant amounts have already been allocated. Perhaps most significantly, the University has hired one of the nation's most respected law librarians, Roger Jacobs, who is a professor of law, as director of the law library at Notre Dame. Professor Jacobs, who until 1985 was the Head Librarian of the Library of The United States Supreme Court, has served as president of both the American and the Canadian Associations of Law Libraries. His experience will be critical to the development of a research library. He has already hired a talented and service-oriented library staff to assist both faculty and students. As director of research and law librarian, he has the goal of building the Kresge Law Library into, in his words, "one of the nation's best."

In future years, the Law School will continue to pursue its traditional mission of preparing students to become lawyers who combine technical competence with compassion and a conscience. The foundation to do this extends back to the nineteenth century and is rooted in the values and spirit of the institution. The contemporary environment, however, is quite different from the past. Scholarly research and professional activities outside the classroom have assumed much greater significance, the success in these areas serving to enhance the standing of the Law School within the legal community at large. During the next decade, the Law School has a dual challenge: retaining its distinctive character and continuing to improve its national impact.

PROFILE

DEAN DAVID T. LINK

THE LAW SCHOOL

WHEN DEAN DAVID T. LINK talks about the Law School, he emphasizes the distinctive nature of a Notre Dame legal education and the "tremendous sense of change" in the Law School since 1970. Link bases the assessment on a diversity of experience in three different capacities at the Law School. He is a Notre Dame law graduate (class of 1961), a professor (since 1970), and the dean (since 1975).

Link, who also received his bachelor's degree from Notre Dame's College of Commerce in 1958, sees "an orientation towards the value questions involved in the law" as the distinguishing characteristic of the Law School. "The moral and ethical questions are raised here with the same intensity that the substantive and procedural issues are discussed," he says. "There are simply very few law schools that emphasize this aspect to the same degree. That does not mean that I would not like to see this emphasized even more, and our new curriculum plan suggests ways that will happen."

A teacher of several classes that focus on legal ethics and professional responsibility, Link believes that faculty members and students have to be careful in considering the value questions that surround the law. "We should not indoctrinate students with some set of pat answers," he notes. "Ethical questions are not that easy and moral philosophy is very personal. But we try to get people to explore all sides of the moral and ethical dilemmas that confront both the lawyer and the lawyer's client."

Teaching future lawyers how to develop a professional and ethical relationship with clients is a fundamental concern for Link, who was a trial attorney and administrator in the Department of the Treasury in the 1960s before becoming a senior partner in a large Chicago law firm. He is currently on a leave of absence from the firm of Winston and Strawn. His experience also involves significant civil rights work. He served on two Human Relations Commissions, participated in civil rights litigation, and is the author of model fair housing legislation. Link remarks, "A lot of people don't realize it, but in the code of professional responsibility for lawyers there is a responsibility put on the lawyer to raise the moral questions with his client. Not many lawyers do. Not many lawyers were ever trained to do that. Lawyers who have gone to Notre Dame are trained to raise the moral questions with their client. I hope no one will leave this law school without knowing how to do this."

The unique nature of studying for a year abroad at the London Law Centre is another distinctive feature of the Law School. This program, which has no counterparts in American legal education, is significant for several reasons, according to Link. "There's a growing need for people with knowledge in international and comparative law because many legal questions are now going beyond the border, and many important issues have major legal aspects, like arms treaties, immigration issues, and world hunger questions. We need more people interested in the world's problems who are trained in more than one legal system. But, even beyond that, this type of training is helpful to the lawyer who never does international and comparative work. Studying in London develops creativity. One of the problems with the legal profession in this country is that many people have been trained in only one system and they don't know there are different ways of doing things." Link notes that several issues facing the American legal system—for example, the value of jury trials in deciding civil suits and whether losing parties should pay legal expenses in certain circumstances—have already been confronted in foreign countries. Lawyers with backgrounds in international and comparative law are better equipped to understand and to resolve these domestic legal concerns.

Many of the changes affecting the Law School since 1970 involve growth: Two major building expansions. Enlargement of the library collections. Significant increases in the student body and faculty. The establishment of new research centers. A greater number of scholarly publications

The Law School 131

either written by faculty members or published under the auspices of the Law School. More participation by students and professors in legal proceedings and in other professional activities.

Although their number is larger, Dean Link sees few qualitative differences between law students today and those who came to Notre Dame before 1970. "As we have expanded the student body size, we have maintained great depth of quality. We don't get very many students who cannot perform at a very high level. I don't think we're getting any better top students because we couldn't. We were always getting some of the best legal talent in the country. As we've expanded we've been able to maintain that quality deep in the class.

"There's also a greater diversity of students coming to Notre Dame to study law. Students come here from every part of the country and from foreign countries. We send them out into every environment and have one of the most diversified placements of any law school. We have graduates in most major law firms, in government positions, and in small general practices. Some of our graduates are engaged in public service and others are in teaching."

Link credits the maintaining of student quality and diversity of ambition to several factors, but he thinks a modification of the admissions procedures is largely responsible. Standardized tests and other indicators of intellectual ability are but some of the criteria in selecting a potential law student. Leadership qualities and existing signs of value orientation play key roles in evaluating an applicant. Link works with an admissions committee, but he is one of the few law deans in the country who personally makes the final decision on each student. "I can think of only one more important thing I do," he says. "That, of course, is my role in the selection of the faculty."

In choosing a faculty today, the Law School seeks men and women who possess more diversified talents and ambitions from many of their predecessors. Scholarship and professional activities to advance the law now receive greater emphasis than before. Link, the co-author of a three-volume series of books on *Law of Federal Estate and Gift Taxation* and the chairman of several significant committees of the American Bar Association and the Federal Bar Association, describes his current faculty as being composed of "teacher-scholars." He notes that the Law School has "always had a reputation of being a good teaching institution. Now we are publishing at a rate comparable to any law school in the country. We have become a very good scholarly place. We've done that, interestingly enough, despite warnings from people that we might sacrifice quality in teaching. There is no evidence that we in any way sacrificed good teaching."

The scholarly productivity of recent years has been a major factor in enhancing the Law School's national reputation, according to Link. Notre Dame is also working to become a University with a nationally recognized legal research center with noted library collections open to all scholars in such areas as human rights and jurisprudence. Doubling the library's size and appointing Roger F. Jacobs as the director of research and librarian are efforts to achieve this goal. As Link says: "Why does Roger Jacobs, the librarian of the United States Supreme Court, leave what is probably the most prestigious job to get involved with us? Well, his coming here tells something about what people believe is the future of this place. Roger believes he can make Notre Dame one of the nation's best research centers."

In Link's opinion, the future standing of the Law School depends on strengthening long-term commitments to teaching and to ethical examination of the law, sustaining the current emphasis on research,and continuing the selective process for choosing the best possible student body and faculty. The impact of completing such work has wide ramifications. "If we're really as good as we think we are and if we really have a special message in values, then we should be training all kinds of people for all kinds of practices," Link states.

"From the big firm lawyer to the solo practitioner, from the business specialist to the legal services litigator, from the lawyer representing the Chase Manhattan Bank to the one going to the Peace Corps, we want Notre Dame lawyers, exposed to the value system that is a part of this place, involved. And our faculty's scholarship should also reflect a deep concern with moral and ethical values. The Notre Dame law message is a special message, and we should carry it to all segments of society."

*Notre Dame Memorial Library*

# The Graduate School

THE AWARDING of post-baccalaureate degrees by the University of Notre Dame dates back to the commencement exercises of 1859 and the conferral of two master's of arts. During the nineteenth century, however, many of Notre Dame's graduate degrees were honorary awards for distinctions accomplished outside of the classroom. What actually happened in graduate education between 1859 and 1882 is not completely clear today, as there was no differentiation made between honorary and earned degrees.

The University approached post-baccalaureate instruction in a more formal way during the first two decades of the twentieth century. A Committee of the Faculty on Graduate Study was established in 1905, and the Summer School, with several programs beyond the bachelor's degree, was created in 1918. Until 1932, when what is now known as the Graduate School was formally organized, the Summer School constituted Notre Dame's principal work in advanced education. Many of the summer students were women, particularly nuns and lay teachers, making the Summer School the first academic entity at the University to admit women.

Because of the success of the Summer School, several hundred master's degrees were awarded between 1920 and 1932. Doctoral programs also existed in several departments, and during the 1920s a total of twenty-one doctorates were conferred in Ancient Languages, Education, English, Economics, History, Philosophy, Politics, Chemistry, and Metallurgy. However, in the early 1930s, University administrators began to question the merits of the numerous master's and doctoral programs. Was Notre Dame prepared to offer advanced work in so many disciplines? Were the curricula of sufficient rigor, depth, and breadth? Did the University have the wherewithal to enable students to complete the original research required for successful dissertations? Assessing the academic development of Notre Dame in 1960, Rev. Philip Moore, C.S.C., a former Dean of the Graduate School, wrote: "Looking back today upon the library resources and other conditions essential to genuine graduate work, especially on the doctoral level, we must conclude that in the 1920s Notre Dame was over-ambitious or overextended in most of the fields in which advanced programs of study were offered." Father Moore knew his subject first-hand. University historians credit him with being the principal architect of and driving force behind graduate education at Notre Dame.

Besides the creation of the Graduate School in 1932, the University took other measures to strengthen its work in post-baccalaureate education. The number of degree programs found worthy of continuation was reduced substantially. Doctorates were available in only Systematic Botany and Organic Chemistry in 1932. Students were limited to pursue a master's in thirteen areas: Boy Guidance (later called Social Work), Classics and Modern Languages, Economics and Politics, Education, English, History, Music, Philosophy, Sociology, Biology, Chemistry, Mathematics, and Physics. To help make advanced education distinctive and separate, all of the departments composing the Graduate School started to identify their courses as being "strictly" or "primarily" for graduate students.

The reassessment and planning that took place in the early 1930s helped build a foundation for the Graduate School as it exists today. From that time on, departments had to prove that their teaching and research met the requirements of advanced education. As deans and chairmen substantiated their cases, new graduate programs were added to the curriculum. Later in the 1930s doctoral studies were approved in Metallurgy, Physical Chemistry, Philosophy, Mathematics, Physics, and Politics.

Although World War II interrupted the expansion of graduate education, the University in 1944 attempted to upgrade the standing of the Graduate School by appointing its first dean and by creating a policy-making body, the Graduate Council. When the war was over, the Graduate School was prepared to continue the development that began in the 1930s. The number of professors with earned doctorates from respected universities rose dramatically. The influx of "refugee scholars" who were escaping from Germany and Eastern European countries helped to foster a climate for serious, advanced instruction and scholarship that was similar to the intellectual environment to which they were accustomed. Library resources and laboratory facilities grew. Sponsored research programs leading to publications in academic journals became integral to the life of the campus. All of these circumstances converged at the same time, greatly contributing to graduate development. The opportunities for doctoral study were enhanced, and more disciplines and areas—like English, History, Sociology, Engineering Mechanics, and Medieval Studies—now offered doctorates. Between 1946 and 1951, during the University presidency of Rev. John J. Cavanaugh, C.S.C., the students enrolled in the Graduate School jumped from 96 to 450, and Notre Dame formally established two research-oriented centers—the Medieval Institute (in 1946) and the LOBUND Laboratory (in 1950)—which brought wider outside recognition of the commitment to post-baccalaureate education.

During the 1950s and 1960s, the Graduate School continued to grow and to become more central to the University as a whole. In an effort to consolidate and to strengthen graduate instruction and academic research, the Office of Advanced Studies was created in 1971. The Vice President for Advanced Studies rather than a Dean assumed the leadership of the Graduate School. The Vice President also became responsible for overseeing all of the research and sponsored programs of the University.

In contrast to 1932, when the Graduate School was founded and had two doctoral and thirteen master's programs, today there are twenty-four doctoral and thirty-three master's programs, operating within four distinct divisions: Humanities, Social Sciences, Science, and Engineering. Outside support for research and sponsored programs has risen from $735,000 in 1951–52 to the current level of $17 million per year.

In a statement about the University study and self-assessment "Priorities and Commitments for Excellence: Report of the Provost to the President," Thomas P. Carney, Chairman of the Board of Trustees of Notre Dame until 1986, wrote in 1983: "As a governing board, the trustees recognize graduate studies and research as having the greatest potential for new levels of excellence at Notre Dame." Recognizing this potential, the University in recent years has focused greater attention on and devoted additional resources to post-baccalaureate education and advanced scholarship. The Graduate School now concentrates on programs of study that lead to doctorates or to what are considered the terminal, professional master's degrees, like the Master of Divinity, the Master of Fine Arts, or the Master of Architecture. Of the approximately 1,350 students enrolled in the Graduate School, one-half are pursuing doctor-

---

*ALFRED J. FREDDOSO*
*Dept. of Philosophy*

*Notre Dame's aspiration to be Christian and, more specifically, Catholic is its central defining feature. Even though the University is at present failing in certain crucial respects to live up to that aspiration, it is nonetheless true that the Catholic character of Notre Dame serves to enhance the intellectual freedom of many of us in philosophy. In this respect the environment at Notre Dame resembles that of the great medieval universities, where the effort to articulate deep and comprehensive visions of the world was not impeded by artificial barriers separating philosophy from theology.*

*Radiation Research Building*

ates and two-thirds are working full-time for their degrees.

Several other factors are involved in strengthening the Graduate School. Having endowed professorships throughout the divisions allows students (and other faculty members) to work with scholars who are widely recognized for their achievements in their fields. The University-wide commitment to creating "a single faculty" with professors who are strong as teachers and researchers also helps to create the necessary environment for advanced studies and its fostering of new knowledge. In addition to these faculty-related advances, graduate students can now take advantage of greater financial opportunities. The number of fellowships and assistantships has grown substantially since 1971, and the levels of support have increased. Travel grants from the Albert Zahm Research Travel Fund and the Graduate Student Union make it possible for several doctoral students each year to do research for their dissertations at libraries with special holdings in this country and abroad. These travel grants have opened up new research possibilities for students and enhanced the quality of dissertations being completed at Notre Dame.

As the work of the Graduate School has become more widely known, more potential students are seeking admission than ever before. This larger pool of applicants enables the University to select candidates with the most promise, and this, in turn, contributes to the overall improvement of the Graduate School. In recent years, according to surveys of the Council of Graduate Schools, Notre Dame's graduate enrollment and the number of applicants to graduate programs have exceeded the national averages for both public and private institutions. At a time when educators across the country are trying to come to terms with a decline in graduate education—a vast difference from the 1960s and early 1970s— Notre Dame's Graduate School is experiencing modest growth, and there is an eventual goal of 1,500 students. At the present time the largest doctoral programs in each of the four divisions are Theology (Humanities), Economics (Social Sciences), Chemistry (Science), and Chemical Engineering (Engineering).

An average of ninety doctorates are awarded annually, placing Notre Dame among the top fifty American universities in the production of doctorates. From 1945 through 1984, 2,276 graduate students earned their doctorates from the University—43 percent in Science, 24 percent in Humanities, 21 percent in the Social Sciences, and 12 percent in Engineering. Notre Dame awards approximately 300 master's degrees from its Graduate School each year, with the greatest percentage (44 percent) coming from the Humanities division.

The sustained commitment to post-baccalaureate education and scholarly research that has taken place since the early 1970s to the present has brought more recognition to the Graduate

*THOMAS J. MUELLER*
*Dept. of Engineering*

*While there has always been an excellent intellectual environment here, it has continuously improved with the addition of more faculty and students whose focus is scholarship and research. This improvement is the result of the long-term commitment by the University administration to enhance the intellectual environment. An emerging research institution of high quality, Notre Dame also takes the time and effort to study the questions related to moral and social values of today's world.*

School than ever before. In *An Assessment of Research-Doctorate Programs in the United States*, sponsored by the Conference Board of Associated Research Councils and published by the National Academy Press in 1982, Notre Dame's Chemical Engineering program ranked in the top twenty-five percent of all such programs in the country. In this study, Chemical Engineering was rated nineteenth of seventy-nine programs. Six other programs—Mathematics, Chemistry, Zoology, Electrical Engineering, Mechanical Engineering, and Philosophy—were ranked in the top fifty percent. These ratings signify marked progress in outside recognition since the previous assessment of 1969. In that study the University did not have a single doctoral program in the top fifty percent. (Neither the 1982 assessment nor the earlier one addressed some areas of University strength or achievement, like Theology and Metallurgical Engineering.)

Although statistical ratings of doctoral programs have value, they can also be somewhat misleading. Unlike many American universities that receive higher rankings because of their heavy and historic emphasis on research, Notre Dame seeks balance between teaching—on both the undergraduate and graduate levels—and research. Most of the faculty members at Notre Dame teach at least twice as many courses per year than do professors at public and private institutions with a research orientation. As a result of this emphasis on teaching, the majority of faculty members don't have the same amount of opportunity to pursue scholarly work as academics at many of the more highly rated schools with graduate programs. This situation, however, benefits the students and enhances the teaching mission of the University. Graduate students assist faculty members in their classes and research; however, few advanced students actually teach undergraduate courses. That responsibility primarily belongs to the full-time members of the teaching-research faculty.

A continuing aspect of the Graduate School that extends back in time to the beginning of serious post-baccalaureate instruction at the University is the Summer Session. Although summer programs at most colleges and universities emphasize classes for undergraduates, Notre Dame's Summer Session has always been predominantly designed to foster graduate education, and the vast majority of students enrolled during the summer are pursuing either a master's or a doctoral degree. For example, in 1984, a total of 1,654 graduate students as compared to 457 undergraduate students enrolled in the Summer Session. The number of graduate degree candidates was 1,051, with the others being listed as visitors, unclassified, and auditors.

The Department of Theology in Arts and Letters and the Institutional Administration Program in Business Administration conduct graduate classes and workshops that involve half of the students participating in the Summer Session. Theology and the Institutional Administration Program each offer curricula of approximately thirty different advanced courses in specific areas of specialization. Theology, for example, focuses on theological studies and liturgical studies. Institutional Administration, which leads to a master of science in administration, provides professional training for people responsible for managing not-for-profit institutions. Specialties include health care, education, financial administration for religious communities, and work for welfare agencies.

Both Theology and Institutional Administration enroll a large number of priests, nuns, and brothers. Until the 1960s, the religious were the primary constituency for graduate education during the summer session at Notre Dame. As priests, nuns, and brothers have in recent years had the opportunity to attend public institutions that in many cases are closer to their homes, the percentage of religious in the Summer Session has declined to just under an average of twenty-five percent.

The Summer Session has historically played a part in the development of the Graduate School, and it will continue to emphasize advanced study in the future. The Graduate School as a whole, though, faces the challenge of improving the quality of its doctoral programs at the same time when there is a national decline of interest in doctoral studies. But the maturity and recognition that have been achieved since the early 1970s are necessary first steps to meet that challenge. Advanced studies and research have now taken root throughout the University, and they are leading to the creation of one faculty that balances teaching and scholarship. During the remainder of the 1980s and beyond, the future of the University in its continuing quest for excellence will be inextricably linked to the Graduate School and how it faces its challenge.

PROFILE

VICE PRESIDENT ROBERT E. GORDON

THE GRADUATE SCHOOL

LOOKING BACK on his years as the Vice President for Advanced Studies, Robert E. Gordon describes the past and present in vivid terms. "It's really a difference between night and day," observes Gordon, who has supervised graduate instruction, research, and sponsored programs at Notre Dame since 1971. "The graduate programs are coming of age."

The Professor of Biological Sciences and former Associate Dean of the College of Science is the first Vice President for Advanced Studies in the University's history. The position, according to Gordon, was created to deepen Notre Dame's commitment to post-baccalaureate education and to strengthen the relationship between teaching (on both the graduate and undergraduate levels) and scholarly research throughout the University. "It was not without thought that the office of the Vice President for Research and the office of the Dean of the Graduate School were combined into a single Office of Advanced Studies," he comments. "What was sought by this meshing of research and advanced study was that the two activities should be definitely related to one another. We aspire to be a research university in which teaching, scholarly research in its broadest sense, and service in the Christian sense are all interwoven in a fabric permeated by Catholic values."

Since Gordon assumed the Vice Presidency, his Office has instituted several programs to advance post-baccalaureate work. Financial support for graduate students has increased markedly. More people are receiving fellowships and assistantships than ever before, and the value of these awards has risen substantially to be competitive with other universities. In addition, advanced students, most frequently doctoral candidates, are now able to apply for travel grants from the Zahm Research Travel Fund. Approximately a dozen such grants each year underwrite dissertation and thesis research trips to libraries and laboratories in this country and abroad. Travel awards are also available for graduate students who are presenting papers at scholarly meetings.

Besides these opportunities for students, the Office of Advanced Studies has inaugurated a number of programs to assist professors in their research. Faculty development funds, travel grants, and money to purchase necessary equipment help to stimulate and support scholarly work and research, especially in its formative stages. Moreover, the Office provides information to both graduate students and faculty members about scholarships, fellowships, and funding opportunities available from public agencies and private foundations.

Gordon believes that these measures and others taken by the University are responsible for improvement throughout the Graduate School. "I think the institution is maturing," he says. "The word is out in the academic community that Notre Dame is building a faculty with a deepened commitment to scholarship. The interaction of faculty with students is really producing some fine research. Of course, there is a difference between graduate and undergraduate education. Scholarship, the mastery of an existing body of knowledge, underlies all of teaching, whether it is graduate or undergraduate. But the participation in the research process—the discovery of new knowledge

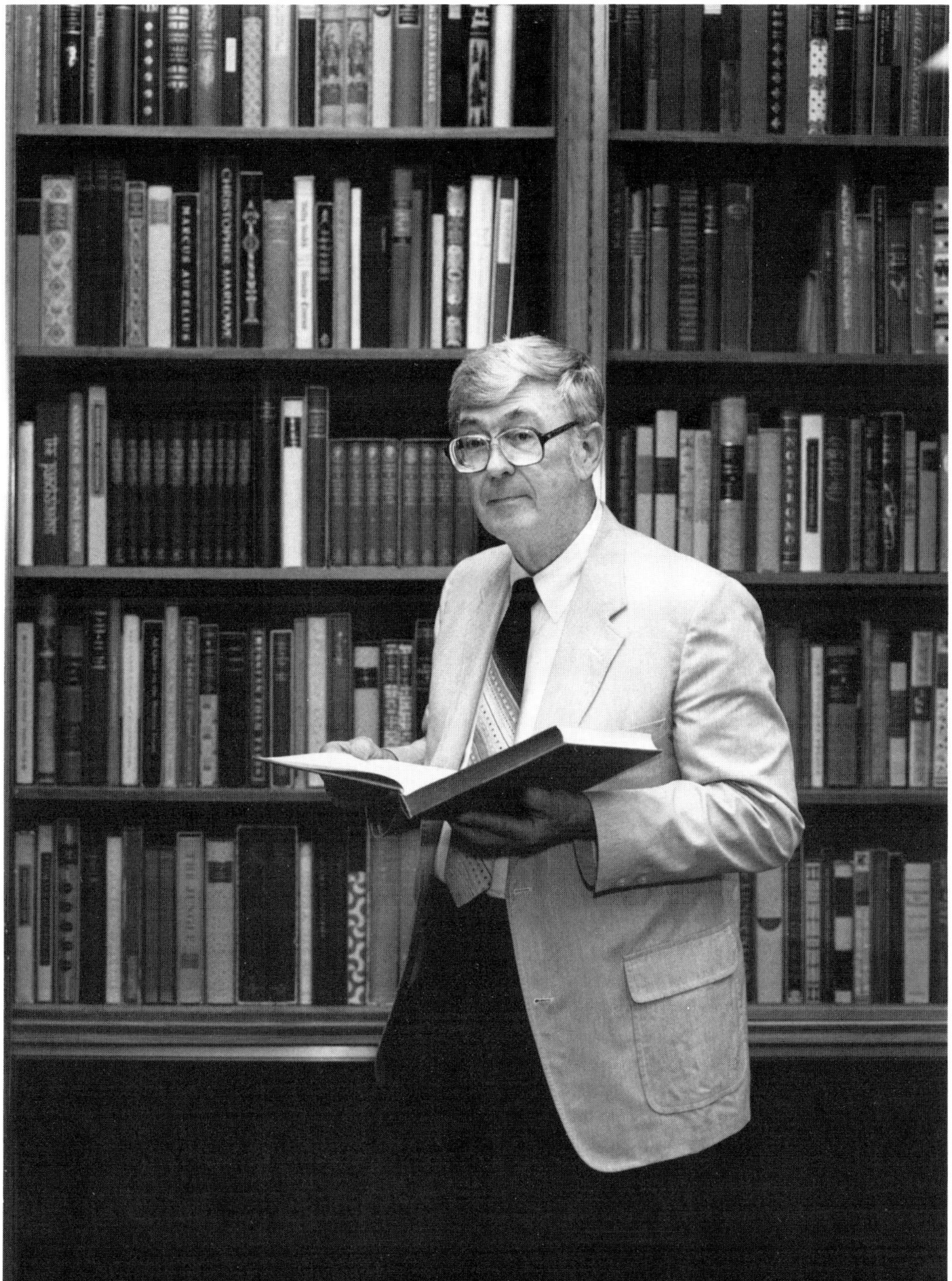

—is a form of teaching characteristic of graduate education. Indeed, it may be the heart of it. So when you think about improvement at the graduate level, you have to look at the research activity that's going on at the University. There's a whole new dynamic on the part of the faculty, and I think the research record speaks of this loud and clear."

Comparing the present to the past, Gordon believes that "scholarship, research, and teaching are now hallmarks of Notre Dame." He credits the maturation of faculty hired in the 1950s and 1960s as well as the appointment of endowed professorships as being important to the University's scholarly reputation. "The concept of the chaired professor is having a major impact here. Not only is it bringing into the faculty people who are distinguished in their disciplines, but it has caught the attention of the academic world. I believe this registers in the minds of many that this University is making a serious commitment as a research-teaching institution. Thus, many bright young people—students and faculty—come here more readily than they did in 1971."

Greater participation by professors throughout the University in professional service activities related to their fields is another difference between the early 1970s and now, according to Gordon. "Our faculty have become more active in leadership roles in their disciplines and in national organizations in this period of time. This, too, gives visibility to the University."

For his own part, Gordon has been active (as either an officer or a board member) in several organizations to advance higher education and in numerous scientific societies. Among his responsibilities during the past few years, he has served as a director or trustee of the Council of Graduate Schools in the United States, the Association of Catholic Colleges and Universities, the Universities Research Association, Biological Abstracts, and the Graduate Record Examinations Board. He was the Chairman of the Council of Graduate Schools in 1984–85. Gordon has also been a fellow of the American Association for the Advancement of Science since 1964 and a member of the American Institute of Biological Sciences since 1965. He was the President of the Institute in 1976. In addition, Gordon, who joined the Notre Dame faculty in 1958, has published over fifty articles and reviews in scholarly journals, and he served as editor of *The American Midland Naturalist* from 1958 to 1964.

In his role as Vice President of Advanced Studies, he is particularly concerned with the Graduate School and with developing new research programs. Gordon, however, recognizes the necessity for maintaining a balanced approach to scholarship, research, and teaching throughout the University. "My major concern in building the Graduate School at Notre Dame is that we do it without compromising in any way our commitment to undergraduate teaching. And I think it can be done. You just have to make sure that everyone is sensitive to the time demands of the several activities and programs accordingly."

Despite the numerous efforts that have been taken since the early 1970s to improve the quality of the faculty and the graduate student body and the work they do, Gordon singles out one significant area that requires additional support. "You can bring great minds here, both faculty and graduate students. But that is not enough. Just as the greatest sculptor in the world can't do a thing with a piece of rock unless he or she has the tools to work with it, faculty need a number of tools to pursue scholarship and research. We have good spatial tools; offices and laboratories are in general good. But we really need to work on the library. It is spotty at best. And we also have an equipment problem on campus. The machines of the 1960s in the experimental fields are aging; we need state of the art equipment and facilities."

Improving library holdings and acquiring additional equipment are two goals for the future. Another involves a modest increase in the size of the Graduate School—from 1,350 full-time students to 1,500. According to Gordon, "You don't build a graduate school with great leaps forward. You do it by steady growth. When we reach the point of 1,500 students, we're going to be bursting at the seams."

More students and more "tools" are tangible objectives in the development of the Graduate School. Of even greater importance, in Gordon's opinion, is the fostering of a continuing commitment to quality on the part of all who come here. The maintenance of high qualitative standards in admission, in scholarship, in teaching and research, are necessary if Notre Dame is to become "one of the major research-teaching universities in the United States."

# *Tomorrow*

DURING THE EARLY 1970s and the first three years of this decade, the University itself became the object of intense study. At both times formally appointed committees collected data, conducted meetings, drafted working papers, and prepared detailed reports (for review and action by the Board of Trustees) describing the current state of the University and charting its future. People representing every segment of the Notre Dame community participated in each inquiry, and the final published reports were candid in their appraisals and specific with their recommendations. Although all aspects of life at the University received attention during the two long-term studies, assessing the quality of existing academic programs and proposing definite measures for future achievement in teaching and research were principal concerns. These efforts of looking inward led Notre Dame as an institution to look outward as well—to the possibility at some point of fulfilling Father Sorin's original dream.

The first extensive effort to study the University and determine its direction was conducted by the Committee on University Priorities in 1972 and 1973. Rev. James T. Burtchaell, C.S.C., the first person appointed as Provost of the University—he served from 1970 until 1977—was chairman of the Committee and the author of the formal report. In the introduction he outlined the main objectives of the Committee's work: "The charge to this Committee is best expressed in the broadest terms: to study the present and, especially, the future of Notre Dame in an effort to determine what are the most important and indispensable elements of our total mission, the most essential as contrasted with that which might have seemed desirable under other circumstances. We cannot have the best of all worlds, but we must plan on principle to achieve what is best for us in our present world, what we can do superbly and what will in the foreseeable future likely be a mediocre or second-rate performance on our part, for a variety of reasons." Throughout its study and assessment of the University, the Committee focused on "the importance of clearly seeing and saying what is of first importance at Notre Dame" during the difficult economic period of the 1970s.

The final report, issued in 1974, set Notre Dame's agenda for the rest of the decade and also became a blueprint for what at the time was the most ambitious capital fund-raising campaign in the history of Catholic higher education. This campaign raised $180 million, $50 million more than the original goal. As a result of the drive, the University's endowment was doubled, with the bulk of these gifts underwriting endowed professorships and increasing financial assistance to students. Some of the other gifts created the Helen Kellogg Institute for International Studies, the Thomas and Alberta White Center for Law and Government, and the Charles and Margaret Hall Cushwa Center for the Study of American Catholicism, and broadened the work of the Institute for Pastoral and Social Ministry. Academic and residential buildings resulting from this campaign include the Fitzpatrick Hall of Engineering, the Stepan Chemistry Hall, the Snite Museum of Art, Pasquerilla East and West (two residence halls for women), and the O'Hara-Grace Townhouses (graduate student apartments).

Beginning in the Fall of 1980, the Priorities and Commitments for Excellence Committee embarked on a second and even more comprehensive study of the University and its potential, particularly during the 1980s. In the final report, which was approved by the Board of Trustees in May of 1983, Professor Timothy O'Meara, Provost and author of the report, wrote: "The University of Notre Dame finds itself on the threshold of becoming a great university, and all our efforts should be directed towards crossing this threshold." With this statement as an overarching theme, the report considers the total spectrum of University life—its Catholic character, teaching and research, student affairs, building needs, library and computing requirements, and athletics. The detailed analysis of these and other concerns led to thirty-nine recommendations, some with as many as nine distinct sub-sections. In several ways the report serves as a guidebook to take Notre Dame across "the threshold" and to a new level of recognition and accomplishment.

All of the report's recommendations embody definite goals for the future. Many of these "priorities and commitments" find their expression in either new activities or the enhancement (frequently with expansion) of existing undertakings. Since the publication of the report, additional planning has produced an agenda of objectives more formidable than anything Notre Dame has ever attempted. Some of the goals include:

—Achieving a total of one hundred fully endowed professorships and establishing new programs to enhance the opportunities for research by the entire faculty,

—Developing a system of scholarship and fellowship support to assist larger numbers of talented and worthy undergraduate and graduate students,

—Upgrading the collections of the University Libraries to facilitate more research and graduate study on campus,

—Improving the possibilities for using computers in research, instruction, and administration through the acquisition of both new hardware and software,

—Providing an endowment for the Snite Museum of Art to help support the operation of the museum and enlarge its collection,

—Insuring the intellectual vitality of Notre Dame Press by inaugurating new programs to underwrite the publication of additional scholarly books of merit,

—Launching several new centers to foster more research and instruction in specific fields, such as a Theology Center, a Microelectronics Research Center, and an Aerospace Research Center,

—Strengthening and broadening the work and activities of many of the existing centers and institutes, especially the Institute for Scholarship in the Liberal Arts, the Institute for Pastoral and Social Ministry, the Center for Social Concerns, LOBUND Laboratory, the Environmental Research Center (located near Land O'Lakes, Wis-

*Tomorrow* 145

consin), and the Center for Research in Business,

— Building a new classroom facility, two new residence halls for women undergraduates, and new apartments for graduate students, as well as adding new social and recreational facilities at the La Fortune Student Center and the Athletic and Convocation Center,

— Renovating extensively two of the most historically significant buildings on campus, the Main Building and Sacred Heart Church.

Completing an agenda of such magnitude will require several years of work and the mounting of the largest capital fund-raising campaign ever attempted by the University. However, some of the ideas for the future are already becoming reality. On December 13, 1985, Father Theodore Hesburgh announced that the University had received a gift of $6 million from Joan B. Kroc, the widow of the founder of the McDonalds Restaurant chain, to establish an Institute for International Peace Studies. Begun in 1986, the Institute, the first of its kind in the world, is directed by John J. Gilligan, the former governor of Ohio and currently the Francis J. O'Malley University Professor at Notre Dame. Activities of the interdisciplinary Institute include coordinating of undergraduate and graduate courses in peace studies; developing a comprehensive research program on the relationships among human rights, justice, and peace; sponsoring lectures, seminars, conferences, and publications that bring eminent scholars to campus, and establishing peace fellowships for graduate students from several nations, such as the Soviet Union and the People's Republic of China. The various activities of the Institute for International Peace Studies have the common objective of finding ways to maintain peace and justice in a world threatened by nuclear weaponry.

Notre Dame will be 150 years old in 1992. What was once a modest school on the American frontier has become an internationally known university that explores new frontiers of knowledge in the liberal arts, science, engineering, business, and the law. Since its founding in 1842, dreams about the future have been as much a part of Notre Dame as considerations of its past. One dream, however, has endured, helping to guide the University's growth and development. Back in the nineteenth century, Father Sorin said: "It may not be a university yet, but if there is ever to be a great Catholic university in America, it will be here." That dream—expressed without hesitation and with challenging clarity—persists and still provides direction.

What about tomorrow? What will Notre Dame be like as the Twenty-First Century begins? Father Hesburgh provides this view of the future: "I think in the year 2000 we should have an endowment well beyond a half-billion dollars. Once it gets past a half-billion dollars the endowment will continue to grow very, very fast. We should have one of the top ten or fifteen educational endowments in the land, in the world for that matter. That would be the first thing, and then it will be very heavily oriented towards, I hope, four things: Endowed professorships, endowed scholarships for needy and excellent students (now we are only able to take care of needy students) and for supporting library and computer studies, which are two enormous costs that simply can't be taken out of tuition. Then I would think in the year 2000 our student body would continue to get better and that we would have then finally a very good balance and working relationship with St. Mary's, and a good balance between men and women in this total social community.

"I would hope by the year 2000 that we would be much closer to that ultimate goal of being both a great university and a great Catholic university. I would hope that this would be a kind of Catholic center that serves the Church in many ways that only a university can serve it, both in providing a synthesis between faith and culture and between reason and faith which is the university and the Catholic component of all our efforts. I would hope that there would be absolutely superb Philosophy and Theology Departments, with great books emerging from them that would have a worldwide effect, not just a national effect. I would hope that our international efforts, especially in this continent, would have grown apace. I would hope that our peace efforts would make us one of the centers for study of peace internationally, even having effects on the creation of peace—if the world hasn't been blown up before that.

"I would hope that we would be pointing with pride at some fantastic graduates. I look at some of these young people around here who are so bright and learning so much. They are going to be leaders who influence the complex world around them. That really is the justification of the academy, the reason we have universities. In brief, we are going to have a great Catholic university, and that's what the whole thing is about."

# *Acknowledgments and Sources*

THE FIRST—and largest—debt of gratitude goes to Professor Timothy O'Meara, Provost of the University. When he proposed the possibility of writing a book about the intellectual and cultural life of Notre Dame, he said: "Do whatever it takes." From the initial meeting (in early 1983) until the date of publication, Professor O'Meara remained actively involved and true to his word. He was most generous with his time and resources each step of the way.

Rev. Theodore M. Hesburgh, C.S.C., University President, and Rev. Edmund P. Joyce, C.S.C., Executive Vice President, kindly provided their thoughts and reflections about Notre Dame since 1952, the year both assumed their administrative positions. These interviews were particularly valuable to understanding the University's progress during the past thirty-five years and its potential for the future. To a great degree their innumerable accomplishments make this book possible.

The following six people—Michael J. Loux, O'Shaughnessy Dean of the College of Arts and Letters; Francis J. Castellino, Dean of the College of Science; Roger A. Schmitz, McCloskey Dean of the College of Engineering; Frank K. Reilly, Dean of the College of Business Administration; David T. Link, Dean of the Law School, and Robert E. Gordon, Vice President for Advanced Studies—were largely responsible for seeing to the completion of the chapters about their Colleges and Schools. They arranged time for several in-depth interviews, and they encouraged their colleagues to provide essential information. Moreover, they read not only the various drafts of the chapters about their Colleges and Schools but also the manuscript as a whole, offering useful comments to improve the final version.

Rev. Edward A. Malloy, C.S.C., Associate Provost, and Isabel Charles, Assistant Provost, made numerous suggestions as the book was being written, and their help was especially valuable. In addition, Father Malloy participated in several planning meetings about the volume, and his thinking significantly shaped how the project was approached. Dr. Charles was also responsible for working closely with the faculty members whose statements and pictures appear throughout the book.

Thomas J. Stritch, Professor Emeritus of American Studies and a faculty member at Notre Dame since 1935, graciously provided his counsel on many occasions about the University he knows so well. His keen memory about events and people helped bring the past to life, and he kindly commented on the entire book as it was being completed.

Richard W. Conklin, Assistant Vice President for University Relations and Director of Public Relations and Information, helped to define the book from the beginning, and he generously provided editorial suggestions about all of the chapters and profiles.

Besides those already mentioned, the following people granted interviews (in some cases several) or provided information. I am sincerely grateful to them all:

In the College of Arts and Letters—Professor Nathan Hatch, Associate Dean, and Alven Neiman and Robert J. Waddick, Assistant Deans; Professor Donald P. Costello, Professor Edward Fischer, Professor Thomas J. Schlereth, and Professor Ronald Weber, all of the Department of American Studies; Professor Kenneth Moore of the Department of Anthropology; Professor Frederick Beckman of the Department of Art, Art History, and Design; Professor Mitchell Lifton of the Department of Communication and Theatre; Professor Charles Wilber of the Department of Economics; Professor Edward Kline of the Department of English; Professor Michael J. Francis and Professor John Roos of the Department of Government and International Studies; Rev. Thomas E. Blantz, C.S.C., and Professor Philip Gleason of the Department of History; Rev. Leonard Banas, C.S.C., and Professor David Ladouceur of the Department of Modern and Classical Languages; Professor Calvin Bower of the Department of Music; Professor Richard Foley and Rev. Ernan McMullin of the Department of Philosophy; Professor Frederick J. Crosson and Professor Walter J. Nicgorski of the Program of Liberal Studies; Professor Thomas Whitman of the Department of Psychology; Professor Andrew Weigert of the Department of Sociology; Professor F. Ellen Weaver of the Department of Theology; Rev. Ernest Bartell, C.S.C., Executive Director, and Albert LeMay, Program Coordinator, of the Helen Kellogg Institute for International Studies; Professor David C. Leege, former Director of the Center for the Study of Contemporary Society; Professor Jay Dolan, Director of the Charles and Margaret Hall Cushwa Center for the Study of American Catholicism; Professor Ralph McInerny, former Director of the Medieval Institute and Director of the Jacques Maritain Center.

In the College of Science—Professor George B. Craig, Professor Theodore J. Crovello, and Professor Morton S. Fuchs, all of the Department of Biological Sciences; Professor Thomas Fehlner of the Department of Chemistry; Rev. Michael J. Murphy, C.S.C. of the Department of Earth Sciences; Professor John Derwent, Professor William Dwyer, and Professor Warren Wong, all of the Department of Mathematics; Professor Paul Kenney and Professor Walter Johnson of the Department of Physics; Rev. Joseph L. Walter, C.S.C. of the Department of Preprofessional Studies; Professor Morris Pollard, Director of the LOBUND Laboratory, and Professor Robert H. Schuler, Director of the Radiation Laboratory.

In the College of Engineering—Professor Thomas J. Mueller, Director of Engineering Research and Graduate Studies; Professor Albin A. Szewczyk of the Department of Aerospace and Mechanical Engineering; Professor James Kohn and Professor Arvind Varma of the Department of Chemical Engineering; Professor William G. Gray of the Department of Civil Engineering; Professor Anthony Michel and Professor Michael K. Sain of the Department of Electrical and Computer Engineering; Professor Gordon Sargent, formerly of the Department of Materials Science and Engineering, and Professor Robert Amico of the School of Architecture.

In the College of Business Administration—Professor Yusaku Furuhashi, Associate Dean; Professor Leonard Savoie of the Department of Accountancy; Professor Howard Lanser of the Department of Finance and Business Economics; Professor John Houck, Professor Lee A. Tavis, Professor Robert Vecchio, and Rev. Oliver F. Williams, C.S.C., all of the Department of Management; Professor Michael Etzel and Professor John Malone of the Department of Marketing; Professor C. Joseph Sequin, Director of the Master of Science in Administration Program; Larry G. Ballinger, Director of the Master of Business Administration, and Arnie F. Ludwig, Director of the Executive Programs Division.

In the Law School—Professor Joseph Bauer, Associate Dean; Professor Fernand N. Dutile; Professor Douglas W. Kmiec, Director of the Thomas J. White Center on Law and Government; Professor Patricia O'Hara; Professor Kenneth F. Ripple; Professor Robert E. Rodes; and Professor James Seckinger, Director of the National Institute for Trial Advocacy.

In the Graduate School—Chau T. M. Le, Assistant Vice President for Graduate Instruction; Professor John O'Fallon, Assistant Vice President for Advanced Studies and Director of the Summer Session, and James H. Powell, Director of Graduate Admissions.

In the University Administration—Rev. David T. Tyson, C.S.C., Vice President for Student Affairs; Kevin Rooney, Director of Undergraduate Admissions; Wendy Clauson Schlereth, University Archivist; Robert C. Miller, Director of University Libraries; James R. Langford, Director of the University of Notre Dame Press; Walton R. Collins, Editor of *Notre Dame Magazine*, and Jerald Janicki, Michael P. Kenahan, and Daniel Reagan, all of the office of University Relations.

Although most of the information for this book came from interviews with and documents offered by the people named above, several books were valuable in providing the necessary background and historical context. These volumes include *Notre Dame: One Hundred Years* by Rev. Arthur J. Hope, C.S.C.; *The University of Notre Dame: A Portrait of Its History and Campus* by Thomas J. Schlereth; *Academic Development, University of Notre Dame: Past, Present, and Future* by Rev. Philip S. Moore, C.S.C.; *A Century of Law at Notre Dame* by Rev. Philip S. Moore, C.S.C; *The Notre Dame Ethos: Student Life in a Catholic Residential University* by Rev. David E. Schlaver, C.S.C.; *Notre Dame: Reminiscences of an Era* by Richard Sullivan, and *The Hesburgh Papers: Higher Values in Higher Education* by Rev. Theodore M. Hesburgh, C.S.C.

Articles in *Notre Dame Magazine*—especially those by Kerry Temple and Thomas J. Stritch—

were also most useful. In addition, papers and other materials in the collections of the University Archives and in the Department of Public Relations and Information provided essential information.

James R. Langford, Director of the Notre Dame Press, has been a publisher's publisher since this book was first proposed. He has lent his imagination and support to the project in ways that a few words can't repay. He also engaged and worked closely with three people deserving considerable recognition. Stephen Moriarty, who possesses an artist's eye, took all of the photographs in this volume. Donald Nelson creatively designed the book, selecting and placing the pictures (no small chore given the hundreds taken) and arranging the type. Carole Roos, who edited the book, made several valuable suggestions about the text.

At one time or another four talented processors of words—Ann Bromley, Jo Ann Gabrich, Joseph Pupel, and Bobbi Thompson—worked their magic on the handwritten pages they were given. They deserve the sincerest of a scribbler's salute.

Finally, Judy Schmuhl not only provided the ideal domestic environment during the many months this book was a husband's consuming preoccupation. She also listened attentively and offered advice as each chapter and profile came into being.